Routledge Guides to the Great Books

# The Routledge Guidebook to Plato's *Republic*

Plato, often cited as a founding father of Western philosophy, set out ideas in the *Republic* regarding the nature of justice, order, and the character of the just individual, that endure into the modern day. *The Routledge Guidebook to Plato's* Republic introduces the major themes in Plato's great book and acts as a companion for reading the work, examining:

- the context of Plato's work and the background to his writing
- each separate part of the text in relation to its goals, meanings and impact
- the reception the book received when first seen by the world
- the relevance of Plato's work to modern philosophy, its legacy and influence.

With further reading included throughout, this text follows Plato's original work closely, making it essential reading for all students of philosophy, and all those wishing to get to grips with this classic work.

**Nickolas Pappas** is Professor of Philosophy at the City College and Graduate Center of the City University of New York, where he regularly teaches courses on Plato's philosophy.

# ROUTLEDGE GUIDES TO THE GREAT BOOKS

## Series Editor: Anthony Gottlieb

*The Routledge Guides to the Great Books* provide ideal introductions to the work of the most brilliant thinkers of all time, from Aristotle to Marx and Newton to Wollstonecraft. At the core of each Guidebook is a detailed examination of the central ideas and arguments expounded in the great book. This is bookended by an opening discussion of the context within which the work was written and a closing look at the lasting significance of the text. *The Routledge Guides to the Great Books* therefore provide students everywhere with complete introductions to the most important, influential and innovative books of all time.

Available:

*Aristotle's Nicomachean Ethics* Gerard J. Hughes
*Hegel's Phenomenology of Spirit* Robert Stern
*Heidegger's Being and Time* Stephen Mulhall
*Locke's Essay Concerning Human Understanding* E. J. Lowe
*Plato's Republic* Nickolas Pappas
*Wollstonecraft's A Vindication of the Rights of Woman* Sandrine Bergès
*Wittgenstein's Philosophical Investigations* Marie McGinn

Forthcoming:

*De Beauvoir's The Second Sex* Nancy Bauer
*Descartes' Meditations on First Philosophy* Gary Hatfield
*Galileo's Dialogue* Maurice A. Finocchiaro
*Hobbes' Leviathan* Glen Newey
*Mill's On Liberty* Jonathan Riley

Routledge Guides to the Great Books

# The Routledge Guidebook to Plato's *Republic*

## Nickolas Pappas

**Routledge**
Taylor & Francis Group

LONDON AND NEW YORK

First published as 'Routledge Philosophy Guidebook to Plato
and the *Republic*' 1995
Second edition published 2003
This edition published as 'The Routledge Guidebook to
Plato's *Republic*' 2013
by Routledge
2 Park Square, Milton Park, Abingdon, Oxon OX14 4RN

Simultaneously published in the USA and Canada
by Routledge
711 Third Avenue, New York, NY 10017

*Routledge is an imprint of the Taylor & Francis Group, an informa business*

*British Library Cataloguing in Publication Data*
A catalogue record for this book is available from the British Library

*Library of Congress Cataloging in Publication Data*
Pappas, Nickolas, 1960–
The Routledge guidebook to Plato's Republic / Nickolas Pappas.
p. cm. – (The Routledge guides to the great books)
Includes bibliographical references (p.).
1. Plato. Republic. I. Title.
JC71.P6P365 2013
321'.07–dc23
2012014793

ISBN: 978-0-415-66800-2 (hbk)
ISBN: 978-0-415-66801-9 (pbk)
ISBN: 978-0-203-09420-4 (ebk)

Typeset in Garamond
by Taylor & Francis Books

# CONTENTS

# Series Editor's Preface

"The past is a foreign country," wrote a British novelist, L. P. Hartley: "they do things differently there."

The greatest books in the canon of the humanities and sciences can be foreign territory, too. This series of guidebooks is a set of excursions written by expert guides who know how to make such places become more familiar.

All the books covered in this series, however long ago they were written, have much to say to us now, or help to explain the ways in which we have come to think about the world. Each volume is designed not only to describe a set of ideas, and how they developed, but also to evaluate them. This requires what one might call a bifocal approach. To engage fully with an author, one has to pretend that he or she is speaking to us; but to understand a text's meaning, it is often necessary to remember its original audience, too. It is all too easy to mistake the intentions of an old argument by treating it as a contemporary one.

The *Routledge Guides to the Great Books* are aimed at students in the broadest sense, not only those engaged in formal study. The intended audience of the series is all those who want to understand the books that have had the largest effects.

AJG
October 2012

# PREFACE

## INTRODUCING PLATO

In the first place Plato needs no introduction because everyone knows his name; but also in another respect, because his dialogues make such an effort to present and explain themselves to their readers. Plato motivates the questions his characters examine, explains the terms they use, and sketches the connections among disparate issues. Indeed the most gentlemanly thing about this most gentlemanly of writers may be his willingness to introduce himself, without a trace of pompousness, to utter strangers. This is why readers can still enter into the dialogues eighty generations – close to thirty-five lifetimes – after Plato wrote them.

Even so most readers prefer to have a guide at hand when they approach Plato's works, especially one as large and difficult as the *Republic*. The dialogue form becomes an obstacle if you want to get an overview of the territory covered, to worry a single point in greater detail than the conversational setting allows, to isolate the premises of an argument and discover which ones are doing the work, or to find different ways of putting a single Platonic point and see what consequences follow from each restatement. The important issues in Plato's long dialogues appear and vanish: Plato raises one point only to digress to another, or to attend to a detail of his argument. Eventually the originating issue comes up again, but transformed or disguised. The reader who feels lost among the turns of conversation may wish that Plato had also written a few pedestrian treatises covering the same ground as the dialogues, but more explicitly, and when it is necessary more tediously.

This book is designed as an accompaniment to Plato's *Republic* for the benefit of any reader who has sometimes felt confused by its brilliant liveliness. For the most part I have stayed close to Plato's own arrangement of his arguments. At each point I spell out his position, then stop to analyze, criticize, or expand on it. I depart from Plato's expository order only in discussing Books 5–7, which I go through once with an eye to the political theory, then again looking only at the metaphysics. Thus most of this book is an exposition of the text, with pauses for further discussion. Later chapters refer back to relevant earlier sections, to facilitate the task of putting together different treatments of a subject into a unified whole.

Toward the same purpose of keeping the dialogue as a whole in mind, I have identified what I consider fundamental premises or assumptions in the *Republic*'s argument, and collected them in the book's appendix, both so that I can allude compactly to important Platonic claims, and so that the reader can see steps in the first books of the *Republic* as they function in the later books. Finally, Chapters 10–12 return to certain general issues that profit from being discussed with reference to the entire *Republic*. They are brief, as they had to be to keep this from becoming some other book, but as first approaches to the issues they show how one may review the whole dialogue.

In addition to bringing forward the *Republic*'s overarching structure, I have emphasized the complexity of its relationship to ordinary thought. It is easy to fall into thinking of Plato as the philosopher of otherworldly ideals, in politics therefore utopian, in ethics a propagandist for a species of 'justice' that has nothing to do with anything people call justice in their ordinary lives. But the *Republic* takes great pains to keep its arguments intelligible to readers who are not trained philosophers, even when advocating a perspective of theoretical reason that would leave ordinary thinking behind. This duality of purpose makes for a productive tension in the dialogue, clearly spotted when Book 1 moves from a behavioral definition of justice to an internal one, or when Book 4 tries to accommodate its psychological interpretation of virtue to the ordinary variety, or Book 5 distinguishes the philosopher from other putative lovers of knowledge. The tension between popular thinking and philosophical thought is most dramatic in the *Republic*'s ambivalence about the nature of reason (especially in Book 9); but it is also at play in Socrates' repeated strategy of double arguments, in which he follows a theoretical justification for a view with one that the nonphilosopher can follow. While Plato certainly does reach conclusions that at points deny the worth of daily experience, those conclusions gain their power from his effort to motivate them from within daily experience.

In the interests of a smoother read, I have omitted the traditional references that would acknowledge the intellectual debts I have incurred in writing this book. Instead and more informally I close each chapter with a list of the books and articles that most informed its interpretations; I consider these the best places for the reader to go first in moving beyond what I have said. The book's bibliography likewise serves the two purposes of identifying the sources I have most relied on, and directing the reader's own further investigations.

Some sources are worth referring to more than once. This book was specially helped by Julia Annas's *An Introduction to Plato's Republic* and Nicholas White's *A Companion to Plato's Republic.* The reader who knows these excellent works will spot my extensive borrowings from them. In addition to these, the books on the *Republic* by Cross and Woozley, by Murphy, and by Nettleship guided my interpretations and presentations.

All quotations from the *Republic* come from Allan Bloom's translation. I depart from his usage in my discussion only in referring to 'reason,' as he often does not, and to Plato's 'Forms,' as he never does.

## THE PRESENT BOOK

I have revised this book twice since first writing it twenty years ago. The second edition appeared in 2003, this version another ten years later. The second edition made some change to each page, and larger changes to the chapters at the book's end, with new discussions of beauty, political paternalism, and the way the conception of reason evolves as one reads through the *Republic*.

The second edition also reflected further on the guardians' natures, emphasizing that with his comparison between the city's rulers and dogs, Plato draws on the fact that domestication produces animals you cannot call either exactly natural or exactly artificial. A city founded on convention or artifice alone is doomed to fail, as Thrasymachus argues, because its moral prescriptions contradict human nature. Dog breeding shows Plato a way to bridge the gap between natural processes and cultural values, so that instead of undoing a society the laws of nature can underwrite it.

This version has undergone much more alteration. Substantial portions are new, such as the comments on Gyges in Chapter 3, the philosophers' reluctance to rule (Chapter 6), degrees of understanding (Chapter 7), the painter's ranking below the maker, and the myth of Er (both Chapter 9). Much has been added to Chapter 10 on the *Republic*'s ethics and politics. A new part of Chapter 5 reviews the current debate between deflationist and realist interpretations of Plato's theory of the soul.

This is not to mention the first chapter of the present book, three-fourths of which was written for this edition; or the last chapter, all new. These bookend chapters sketch out historical contexts for the *Republic* and its later reception. The result is a book that does at least two things better than its predecessors: situate the *Republic* in its time and in the subsequent intellectual history of the West; and spell out the main interpretive debates that surround the *Republic* today. I hope that readers who found the earlier editions clear and patient in their expositions continue to see those virtues in the present edition, together with its increased scholarly timeliness and historical responsibility.

## MANY THANKS

I first learned Greek with William McCulloh; I first read the *Republic* under Cyrus Banning, and Plato systematically in the classrooms of Eugen Kullmann and Thomas Short. In graduate school I am grateful to have studied ancient philosophy with Martha Nussbaum and Steven Strange. I hope that this book is a credit to my teacher Stanley Cavell, to whom I owe my deepest understanding of what a philosophical theory is, wants to be, and perhaps ought not be.

Among my peers I must include three by name: Kirk Fitzpatrick, Burt Hopkins, Brian Seitz. And I am particularly grateful to Michael Pakaluk for reading a long section of the first draft and helping me improve it.

I have now spent a quarter century teaching the *Republic*, to more good students than I could list. At Hollins College, Jennifer Norton and Caroline Smith made special contributions to this book. Some names from City College come to mind because their comments sent me back to my book to jot down ideas for changes: Shontanu Basu, Gloria Bragdon, Joseph Brown, Keegan Goodman, Amalia Rosenblum, Stephen Sykes. At the CUNY Graduate Center, I want to thank my students Brandon del Pozo, Mary Clare McKinley, and especially Daniel Mailick. I must also mention Professor Ruth Bevan of Yeshiva University, in New York, and her political science honors students.

Much of the time that I needed to complete this new edition was made possible by Dean Geraldine Murphy, who deserves special thanks – not just for this help, but for this on top of her many services to City College.

# Part I

## GENERAL INTRODUCTION

# 1

# PLATO AND THE *REPUBLIC*

The broad historical context to Plato's life, which is also the context essential to understanding the *Republic*, includes the Athenian Golden Age, a fifty-year period of military power and cultural activity; democratic government, which was established in Athens around 508 BC and only rarely interrupted until after Plato's death; the Sophists, and the philosopher Socrates who was sometimes mistaken for a Sophist, more often his activity in contradistinction to theirs; and the philosophical tradition that investigated the universe and reality in the centuries before Socrates.

This chapter will sketch Plato's Athens as the scene of these phenomena and movements, then situate Plato in the Athenian context. Then it will be possible to say a few words about the Platonic art of writing in general and specifically about what modern readers consider his greatest work, the *Republic*.

## HISTORICAL BACKGROUND

### ATHENS IN THE GOLDEN AGE AND AFTER

A long stretch of the fifth century saw Athens' greatest achievements. By 479 the city had established an unprecedented democracy, and working together with Sparta had twice stopped the Persian Empire from conquering Greece. For fifty years after Persia's retreat, Athens built its own grand alliance, first with the alleged purpose of defending against the return of the Empire, then to resist encroachments by the Spartan alliance that rivaled the Athenian group for control of Greek territory. The alliance was supposedly a mutual-defense pact, but from an early date almost all the other cities involved found it more convenient to let Athens provide the defense of the group and to pay a cash tribute instead. Athens in turn built the fleet and trained the infantry that it took to defend the alliance, and made good use of the funds from its allies. Soon enough the alliance functioned as an empire, for the member states learned that Athens would not let an ally withdraw.

The alliance brought Athens prosperity and a fair measure of peace. During the years between the decisive stand against Persia at Plataea and the beginning of war between Athens and Sparta in 431, Athens built its great temples and a huge harbor at Piraeus, perfected the dramatic forms of tragedy and comedy, and otherwise encouraged the arts, scientific speculation, and general intellectual inquiry. The war, the protracted struggle against Sparta that has long been known as the Peloponnesian War, brought the end of this grand era. Off and on for twenty-seven years, Athens squandered the prestige and wealth it had amassed since the end of the Persian War.

At first the city much exceeded Sparta in wealth, in number of allies, and in the naval power that had recently become decisive to warfare. Athens felt confident of victory. But early on the great democratic leader Pericles died; and after some years of mixed results on the battlefield and a welcome truce, Athens attempted a huge military expedition to Sicily in 415. It was an overreaching move and a doomed invasion. Nearly all the participating Athenians were killed and their fleet destroyed. The war would drag on for a decade after the Sicilian Expedition, but Athens was on the defensive now, and finally had to accept humbling terms from the Spartans in 404.

For close to a year after this loss, Athens was governed by a pair of dictatorial committees that were known together as the Thirty Tyrants. Plato's own relatives Critias and Charmides belonged to this group; in fact they were among its most bloodthirsty members, who made an easy transition back to democracy impossible. But the democratic forces did prevail, and Athens continued as a democratic, autonomous city until after the death of Plato.

## ATHENIAN DEMOCRACY

Plato saw the democracy close up. Except for a brief oligarchic coup when he was a teenager, the Thirty Tyrants created the only break in democratic governance that he would have seen. Athens ran itself according to principles of direct democracy and defined itself as a place of equal political rights for its citizens.

Plato's dialogues regularly refer to the fact that Athens is a democracy, especially the dialogues that focus on politics as the *Republic* does. With few exceptions the references are negative, sometimes suspicious of this inefficient way to run a city, more often repelled by the corruption that democracy represents. Plato is called a reactionary for his attitude toward democracy, or at least that vaguer thing a 'conservative'; but while this description does capture something about his distaste for contemporary politics and his yearning for old-fashioned values, Plato rarely advocates a simple return to the good old days. From enlightened governance to structured education, his political proposals contain as many new ideas as rehashes of old customs. For better or for worse Plato envisions a society that resembles no society known thus far, more than it resembles any past version of Athens.

Above all Plato has a talent for not saying what you might expect him to. This is another reason not to call him a conservative, because such labels presuppose someone's attachment to a known cluster of beliefs. Plato sounds like a traditionalist about the warrior class that runs his new city; then he seems to be the most progressive Greek of his time when he advocates including women in that class, or having philosophers govern the warriors.

The Athenian democracy itself is not always what the modern residents of democratic societies expect. Democracy means the general public's right to vote. But in almost all democracies today, the public votes to elect its political leaders and representatives. The Athenian public mostly voted, in the frequently convened assembly, to enact legislation. A few public offices were elected ones, the most important of these being the ten generals who commanded Athenian troops; but most offices were chosen by lot. Five hundred citizens were selected at random each year to represent the complex districts of Athens in its *boulê* 'council,' which prepared legislation for assembly meetings and formed executive committees to administer the city's daily business. The assembly met too frequently to be superseded on substantive matters even by this important council, and the assembly's quorum of 5,000 ensured that legislation reflected the will of at least a very large minority of the population. Thus the actions of the state had more to do with the immediate wishes of its voting public than the actions of modern democracies have to do with their publics' wishes.

It is a restriction on Athenian democracy, of course, that only a fraction of its inhabitants were voting citizens. Slaves, resident aliens, and women made up a large neglected percentage of the whole. This innocuous word 'population' should always be qualified as 'free adult-male citizen population' when describing the Athenian government. Calling it 'direct democracy' to contrast with modern representative democracies should not be taken to imply that all the people participated.

Scholars of ancient thought observe that the first political theory came into existence in the Athenian democracy; unfortunately (paradoxically) the theorizing that came out of the democracy all seems to have argued *against* democracy. From the pamphleteering *Constitution of Athens* whose unknown author is now called the 'Old Oligarch,' through the portrayal of Athens in Thucydides' *History of the Peloponnesian War* and Plato's dialogues, to Aristotle's *Politics* and the work *Athenians' Constitution* probably written by a member of Aristotle's school, a century's worth of observations on

Athenian democracy viewed that form of government with greater or lesser contempt but never approval, more suspicion or less but never trust. The arguments brought against Athenian democracy by this disapproving tradition influenced later readers so strongly that, until well into the twentieth century, modern scholars joined the ancients in declaring the Athenian democracy inefficient, fickle, and lawless; they looked back more fondly on the armed camp that was Sparta as forebear of the West than they did on unreliable democratic Athens.

The Athenian intellectuals' own arguments against democracy may be unfortunate, but they are not inexplicable. Perhaps for the first time in history, a culture's intellectual elite did not belong to its governing class or serve that class. This is an astonishing development: the alienated thinker, the elitist expelled from the halls of power. However wealthy and educated they were, the intellectuals of Athens were not, as ancient intellectuals before them had been, advisers to kings or sloganeers on the kings' behalf. Lacking political power, they were reduced to developing arguments that would win their readers' agreement, or rhetoric that seized the readers' hearts, because they could no longer simply command agreement.

In other words political theory came into existence because democracy marginalized its elite writers. The theory those writers produced was undemocratic not by an unhappy coincidence of history but as a token of the democracy's power.

The historian Thucydides emphasizes the irresponsibility in Athens. When the news sank in that the Sicilian Expedition had been destroyed, the Athenians blamed the politicians who had convinced them of its merits, 'just as if they had not voted for it themselves' (*History of the Peloponnesian War* 8.1.1). Another episode in his chronicle shows the chilling difference this democratic irresponsibility could make. Thucydides tells of the day in 427 (coincidentally the year of Plato's birth) when an angry assembly voted to kill all the men of Mitylene and enslave its women and children, after that city had unsuccessfully tried to withdraw from the Athenian alliance. Next day, even as the ship sped to carry out liquidation, the men in the assembly changed their minds and sent a second ship speeding after the first one to rescind the deadly order, and execute only the revolt's leaders (*History of the Peloponnesian War* 3.36–50). The will of the people had changed overnight.

While other antidemocratic authors stressed the capriciousness of democracy, its disrespect for moral standards, or the downright wrongness that some saw in treating unequal people as equals, Plato's dialogues emphasize what is *unreasoning* about democracy. Democratic deliberation gives no weight to expert opinion but treats every vote as equal to every other one, no matter how ignorantly a citizen votes. The most knowledgeable speakers do not always prevail; if anything they tend not to. Knowledge, wisdom, expertise lose to guesswork and personal interest – to bodily desire, old wives' tales, and newfangled speculation. Although the dialogues show aristocrats and oligarchs letting their own selfish opinions likewise run roughshod over temperate deliberation too, Plato does not oppose philosophical governance equally to all other regimes. Most of all he pits philosophy against democracy. The *Republic*'s proposal that philosophers rule the good city is the ultimate expression of Plato's call for expertise in governance over against the ignorant governance practiced by democracies.

Other differences between the constitution that the *Republic* calls for and the type that Plato grew up observing are more indirect. Consider imperialism, which in today's political vocabulary is practiced by political and economic elites. It is seen as the work of capitalistic nations, which behave undemocratically as they dominate other countries. It is commonly assumed that in a representative democracy the 'conservatives' and the rich and powerful will support a bellicose foreign policy, while progressives and other liberals, and the poor and disenfranchised, argue for peace and coexistence with the state's alleged enemies.

In Athens the opposite happened. The city's wealthy families were the first to tire of war with Sparta, a war in which they bore a disproportionate burden of the cost, e.g. by having to pay for the new ships of Athens' fleet. Many aristocrats sympathized with Spartan culture. The poorest citizens, on the other hand, could earn a subsistence wage by rowing the navy's ships; and the large alliance of cities that this navy permitted Athens to lead – an alliance that increasingly resembled an Athenian empire – brought a wealth of tribute money to the city. That money found its way to the general population by funding pay for jury duty and pay for attendance at the assembly, the modernization of the city's harbors (which meant many days' wages) and the temples on the Acropolis (again, wages for many workers). Both the empire and the long war benefited the city's urban voters. Plato joined other wealthy Athenians, and the property-holding farmers who were neither wealthy nor poor, in hoping for a city that held itself aloof rather than embroil itself in alliances, and especially a kind of city that did not float that symbol of democratic aggressiveness the navy.

Democracy was far from the standard form of government for these independent Greek cities. Many of them did operate according to some version of a democratic constitution, and by the fifth century monarchies had largely disappeared, but most cities were either run oligarchically – by the wealthiest minority – or tyrannically, by a single dictator who had seized power. The extreme opposite to Athenian democracy seems to have been Sparta, whose reputation for boot-camp austerity is as widespread as the picture of Athens as freethinking. The warrior-citizens of Sparta lived abstemiously, spending their lives training for battle. Within their home city they kept the majority of the population, the Helots, working the land as cowed serfs. Beyond the horizons of their own land they enjoyed a reputation as the most fearsome and successful fighters in Greece.

Most Athenians who criticized its democratic institutions – this especially includes Socrates – sympathized with Sparta and wished that their society could be more Spartan. Socrates wore simple clothes and walked barefoot not because he was impoverished (his reputation for poverty seems to have been exaggerated), but because this was how Spartan men dressed, insensitive to bad weather and careless of personal luxury. Such sympathies only grew when Sparta finally won the long and brutal war between the cities, for that victory appeared to have demonstrated the superiority of the Spartan state.

Plato does not appear to have affected Spartan manners or wardrobe, but he did take Sparta as one of his models when designing the *Republic*'s city. His city differs from Sparta in important ways, but the permanent separation of productive workers from soldiers, and those soldiers' lives in barracks, closely resemble, if not actual life in classical Sparta, at least that life as sympathetic Athenians envisioned it.

## THE SOPHISTS AND SOCRATES

The wealth of Athens made it the most desirable stopping point for the Greek world's itinerant intellectuals. Poets traveled from city to city; so did rhapsodes, who recited and interpreted the epics of Homer; so did those all-round experts known as Sophists.

When the Sophists arrived in Athens they saw that they could fill a void in the locals' education. In Athens of the early classical age, schoolboys memorized passages from Homer, learning writing syllable by syllable in the process. Once they could read and write and knew a fair quantity of Homer, their formal education was over, maybe at the age of twelve.

A society that farmed and warred did not need more education. Doctors, carpenters, musicians, and other experts received their specialized training as apprentices. But as Athens became more complex, wealthy families sought out teachers for their adolescent sons who could prepare them for public life. At first such preparation meant all-round tutoring that would turn a literate boy into a man of culture. The Sophist Hippias appears in the pages of Plato, in one of the dialogues that bear his name, boasting of the wide range of subjects he could teach: astronomy, genealogy, and grammar.

Learning from a universal expert must have seemed glamorous. The word for these smart men, 'Sophists,' is still at work in the English word 'sophisticated.' But of all the skills that made a young gentleman impressive, it soon emerged that the one most useful in the city's growing democracy was skill at public speaking. The assembly held all policy-making authority in Athens; and the assembly's laws were enforced in the courts, in which both criminal cases and lawsuits were tried. One citizen would bring charges against another and they both argued their cases before large juries, from 51 jurors in routine cases to 501 or even more when someone faced a capital charge (as Socrates did in the year 399).

The origins of the Athenian judicial system are obscure, but one significant factor in its development was Pericles, who introduced pay for jury duty. This pay was not lavish, but like the allowance for attendance at the assembly, which encouraged farmers to make the long walk into town for meetings, jury pay brought citizens into the courthouse who had not been part of the process. And now that would-be plaintiffs and defendants addressed large crowds of barely educated men in trials – as political leaders did in the assembly – persuasion became a greater challenge than ever. What arguments would move the assembly to pass a law against its immediate interests? The story goes that Athens spent a windfall of silver from its public mines on the fleet that would defeat Persia (and would eventually subject half of Greece to Athenian power) only because Themistocles tricked the assembly into thinking this fleet was needed for defense against nearby Aegina. Did a successful political career mean that someone had to whip up overt lies like that one twice a month? Was this another cost of democracy, that the elite had to achieve through fine speeches what their ancestors had accomplished by force?

Similar challenges faced the private citizens who brought charges in court or defended themselves against accusations. The Athenian courts had no judges to manage the proceedings and no professional attorneys representing clients. First the man bringing the charges spoke before the jury, identifying the law that the defendant had allegedly broken and introducing witnesses to substantiate his case. The defendant replied with his own speech and witnesses, everyone on both sides speaking under time constraints. Finally the jury voted on its verdict, and when the defendant was found guilty they voted a second time to determine the sentence.

In the courthouse as in the assembly, the ability to speak gracefully and persuasively could mean the difference between triumph and ruin. Hence the quick rise in importance of experts at rhetoric, if also suspicions about their powers. In developed societies today there is a widespread assumption that private citizens need clever lawyers, while political success depends on advertisers. People express contempt for lawyers and advertisers while also considering them supremely efficacious, even magically so. This is not a bad approximation to how Athenians perceived skilled public speakers. What those people did was somehow not real and yet it worked, and (perhaps just because it was not based on honest labor or brute force) it worked thanks to undetectable powers. So no one wants such people in the city when thinking about the city as a whole, and yet each person wants the advantage that comes of consulting such magical experts. And in ancient Athens the sons of rich and powerful people studied with Sophists to become persuasive speakers themselves.

To some Athenians, Plato's friend Socrates (469–399) was one more Sophist. It is telling that for all the differences among the portrayals of him that still exist, all three take a stand on this question, either calling Socrates a Sophist or denying that he could be one.

The factual evidence about Socrates is varied, however, coming as it does from three different sources: Aristophanes the comic playwright, Xenophon the gentleman soldier and author, and Plato. Aristophanes is the earliest, satirizing Socrates in *Clouds* before Plato and Xenophon had even learned to read. It is not known why a private citizen should receive such ridicule. Socrates had apparently come to the public's attention the year before, during an ignominious Athenian retreat after a battle. Even though he stood out for his dignified courage, Socrates was so eccentric that the public must have started gossiping about him; and Aristophanes baked gossip, scraps of fact, and the man's odd appearance into the memorable slander that is the *Clouds*. In that play Socrates runs a deranged school whose curriculum – part blasphemy, part wordplay, part lunatic science – works together to fuel attacks on traditional morality. Any student who pays can learn rhetorical tricks for eluding creditors and escaping moral sanctions.

At best *Clouds* is based on partial information. And even if Aristophanes has no special animus against Socrates, he wants someone to represent 'dangerous new ideas,' and willingly sacrifices his characters on the altar of a joke. He has surely defamed Socrates. Plato and Xenophon offer the alternative, authors who know Socrates and want to present him, if anything, as better than he really was. In the dialogues that Xenophon wrote, Socrates is an upright character, perhaps politically subversive (depending on how one interprets these works), but uninterested in the far reaches of theory. Socrates is a man of great integrity in Plato's dialogues as well, but in addition he is one who develops abstruse, innovative theories about morals and reality. Plato portrays a Socrates sometimes interrogating his fellow Athenians about their moral practices and theories, sometimes leading his co-conversationalists through the steps of elaborate ethical and metaphysical theories.

In some ways the three visions of Socrates overlap. There is a core of fact about the legendary figure. It seems undeniable that Socrates existed and was put to death, almost as certain that young Athenian men kept company with him and learned something from his company. Because the city executed him, it also seems safe to conclude from all the existing accounts that Socrates made powerful enemies. Finally, all three authors depict him debating the meanings of words with sharp logic; and he either challenges conventional morality or gives the appearance of doing so.

What else is needed to make Socrates a Sophist? Xenophon and Plato both depict him as magnetic in private conversation, skilled at reducing his interlocutors to silence. All three portrayals give him a facility at speech that other people lack. And like the Sophists he mainly talks about questions of value: how to live, what you can know and say about the good life, and how an individual's good life fits or fails to fit with the larger concerns of a community. If Socrates spoke with such uncanny effectiveness on ethical matters, and if (as he admits at his trial) the young men of rich families picked up argumentative techniques from him, then Aristophanes would appear to have some truth on his side. But Xenophon and Plato try to show the distance between Socrates and the dangerous new ideas that the Sophists brought to Athens.

For Xenophon the difference mainly consists in Socrates' moral incorruptibility. No relativism to worry about when Socrates so absorbs the values of the Athenian gentleman. Plato adds an epistemic difference to this ethical one. To put the point generally, he has Socrates pursuing knowledge while Sophists aim at no more than persuasion. Of course Socrates wants to persuade others when he speaks, as much as everyone else does; but Plato says he seeks to persuade those he is speaking to of what he believes to be true.

The Sophists seek to persuade regardless of the truth. They may be opportunists in this respect or nihilists. The opportunistic Sophist persuades not caring whether the view in question is true, while for the nihilist or relativist there is no fact of the matter about its truth. For this type of Sophist – Gorgias and Protagoras were famous examples – persuasion does not triumph over truth but reigns in the absence of truth.

Some of Plato's dialogues directly take on the difference between philosophy's commitment to knowledge about value, virtue, and happiness, and Sophistry's relativistic attitude that values and virtues rest on no more than appearance and cultural propaganda. In Book 1 of the *Republic*, the rhetorician and Sophist Thrasymachus will represent a specially aggressive variety of that attitude, sometimes sounding like an opportunist or cynic and sometimes like a nihilist.

Plato also distinguishes Socratic philosophy from Sophistry on the basis of differences in their practices and methods. Where the Sophists identify themselves as experts in a position to teach what they know (in exchange for sizeable fees), Socrates claims not to know anything and therefore not to be able to teach. He never charges money to those who keep company with him. If the paradigmatic mode of speaking for Sophists is rhetoric, his is dialectic. They shape prose as no Greek had done before them, and the wizardry and the emotional appeal of their language carries the day. Socrates seeks arguments that logically support conclusions; often the goal of his argumentation is a philosophical definition that would display the exact meaning of a word, the kind of word that people tend to use inexactly. Much of the *Republic* for instance will set itself to pursuing the Socratic definition of *dikaiosunê* 'justice.'

In a way, then, Socrates and the Sophists both attach themselves to what the *Phaedrus* calls 'the disputable terms' that express values: good, beautiful, fair, just, wise, brave. But where the Sophists take advantage of those words' slippery meanings and emotive associations, Socrates tries to pin down the meanings and damp the associations. The Sophists sail over the waters of ambiguity; he drains them.

Plato sometimes has Socrates contrast his method with that of the Sophists by saying he does not seek victory, only knowledge.

First-time readers might feel skeptical. This sounds a little like someone punching you while saying this is only to test your reflexes. Even if it does test the reflexes it is still a pounding, and Socrates still metes out defeat even if he mainly wants to test the truth of a definition. Nevertheless the Socratic one-on-one points to another difference from the Sophists that is related to the search for the truth. Sophists play to a crowd, but Socrates works privately. As Plato depicts them the Sophists are on show, writing or declaiming before crowds. Even when a Sophist is exercising the 'eristic' method of demolishing what someone else said, he does so with an audience. (See *Euthydemus*.) Sophists are paid professionals always seeking new students and broad reputations. Socrates works with the set of beliefs held by the specific interlocutor he is examining. There may be no one else present, as in the *Euthyphro* and *Crito*, or one or two people, but even when he has many witnesses (*Protagoras, Symposium*) Socrates relies on the same criterion of argumentative success, namely agreement from his interlocutors, which he sometimes equates with the interlocutors' agreement with themselves. Never mind public opinion, Socrates says in private conversations with his friends, as we will also find him saying in the *Republic* as he recommends startling new ways to run a city.

In Plato's account of the trial that ended Socrates' life, Socrates tells the jury that he has avoided politics in all his years as an Athenian, playing almost no part in this democracy that offered hundreds of participatory roles to its citizens. This seems to have been the case, for Thucydides recounts Athenian history with close attention to everyone in town who mattered, down to Socrates' fifty-ninth year, and never mentions him. Private living had at least one very concrete consequence, if Plato's *Apology* represents the trial's dynamics correctly. For Socrates, who was renowned for demolishing every claim an individual said to him in conversation, is powerless when addressing a jury. Rather than abashing them he rouses them to anger: he has to keep telling them not to shout at him. The jury votes to convict, and Socrates' speech after the vote antagonizes them so much that even some who had voted for acquittal turn around and vote to execute him. Socratic dialectic is not suited to large publics.

The private nature of Socratic philosophizing produces a paradox at the heart of the *Republic*, that it sets about the work of founding a city in a conversation conducted mainly by three men talking among themselves in a private home, sometimes proposing actions that they agree should not be voiced in public. Private agreement suffices to define the structure of this new public entity. Plato might say that this is all philosophical inquiry is capable of doing. Nevertheless this way of proceeding leaves political philosophy a long way from politics and from the very large public served, or dis-served, by politics as usual.

## NATURAL PHILOSOPHY

One element in the intellectual environment mattered to specialists rather than to Athens as a whole. Everyone in Athens lived with its democracy, and most Athenians seem to have known something about Sophists. But the natural philosophy of preceding centuries only occasionally filtered into the public consciousness, even though Plato and his contemporaries felt the need to respond to these predecessors in their own philosophies.

For more than a century before Plato's birth some Greeks had debated the material nature of the universe. Today these nature theorists are known as 'pre-Socratics.' It goes without saying that they could not have understood such a label any more than they could have numbered their years 'BC.' Nevertheless this name 'pre-Socratic' refers to a feature of their thinking that will inform their significance to Plato. For what unites the philosophers of this time is their interest in nature and the universe, subjects that Socrates barely said a word about. They lived long before the disciplinary distinctions that prompt moderns to call this work 'science' and that one 'philosophy,' and many of their hypotheses mark the emergence of natural science as much as they do the start of metaphysical thinking.

Plato does not pay much attention to the first cosmological philosophers, the Milesians or materialists Thales, Anaximander, and Anaximenes, each of whom posited a single element constituting all natural objects. 'All is water,' Thales said, and the intellectual ambition of this pronouncement, turning away from myth and revelation to rational human inquiry, informed much subsequent thinking. But Plato took more inspiration from a philosopher almost as early as the materialists, namely Heraclitus, who described the universe as ceaselessly fluctuating. Things not only changed, according to Heraclitus, they changed into their opposites. What is hot cools; the living die; and from a larger perspective Heraclitus says that such radical changes into contrary states are possible because all things already possess contrary qualities even when not changing. Sea water is undrinkable and a cause of death *and* is life-giving refreshment, depending on whether you are human or halibut. Certain passages in the *Republic* rely on Heraclitus' characterization of the contradictoriness and flux in nature – but with at least one remarkable distinction between the two thinkers, that Heraclitus finds the secret to the natural order in the rhythm of its fluctuations while Plato understands nature's changeability as a problem in need of a solution.

Two other philosophers showed Plato a way out of the Heraclitean predicament. The major figure is Parmenides, in many historians' opinion the most influential of the pre-Socratics. Parmenides found the concept of change incoherent. The *ôn* 'being' he described as an alternative to 'becoming' was a changeless and nearly featureless object. Just as important, this object, understood by the reasoning mind, stood apart from the objects that human beings' senses told them about. He came to his conclusions about being through a logically valid argument – necessary truth he called 'the bonds of justice.' Thus Parmenides introduced two ideas into philosophy: eternal objects, and the quest for a nonempirical method by which one learns about them.

Philosophers after Parmenides worked within the strictures imposed by his arguments. And to some degree Plato responded to Parmenidean thinkers, such as Zeno and Melissus, as well as to the later materialist and atomist thinkers (Anaxagoras, Democritus) whose thinking reflects the influence of Parmenides. But Plato was probably more affected by the last philosopher to be mentioned here, the legendary Pythagoras. He was a shadowy figure even by the standards of these first philosophers, whose work exists only as occasional quotes and anecdotes. Did Pythagoras himself invent the doctrines of Pythagoreanism? Prove the theorem that bears his name? Discover the ratios that produce musical harmonies? Impossible to say.

The founder aside, Pythagoreanism as a school did promote certain beliefs; what is even more certain is that Plato *believed* certain doctrines to be Pythagorean ones and often argued in favor of such doctrines (this aside from whether or not they really came from Pythagoras and his followers). Numerous dialogues, including the *Republic*, defend some version of reincarnation, which was seen as a Pythagorean belief. More pervasive in Plato's thought, though less visible, is the Pythagorean belief in number as the ordering principle of the universe. The world's order was an order of rational numbers and could be apprehended by rational humans.

The Pythagorean world should not be confused with the much simpler world that Parmenides describes. But both conceptions of the universe helped Plato find coherence in nature, even a coherence that would provide some order to human lives: a *moral* coherence.

This last idea returns to the business of Socrates and his relation to the pre-Socratics. Already in the ancient world Socrates was seen to mark a decisive move away from the Milesians and the cosmological thinkers who followed them. He 'brought philosophy down to earth,' it was said, renouncing speculations about the metaphysical structure of the universe in favor of inquiries that centered on human beings and the virtues they ought to pursue. Most of the old philosophy did not matter to Socrates. It *couldn't* matter, because philosophy found its value for him in discovering the essence of human virtue, and philosophers before him had omitted the human (and the virtuous) from their theories. Shortly before dying – or so Plato tells the story in the *Phaedo* – Socrates says he had read Anaxagoras, only to find his great hopes dashed. What he found in the book was a philosophical system that explained everything mechanistically and materially. Despite a nominal mention of *nous* 'mind,' Anaxagoras did not let reason and its pursuit of the good figure into his theory of the world. This theory of everything did not account for human values, according to Socrates, who may have concluded that none of the other cosmologies did either.

In this respect looking back at Socrates as a philosopher requires that we classify the ones before him as 'pre-Socratic,' because he set an agenda for philosophy that departed from that of philosophers before him. Philosophy was pre-Socratic by virtue of its cosmological concerns; Socratic philosophy gave up cosmology for virtue.

From another perspective, the Sophists had created the context in which thinkers made human issues their area of specialization, and as their opponent Socrates proposed treating those issues with the philosopher's rigor and argumentation.

Plato shares Socrates' allegiance to a predominating moral concern in philosophy. His dialogues rarely ignore moral issues even when they emphasize a metaphysical or epistemological question. But Plato incorporates certain pre-Socratic figures into his works in order to keep the moral discussions from taking place in a vacuum. Plato becomes the first systematic philosopher by dint of his attempt to use theories of nature as a foundation for his theory of human existence. Because the universe operates as he thinks it does, it assures him and his readers that the virtues Socrates spent his life examining were no merely human concoctions, not 'socially constructed' as today's buzzword would have it, but reflected an order independent of human social existence.

## THE LIFE OF PLATO

### PLATO IN THE ATHENIAN DEMOCRACY

Given his gigantic status in world history, it might seem perverse to read Plato's life as a series of frustrations; but there were frustrations in his life, and they did shape him.

For one thing Plato was born too late to enjoy the greatest glories of his home city. He watched the city misgovern itself, in his opinion, by clinging to an unworkable democratic tradition. Legend adds a blocked career: Plato supposedly planned to write tragedies, until he met Socrates and gave up poetry for philosophy. In any case he had to give Socrates up soon enough, when Athens executed him. And later, according to some sources, Plato tried to put his political thinking to work by turning one dictator into a philosopher – but he had to give up political practice when that attempt fell through and he barely escaped with his life, and he resigned himself to living on the grounds of the school he founded, neither in Athens nor free of it; not quite a playwright, but something resembling one; not exactly engaged in politics but certainly enmeshed in one new form of political planning.

But some of these events are historically uncertain, and the rest deserve more than a summary phrase. Take Plato's birth in 427, soon after the beginning of the Peloponnesian War. The fact that Athens had gone to war against Sparta did not make the average Athenian believe that now the good times were over, but morale in the city would have changed by the time Plato was a little boy. Pericles had died a few years before his birth, and that death shook the city; what's more, Pericles died during one of the outbreaks of plague that struck Athens between 430 and just about the days of Plato's birth. Whether or not Athenians saw this plague as an omen, it carried away a good portion of their population. And now the war was on, yearly carrying more away.

Picture Plato at thirteen or fourteen, when the news came back to Athens about the disastrous outcome of the Sicilian Expedition; or a couple of years later, during the failed coup that many oligarchs watched with sympathy, and with hope that the city's property holders would negotiate a peace; or Plato in his early twenties when Athens surrendered to Sparta. It would have seemed to him that the entire history of Athens he had witnessed was a progression from bad to worse. Plato would have reached adulthood already wishing for some better political arrangement than Athens had known thus far.

About this time Plato began to join the company of other young aristocrats who associated with Socrates in the streets of Athens, in its central marketplace, and at the gymnasia where the men of Athens exercised. A fairly reliable source tells us that Plato was an able wrestler, even participating in the Isthmian games, which were one of the four most prestigious athletic events in ancient Greece (the Olympics being the foremost of the four). He might have met Socrates at one of the gymnasia around Athens; anyway his uncle Charmides and his mother's cousin Critias were already among Socrates' friends. How closely Plato was drawn into the circle is impossible to say. Even by the less formal standards of the day Socrates was no obvious sort of teacher – nor did he claim to be one – and Plato was no obvious sort of student. Socrates seems to have captured Plato's imagination first as the originator of a kind of philosophical question, and secondly as a symbol of the questing philosopher, who follows an investigation wherever it may lead.

Later writers did embellish the few known facts about the relationship between Plato and Socrates, as with the tale of Plato's youthful ambition to write tragedies. According to the story, he showed his poems to Socrates, who quizzed him about this or that word, until Plato went home and burned everything he had written. No poetry came out of him again.

The story has very little credibility, but everyone repeats it, probably because it would account for some things about Plato: his literary skill, which does not require but is consistent with a talent blocked from finding expression in one domain, and flourishing in another; his antipathy toward tragedy, now seen as the pleasure that Plato had had to forbid himself and went on to deny to others. If anything the story fits too neatly, and its convenient explanation of Plato's writing is a reason to reject it as historical truth.

More usefully, the story reminds us that Socrates was known for his questioning more than for anything else. It was probably the questing philosopher that Athenians first wearied of: Socrates' constant cross-examinations looked like moral skepticism to them. And if the fear of moral skepticism begins in the concern that someone who questions traditional values is capable of anything, the associates of Socrates would have validated that concern. For years Alcibiades had been the great hope for the future, until he talked the city into the Sicilian Expedition; in subsequent years he betrayed Athens more than once. Critias and Charmides orchestrated the regime of the Thirty Tyrants as if they had been spending their time with Socrates learning to hate democracy. The Athenians convicted Socrates of corrupting the youth and introducing new gods into the city, but Plato pretty clearly thinks that those charges masked the real issue, that Socrates challenged the legitimacy of democracy.

## PLATO'S LIFE AFTER SOCRATES

Plato lived to be eighty or eighty-one. He left Athens for about a decade after the death of Socrates, probably because of his own connections with the democracy's enemies. When he returned he bought land near the gymnasium called the Academy; the school he founded there went by the same name. Plato lived there and oversaw the school until his death in 347.

During this time Greece experienced no upheaval of the magnitude of the Peloponnesian War. After Plato's death King Philip of Macedon, a power to the north, would conquer most of Greece and end the era of the autonomous city-states; his son Alexander the Great would spread Greek civilization to the east; but no contemporary of Plato's foresaw those developments.

For thoughtful Athenians of this time, their task was to make sense of the changes they had seen in Athens and in Greece at large. It was an open question how much longer the *polis* would still work. (This word *polis* literally means 'city,' but for the Greeks it designated a self-sufficient political unit, hence is often described as a 'city-state.') Athens had wasted its power fighting Sparta. In 371 Sparta lost an astonishing battle to Thebes. If mighty Sparta could lose, no *polis* was invincible. Should the new alliances among cities grow into pan-Hellenic governments? How much autonomy could each city be expected to give up? And by now Persia had reinsinuated itself into Greek politics, winning a hegemonic control through foreign aid and shrewd diplomacy that it had not been able to achieve with open warfare.

Plato and his fellow members of the Academy participated in Greek discussions about the possibilities for local politics. It is said that the Academy sometimes functioned as a group of political consultants, with members traveling to other cities to rewrite their constitutions. This would have been seen as a fitting activity for political philosophers, for city planners had long been seen as popular heroes. Sparta attributed its constitution to the legendary Lycurgus; Athens had Draco and Solon. Legend aside, Aristotle (*Politics* II.7) tells us of Hippodamus of Miletus, who invented city planning, and who in particular planned the Athenian port of Piraeus. Hippodamus was, according to Aristotle's testimony, a kind of philosopher, being the first nonpolitician to inquire into forms of government.

If a political theorist before Plato had applied himself to the details of city planning, then the Academy's constitutional consultants must have belonged to a recognized tradition. We ought to read the *Republic*'s plan for a new city against the background of that tradition, not as a lone thinker's dream about some impossibly perfect regime, but one contribution among many to a living debate over the future of Greek society.

During this second half of his life that he spent at the Academy, Plato may have left Athens for trips to Sicily, to the Greek city of Syracuse on that island. The available information about these trips comes from the *Seventh Letter*, an unreliable document. (Plato wrote the letter, if it is genuine, to parties involved in Syracusan politics who worried that Plato had played an inappropriate role in the events in question. So even if he did write it, we should read it with caution.) If the account is true, Plato visited Syracuse three times. The first time Dionysius the Elder was tyrant of the city; Plato met the tyrant's brother-in-law Dion, with whom he established an enduring friendship. When Dionysius died and his son, Dionysius the Younger, succeeded him, Dion wrote asking Plato to come again. Dion hoped that philosophers might influence the young and impressionable ruler at the helm of Syracuse into establishing an ideal city. Plato's grand theories of politics and the best city could become reality.

Instead the young tyrant grew hostile and exiled Dion, and Plato fled back to Athens. A year later Dionysius wrote to Plato claiming to have had a change of heart; but although Plato went a third time to Syracuse, Dionysius remained unconverted, had Dion assassinated, and left Plato's sole experiment in establishing his city an undignified failure.

If anything like this misadventure did take place it could help to explain how Plato's politics changed after the *Republic*. The *Laws*, his last work, arrives at a best possible constitution by adapting the constitutions of good regimes that already existed. It does not try as the *Republic* does to wipe the slate clean, and to invent a city out of theoretical truths about knowledge and human nature.

## PLATONIC DIALOGUE

The reader first coming to Plato should not feel obtuse when confronting the dialogues' frequent inconclusiveness, occasional vagueness, and the regular hints that there are other subjects at stake, or other arguments the speakers might go into. Plato has long enjoyed a reputation for elusiveness. His dialogues become clearer after repeated readings, and historical information illuminates some unclear passages. But the dialogues' differences from one another and their self-conscious form leave even experienced readers tentative, at certain points, about what Plato is really saying. Attractive as they are to the new reader, the dialogues call for advance preparation.

## THE DIALOGUE FORM

That story of Plato and Socrates and burning the poems may be pure invention, but it acknowledges certain characteristics of Platonic dialogues: their skilful presentations of character, and the subtle connections they draw between people's lives and the abstract theories those people espouse. The language remains grounded in ordinary speech, but it is ordinary speech made elegant and elastic. The conversations sometimes circle back to a single question, each reappearance of the question deepened by the preceding discussion. More often the participants veer off into the tangents familiar to everyday conversation, except that in these dialogues, unlike real conversations, the tangent has a way of returning to the originating question.

Given the Platonic dialogues' prosaic settings – a courtyard, a wrestling room, a walk around town – and the characters drawn from daily life, the effect is one of bringing intellectual conversations up to the artistic level of high drama.

Though all the dialogues purport to record conversations, they vary in dramatic structure. Some are highly developed dramas, while in others the main speaker is essentially lecturing, with only perfunctory interruptions. Some dialogues present only their characters' words; in others, one character narrates the entire conversation. Still others mix the two forms by enclosing the narrative in a dramatic frame. Socrates occupies pride of place in the dialogues, but in several – *Timaeus, Sophist, Statesman* – he yields the floor to another philosopher; he does not appear at all in the *Laws*. We will see him dominating the *Republic*, which like only two other dialogues is entirely a narration by Socrates; the effect is of an almost confessional immediacy, Socrates in a candid moment of a kind that rarely occurs in Plato.

The dialogues may also be classified according to whether scholars believe that Plato wrote them early or late in his life. Some have traditionally been called Plato's 'early' or 'Socratic' dialogues; others, work of his 'early middle' period; and dialogues like the *Republic*, 'middle' works. For the most part whatever comes later than the *Republic* is deemed 'late'; those late works have a recognizable abstractness, and less literary charm than the average Platonic dialogue, but still a magnificence that sets them apart.

In recent decades many scholars have attacked the general view of the dialogues, the 'developmentalist' view, that underwrites these categorizations. The debate has not been settled yet, but even if the antidevelopmentalists do not prevail readers should not accept the developmentalist position as simple and proven fact. Developmentalism regarding the dialogues asserts that (1) Plato wrote different types of dialogues at different times; (2) linguistic and other features permit us to identify the order in which he wrote his works; (3) both Plato's philosophical doctrines and his authorial methods proceeded through clear stages; (4) the early dialogues are short, inconclusive, and historically accurate about Socrates; while (5) later dialogues from the middle of Plato's writing life depict a Socrates who has transmuted into Plato's mouthpiece, arguing for positive doctrines about Forms, the soul, and the afterlife, with a more tractable, less vividly presented inter-locutor. This is a useful way to group and approach the dialogues, certainly the best way to come at them as a new reader, as long as you do not think it is possible to map every Platonic thought somewhere on the chronology of his life.

## LITERARY ANTECEDENTS

As a writer Plato responded to the new literacy in Athenian life, which is to say not a new acquisition of written language but a general *practice* of reading. The Greeks had had a phonetic alphabet for centuries already, and widespread adult competency at basic reading and writing, but what we may call literary culture had only come into existence shortly before Plato's time. The new practice involved longer, substantive texts that were designed to be read (as opposed to scripts designed to be performed, or records to be stored in archives); it involved copying such works so that one could permanently own a play or book; and reading the works one owned, alone and carefully.

In this new culture of more elaborate writing, several new genres of writing came into existence, of which at least three informed Plato's own decisions about how to write: *tragedy*, *comedy*, and *history*.

## TRAGEDY

Tragedy is the place to begin comparing other written forms to Plato's dialogues, because there is no other form he attacks in the same way. The *Republic* contains Plato's most caustic treatments of poetry and throughout those arguments his main target is tragedy, as if he were going after a rival.

The dialogues provide ample evidence for Plato's consciousness of drama, and consciousness of his status as a dramatist. He frequently has his characters describe the conversations they find themselves in with vocabulary drawn from the stage. To mention only examples from the *Republic*, we have Socrates saying, 'I choose [virtue and vice] like choruses' (580b), calling his account of women's place in the city 'the female drama' (451c), and generally using the words 'chorus' (490c, 560e), 'tragic' (413b, 545e), and 'tragic gear' (i.e. costume: 577b) to characterize the world of which his dialogue speaks.

But we don't need a story about Plato's teenage crisis over careers to understand why he resists tragedy. In Plato's Athens, tragic drama is the prime example of legal and moral reasoning. The *Iliad* and *Odyssey* in all their grandeur remain at a remove from the morality that fifth- and fourth-century Athenians recognize as such; in Athenian tragedy the kings and heroes from archaic myth are brought within the reach of fifth-century legal concepts and anachronistically subjected to fifth-century scrutiny. In other words, tragedy presupposes the moral vocabulary of its own times, and by doing so it engages its audience not in historical thinking ('What would Oedipus have done in those heroic times he belonged to?') but in live moral reasoning ('How would we judge Oedipus today?').

Together with the moral content of tragedy its back-and-forth argumentation, *stichomythia*, let it play the role of moral instructor. During those sections of tragedies in which each character speaks a single line and is answered by another line, the goal is normally persuasion. Characters appeal to general principles (political legitimacy, family obligations) and they cite relevant facts (you killed him; I tried not to). In Aristophanes' *Frogs* the playwright Euripides is made to say that he taught Athenians how to speak. Plato wants people to follow a different model, something more like his own dialogues. Plato may not have invented the dialogue form – Xenophon wrote his own Socratic conversations, and we know that other friends of Socrates also did – but he seems to harbor more ambitions for the dialogues than his predecessors did.

Pitting philosophical dialogues against tragedies does not mean Plato thought his works would be mistaken for tragedies. The characters in the dialogues speak in prose, not verse. The 'plot' involves the motions of ideas: people sit or stand for hours and talk. Dialectic is their action, not the killings and acts of war that occur in Greek tragedy. But Plato's reader should not misunderstand this statelier tempo as an authorial failing, as if Plato aimed at producing a ripping yarn and managed no better than careful logical analysis. Rather Plato wants to retain the exchanges that give tragic drama its vibrancy and its preoccupation with moral matters, but to jettison the fevered emotions of tragedy, the deceptive pleasures of its verse, and all the distracting incident that stops tragedy from really examining major moral principles.

## COMEDY

It is not enough to locate Plato's dialogues in the context of Athenian tragedy, because certain features of the dialogues are too different from any counterpart in tragedy.

Not every tragedy concludes with an 'unhappy ending,' but declines in fortune are common. Plato's dialogues rarely suggest any misfortune or move to unhappiness. More often the participants agree that they have reached their desired conclusion of understanding what they set out to study. In those dialogues that end without conclusions but rather in *aporia* 'perplexity,' Socrates' good cheer about this outcome suggests that even this chaos of ignorance does not have to be a bad thing.

Second, tragedy is the drama of kings and queens and magnificent heroes. Plato's dialogues take place in ordinary settings. Sometimes Socrates talks to a prominent Athenian but not to anything like a king or hero. The high standing of tragedy's characters means that their misjudgment and misfortune constitute misfortune for their entire community; Plato's people, however publicly they live, philosophize within the dialogues as private individuals. (This difference of course flows from one of the differences between Socrates and the Sophists.)

Another point of contrast is harder to pin down but unmistakable. Tragedies stay focused on their main story, or on a pair of main stories. Greek tragedy will lose its effect of inexorability if it digresses. In Plato's dialogues, one conversation about teaching virtue evolves into a geometrical proof. Another one stops to interpret a poem before assessing hedonism. The *Republic*, just before concluding its overarching argument about kinds of unjust cities, veers off to spend one-third of its length detailing the political features of the good city. In general the dialogues tend not to go where they were heading. Like their language, which is artistically supple but always rooted in the rhythms of spoken prose, they simulate human conversation, even if that is human conversation made sublime and brainy.

These differences between Platonic dialogue and tragedy leave it looking closer to comedy. Athenian comedy is not as well mapped out as tragedy, a genre whose more than thirty surviving examples by three undisputed masters let one say what tragedy does and does not do. Eleven comedies do exist intact from the time of Socrates, but they were all written by a single person, Aristophanes, and students of 'Old Comedy' (as the genre is known) are wary lest what they take for a feature of the genre is really only a feature of Aristophanes. If the distant future's art historians had to define twentieth-century painting on the basis of a dozen of Picasso's works and nothing else, they could reconstruct some major movements and concerns, but Picasso's particularity would stand in their way.

Plato seems similar to Aristophanes in the unplotted movement of his dialogues, always ready to take new turns. To modern readers the typical play by Aristophanes looks incoherent at first, even if close study reveals a sly pattern. His plots appear improvised, with an aside in one scene inspiring the scene that follows, not unlike the movement in Plato's dialogues into what can appear to be conversational digressions – even if, again, closer study shows how little in the dialogues is accidental.

There is no denying the difference in manner between Plato's courtly restraint and the absurdist, obscene plays of Aristophanes. Nor could anyone familiar with Plato's *Apology* forget that Socrates blames Aristophanes, as he blames no other individual, for the nasty wrong impression of him that Athenians have formed. What Athenians thought they knew about Socrates they had learned from *Clouds*. Aristophanes slandered Socrates, and the slander inclined the jurors to consider Socrates a dangerous modern thinker before even hearing the formal legal charges.

And yet it is said that Plato admired Aristophanes. More than one ancient anecdote testifies to his fondness for Aristophanic comedy, and Plato makes Aristophanes a character in the *Symposium*. In that dialogue Plato gives Aristophanes an insightful speech about love to deliver, something wiser and truer than any other speech at the dinner except for Socrates' own.

And no discussion of the *Republic* could fail to mention Aristophanes' *Ecclesiazusae*, or *Women in the Assembly*. In this comedy, which Aristophanes staged before Plato wrote the *Republic*, the women of Athens implement a revolutionary new constitution reminiscent of *Republic* Book 5. Women have as much power as men, citizens pool their property and dine together, and even lawsuits disappear. It looks astonishingly as though a comedy by Aristophanes inspired Plato in writing the most radical sections of the *Republic*.

Speaking formally, the most important legacy of Old Comedy for the Platonic dialogue might be the section of a play called its *agôn* 'competition.' Located around the middle of most comedies, this scene pits two figures against one another in a heated debate.

The *Clouds* contains a famous example, with Right Speech and Wrong Speech arguing the relative merits of (respectively) the traditional values that Athenians still remembered, and the freethinking and license now sweeping the city.

Whereas scenes of disagreement can occur anywhere in tragedy, the *agôn* was confined to one part of a comedy. But despite the real moral argumentation that takes place in tragic *stichomythia*, the characters seem to be giving vent to their own views more than they reach a conclusion. The comic *agôn* has a winner. Modern readers sometimes find the passages in a comedy that come after the dispute to have gone slack, because the *agôn* determines the winner of the play's action. Nothing that follows affects that victory. It is a different model of debate from tragic dialogue, in some ways closer to what Plato's characters do.

The *Republic* also feels close to comedy's progress toward rebirth out of the death that has thus far been human social existence. If the eleven surviving examples are any kind of fair sample, the comedy of Aristophanes tells stories of death and regeneration, often with particular attention to making sick or perverted human desires healthy again. Death and deathly states are evoked in language and settings of imprisonment, typically in a cave or other underground place. The comedy's progress takes its protagonist from that enclosure in the earth to a new life outside it.

Of all Plato's dialogues, the *Republic* best illustrates the last of these themes. No interpreter of the dialogue can ignore its metaphors of death and rebirth, especially birth out of a cave or some other underground place. The noble lie (414d–e), the allegory of the cave (esp. 514a, 516a, 516d), and the closing myth of reincarnation (esp. 614d) are obvious examples of this narrative and metaphorical structure.

## HISTORY

The earliest extant Greek history is the work by Herodotus that he titled *Historiai* 'Inquiries.' *Histories* was probably finished a decade or two before Plato's birth. Plato knew something about the book, whose opening sentence he quotes almost verbatim in the *Timaeus*, but he probably spent more time reading Thucydides than Herodotus. Herodotus may have visited Athens but Thucydides was himself an Athenian, having even served as a general. His *History of the Peloponnesian War* appeared when Plato was a young adult, making it temporally as well as spatially closer to home.

The *Republic* alludes to Herodotus at least twice. In Book 2 Plato has Glaucon tell a story about a man named Gyges, the naked body he sees at a crucial moment, and the subsequent train of events that leads to his seizing the throne. Herodotus' *Histories* begins (1.8–12) with someone named Gyges, too. That is a different story, but again Gyges sees a naked body at a crucial moment and again the events that follow end with his overthrowing the king.

More philosophically, Herodotus (3.80–82) depicts three Persian nobles debating how to govern their empire: as democracy, oligarchy, or monarchy? Should the many rule, or the few, or only one? It is hard to believe that the Persians would have entertained any alternative to one-man rule; but considering the *Republic*'s attention to the same question in Books 8 and 9 it is not hard to picture Plato reading this passage and deciding to take the question up in his own writing.

The discussion of constitutions in Herodotus is anomalous, however, and what makes it anomalous is also what suggests that Plato would have taken Thucydides for his model more than Herodotus. The two historians differ in numerous ways. Herodotus ranges over the known world, recounting memorable anecdotes in a straightforward brand of Greek. Thucydides keeps his focus on Athens and its war against Sparta, using knotty, difficult language to describe the complex political and military events that led this war to turn out as it did. But there is also the difference that Herodotus does not spend much time depicting people engaged in debate. The people in his history act more than they talk, and when they talk it is rarely as the three Persians do, each defending a position. When philosophers appear they are more likely to change the path of a river than to spell out a reasoned argument.

Thucydides on the other hand stocks his *History* with debates. Everyone important to his story speaks, and almost everyone who does speak is answered by someone else with counterarguments. Should Athens support Corcyra or Corinth? Should they kill the people of Mitylene? Thucydides develops both sides of the debate and largely avoids authorial comment, not because he has no opinion about the two sides' relative merits but so that his reader will not rush to agree with the author but rather has to think through what is true and valuable in each side's argument.

The people in Thucydides speak at length – opposite extremes to the tragic characters who condense an argument into a dozen syllables. The historical characters do not always analyze one another's arguments and never cross-examine. Still there is a sober development of arguments here that must have inspired Plato. Imagine letting the conversation go on as long as it needed to, not racing as dramas do (and speeches in court) but leisurely on the page, waiting for an elite of educated readers.

Plato has very few incidents to portray, none with the magnitude of the Peloponnesian War; and the debates that he depicts are rarely the kind that will issue in action. But that may be all to the good. When the situation calls on people to act and the actions will be momentous, it is hard to free one's deliberations from bias and self-interest. Let philosophy portray a different kind of debate, one in which no emergency threatens and the participants can move from concrete practical questions to the most theoretical kind, not ending when everyone has spoken once or twice but just beginning then, when the speakers have time to review one another's opinions and their own most warmly held beliefs.

## THE *REPUBLIC*

Probably more people alive have read the *Republic* than any other single work of philosophy. It is the earliest surviving systematic utopia in Europe's history. It also contains the first theory of psychology, the first examination of the origins of government, the first proposals for educational reform, and the first theoretical aesthetics.

But leave aside the 'firsts,' because that praise can apply to fumbling efforts, like the credit we grant to Hero of Alexandria for producing a whirling toy that we now call the first steam engine. Apart from any isolated insight or hypothesis, Plato retains his importance and his broad appeal first because of his thorough mistrust for the world of appearance, and second for his efforts, notwithstanding that mistrust, to show how the world that he called real could affect the merely apparent one.

The mistrust of appearance produces Plato the dualist, who constructed intelligible Forms as metaphysical compensation for the chaos of visible things. The effort to bridge the gap between these Forms and things gives us Plato the systematic philosopher, whose dialogues interweave questions of *value* – the definitions of moral terms, outlines of moral theories, political recommendations – with questions about greater and lesser reality and the methodology of human knowledge. The works for which Plato is best known express his vision that dispassionate inquiry into the nature of reality will ultimately inform a human life. We may say that his greatest importance to the history of philosophy (for better or worse) followed from his tireless effort to bring not just philosophical thinking but out-and-out metaphysics into human existence.

The *Republic* is a classic Platonic dialogue in that it contains the fullest expositions of the doctrines traditionally associated with Plato's name: the theory of Forms, the division of the soul, the condemnation of poetry, and of course the recommendations for political change. And it brings Platonic ethical and metaphysical issues together into one argument more completely than any other dialogue does.

## CHARACTERS AND SETTING

In many respects the *Republic* does not reward a literary reading as much as some of the other dialogues do. Almost all its characterizations and historical allusions come in Book 1, and then practically disappear. So the information here scarcely applies to Books 2–10, whose characters are only Socrates, Glaucon, and Glaucon's brother Adeimantus.

Regarding the setting, scholars have argued for various dramatic dates, the date when the conversation reported in the *Republic* allegedly took place. This date naturally comes before the date of composition, but otherwise is not related to it. The *Republic* was written sometime between 380 and 360; evidence for this date is much more speculative than evidence for the dramatic date.

When did the conversation take place, then? The proposals for the dramatic date range from an earliest possibility of 424 BC to the late extreme of 409, but the two years most frequently argued for are 411 or 410 on one hand, 422 or 421 on the other. The dialogue makes clear that it is summer, with Athens evidently not engaged in fighting. There is a festival in honor of the goddess Bendis (237a, 254a), to all appearances the first Bendis festival ever held in Athens, though it has been argued that the event could have been a revival or larger version of an earlier first festival. Book 2 mentions a recent battle at Megara (368a). This evidence is consistent with both dates, although if the Bendis festival is supposed to be newly inaugurated the earlier date is more likely, say 421; and because the old man Cephalus probably died around 415, 421 is again more likely than 411 unless Plato is guilty of accidental or intentional anachronism.

The summer of 411 would have been a gloomy time in Athens, with the Sicilian Expedition a recent catastrophe; in June of that summer a group of propertied men engineered a coup and tried to install an oligarchy in Athens. Socrates would be fifty-eight years old and probably becoming known as the friend of democracy's enemies.

The more likely suggestion of 421 implies a different atmosphere. Instead of feverishly debating forms of government because Athens is being rocked by constitutional revolutions, the men are considering this problem in the abstract, while living in a stable and thriving democracy. Socrates is forty-eight, having only recently become notorious to Athenians after the performance of *Clouds* two years before, and probably not known for any views or friendships. Athens has less to worry about in 421: a truce is on, the longest interruption that the Peloponnesian War was to know. Athens still looks stronger than Sparta. The truce, called the Peace of Nicias, will last for six more years until Alcibiades and his friends convince Athenians to invade Sicily. The Peace of Nicias is far from perfect – Athens alone came close to outright violations of the truce several times during this period – but the imminent loss of culture, wealth, and constitution that would have haunted a conversation of 411 does not filter into this night's talk. This is an image of philosophy not as response to emergency, but as contemplation in peace and prosperity. Radical thinking goes on in both contexts, usually more freely in an emergency (when people will consider any proposal), though the peaceful, prosperous setting that was the more likely context encourages systematic thinking, the kind we actually find in the *Republic*.

In 421 Plato would have been a child, which means that even if some version of the *Republic*'s conversation actually took place, he could only have learned about it long after the fact. Even an unrealistic early date of composition, 380, puts the writing of the *Republic* more than forty years after its alleged occurrence; on more realistic estimates of when it was written, it becomes exceedingly likely that all the participants in the conversation are now dead.

This gap in time tells us, first of all, that the dialogue is fictional or has been fictionalized. Plato knows as he writes that the conversation of the *Republic* cannot help being overshadowed by our knowledge of what will happen to its characters. Socrates will be executed as a threat to democracy; but as if he had no sense of that danger, he cheerfully proposes a state run by committee, with no political participation for the majority of its citizens. At times his interlocutors warn him that the public will not take kindly to his ideas (e.g. 474a). These warnings let us know that this dialogue serves, as others do, as – among other things – a defense of Socrates.

Polemarchus, one of the first characters to speak in the *Republic*, will also be executed on political charges, as will Niceratus, who is present (327c) but says nothing. The Thirty Tyrants will kill those two and force Lysias (328b), Polemarchus' brother, into exile, when the Piraeus, where Polemarchus and Lysias live with their father Cephalus, becomes the center of democratic opposition.

Cephalus, a wealthy businessman, appears early in the *Republic* (388b), though he soon removes himself from the conversation. His conception of the good life centers around the comforts that his fortune have made possible; but we know, as Plato's original audience would have known, that when the Thirty Tyrants come to power they will seize the family fortune. Significantly, Cephalus and his children are noncitizens and non-Athenians. Resident foreigners in Athens enjoyed some legal protections, but they could not own property, and only rarely became citizens. As a result, Cephalus and Polemarchus describe the good human life without mentioning politics, even though we know as readers that politics will render their conceptions of the good life irrelevant.

We may provisionally conclude that Plato wants the *Republic* to open with apolitical discussions of ethical theory to show how limited those discussions are bound to be. Even the third active participant in Book 1, the rhetorician Thrasymachus, comes from Chalcedon. Although he speaks of rules for life by appeal to a city's rulers, his idea of politics has the cynical tone, the attention only to naked power, that comes of living in a political system over which one has no control.

Thrasymachus is known to moderns mostly through his part in Book 1. He and Callicles, from Plato's *Gorgias*, mount the most critical, most unsentimental, opposition to morality in all of Plato's works. Thrasymachus outdoes Callicles in rudeness: he insults Socrates (337a, 340d, 343a), argues belligerently, sulks when Socrates defeats him. And yet this wild nihilist's challenge to morality takes Socrates the remainder of the *Republic* to answer. The reason is that Thrasymachus understands more than he can defend in logical argument. He is after all a premier rhetorical stylist of his day, even if he is not a philosopher. Plato acknowledges his skill in the *Phaedrus* (267c); Aristophanes takes the trouble to burlesque his oratory; Aristotle credits him with the invention of polished prose rhythm (*Rhetoric* 1404a14). Behind Book 1's hot-tempered, arrogant, and glib rhetorician, we should try to glimpse a man whom Plato respected enough to form into Socrates' most difficult opponent. And all the rest of the way through the *Republic* we should bear in mind that Thrasymachus has stayed to listen to Socrates' reply; when he speaks up again in Book 5 (450a–b), it is to insist that Socrates say more about his political theories. With this interruption of the conversation Plato means to remind us that Thrasymachus is still present to hear and to test everything Socrates says.

For most of the *Republic* Socrates speaks to none of these men, but only to the brothers Glaucon and Adeimantus, who are also Plato's half-brothers. Adeimantus tends to represent pragmatic resistance to Socrates' claims, while Glaucon seems readier to follow Socrates through difficult arguments, and also readier to agree with him. But their personalities hardly emerge at all by comparison with those of Book 1. In this respect Books 2–10 belong with those later dialogues in which characters function as little more than names, whereas Book 1 harks back to the deft characterizations of the *Lysis*, *Protagoras*, and *Charmides*. What matters most about Plato's brothers becomes clear enough: they are morally upright and philosophically sincere, so that their argument against Socrates is posed as the work of devil's advocates.

## THE OPENING SENTENCE

It is worth pausing over the dialogue's first sentence, not because we need to read the whole *Republic* with the same pondering care, but because reading one sentence well can show that Plato's writing rewards the diligent reader:

> I went down to the Piraeus yesterday with Glaucon, son of Ariston, to pray to the goddess; and, at the same time, I wanted to observe how they would put on the festival, since they were now holding it for the first time.

> (327a)

'I went down' is a single word in Greek (*katebên*), the first word of the *Republic*. Socrates descends from the plane of his intellectual existence to explain his views. As the dialogue's opening action makes clear, the threat of force will haunt the participants' high-minded talk of an ideal city: when Polemarchus sees Socrates and Glaucon at the festival, he jokingly threatens that they must remain in town as his guests, since he has more men on his side (327c). Socrates will never persuade him otherwise, because 'we won't listen.' As the *Republic* imagines a perfect city, Socrates faces the problem of how such a city could ever come into existence in this imperfect world; that he comes down to talk about the city, instead of working out its details among trained and sympathetic philosophers, shows that Plato intends to face the issue directly.

'I went down' also looks ahead to the most widely known image in Plato's dialogues, the Allegory of the Cave in Book 7 (514a–517a). Ordinary human existence resembles the fate of prisoners shackled in a sunless cave, while the philosopher is like someone who has escaped from the cave up to the brightly lit surface. After finishing his story Socrates makes its applications explicit: the philosopher must be chosen from among other people, educated, then compelled to return and rule the rest. In this passage Socrates, in explaining the philosopher's chore, repeatedly uses the same verb for 'go down' or 'descend' that he used in the opening to the *Republic* to describe his own arrival at the scene of his discussions (516e, 519d, 520c).

Plato will justify his city the hard way, not by beginning in consensus and clarifying the theory, but by beginning amid radical disagreement and nevertheless finding common ground on which to build his argument.

The 'Piraeus' was destined to become the center of democratic forces in Athens. Again Plato makes his job as hard as possible, for Socrates will try to persuade this audience not only that a type of dictatorship is better than democracy, but that democracy in fact weighs in as the second worst of all political systems.

The Piraeus was also the port of Athens, and contained a different community from the rest of Athens. More than the usual number of itinerant merchants could be found there, and a high concentration of noncitizen aliens, and more than a few criminals. To the extent that political rule implies order, the greater chaos of the Piraeus will again suggest the disorder that threatens a malfunctioning regime.

To these well-known meanings of the Piraeus, I would add a fact that has already come up, that the Piraeus was laid out by Hippodamus, whom Aristotle considers the first to inquire into the nature of the best city. Plato is placing himself in the tradition of municipal reformers but also opposing himself to that tradition, as the first investigator to do the work properly. Thus we shall find him repeatedly digging deeper into the nature of the human soul, and into the nature of all moral value, to find the guiding principles for his political proposals. Anything less will amount only to politics as usual, patchwork reforms and opportunistic compromises.

'Yesterday' is all the *Republic* provides by way of a setting for its speaker. Socrates never indicates to whom he is recounting the previous night's conversation, and aside from this single 'yesterday' he seems to forget that he is addressing an audience at all. (Later in Book 1 he comments that 'it was summer' [350d], an odd thing to say about the preceding day.) The 'yesterday' supplies no interesting context, then, only the reassurance that since this conversation took place so recently, Socrates might more plausibly remember it all.

The 'goddess' to whom Socrates has come to pray, whose festival Athens is celebrating 'for the first time,' is the Thracian moon goddess Bendis.

New gods came rarely into ancient cities, for public festivals were considered the city's endorsements of the worship of a god. The gods protected their chosen cities, so the cities had to take care in turn to protect their gods, especially by not permitting the observance of foreign deities: the cost of welcoming new gods could be the loss of the old gods' protection. Only crises could bring a city to license the worship of new gods. Thus, during the entire fifth century, Athens only twice admitted significant new gods into its pantheon. The other was Asclepius, a Greek hero from the city of Epidaurus, first remembered there as a legendary doctor, then elevated to the status of the god of medicine. Athens recognized him as a god in 420, but the first steps toward legal acceptance of his cult came in 430–429, the years of a great plague.

Asclepius at least was the local hero of a Greek city; Bendis would have struck Athenians as something more exotic, besides being a competitor to the Greek Artemis. At least in the course of the fifth century, there was no other act comparable to the Athenian assembly's decree in 430, that Bendis now belonged with their traditional gods.

What accounts for this alteration to the public religion? Three years earlier, a group of Thracians had received permission to construct a private shrine to Bendis within the city walls. In that same year the king of Thrace entered into an alliance with Athens. The Athenians had known from the beginning of the Peloponnesian War that success would depend on their naval superiority over Sparta. But fleets require timber, which Thrace possessed in abundance; so, after a few more years of war, Athens upgraded Bendis and even planned for her public festival.

This arrangement becomes ironic in light of the fact that in 399 Socrates' prosecutors would accuse *him* of introducing new gods into Athens. The mention of this first-time festival reminds Plato's audience that the city had already introduced new deities, and for mercenary motives. In part this introductory reference to the festival exonerates Socrates from one charge against him.

How many of these implications did Plato mean to resonate in the *Republic*'s opening sentence? We do not have to quarrel about its details, as long as we remain conscious of Plato's careful construction of the *Republic*. Especially at certain passages, when we have to reconstruct arguments out of elliptical remarks and undefined terms, it will help to bear in mind that in Plato's hands even an innocuous aside may contain a crucial premise, or the gloss on another passage.

## OUTLINE OF THE DIALOGUE

The *Republic*'s length and complexity can obscure its overarching structure. The reader needs to bear in mind that the *Republic* essentially consists of a single argument, with a foreword and afterword and a digression in its middle. The central argument comes in Books 2, 3, 4, 8, and 9, with Book 1 to introduce its issues and 10, almost an appendix, elaborating on specific points in the principal argument. These parts of the *Republic* make considerable sense even without the digression of Books 5–7, the political and metaphysical discussion that for the most serious reader constitutes the heart of the dialogue.

The central argument sets itself the task of answering two questions, 'What is justice?' and 'Is justice profitable?' That English word 'justice,' while imperfect, captures two important features of the Greek *dikaiosunê*:

(a) Both terms are primarily used of law-abiding behavior or institutions, especially when law-abidingness also implies regularity, predictability, and impartiality.
(b) Both terms apply in contexts of relations among people. They are other directed, as opposed to a virtue like courage, which may not involve anyone else, or honesty, which has natural applications both in solitary and social contexts.

But whereas these features exhaust the meaning of the English word, *dikaiosunê* goes beyond 'justice' in implying appropriateness. In moral terms, this appropriateness means not wanting or taking more than one ought to have. (The English word approaches such connotations only in nonmoral contexts: the adverb 'just' can mean 'exactly,' and the printer's use of 'justify' means the adjustment of lines of type to equal lengths.) Plato will exploit the sense of appropriateness in *dikaiosunê*; though 'justice' does not capture that overtone, it still works better than any other single word. 'Right' is too vague, with unwanted connotations. 'Fairness' is too anemic and too specific. Moreover, at least some of the inexactness of the translation is the result of Plato's expansion and reinterpretation of the Greek word. Plato would never assume that we already know what justice is. In that case, the failure of 'justice' to fit Plato's usage may prove an advantage; for it will keep us conscious of the ways in which philosophers can reinvent the most ordinary words when they place those words in philosophical theories.

With that clarification in mind, we may schematize the *Republic*'s argument as shown in Figure 1 overleaf.

## SUGGESTIONS FOR FURTHER READING

Some works of ancient history made this chapter possible, and the interested reader will enjoy learning more by turning to those sources.

On the continuing preference for Sparta over democratic Athens in later centuries the definitive work is Jennifer T. Roberts, *Athens on Trial: The Antidemocratic Tradition in Western Thought*.

This chapter's vision of the antidemocratic elite within Athens is indebted to Ober, *Political Dissent in Democratic Athens: Intellectual*

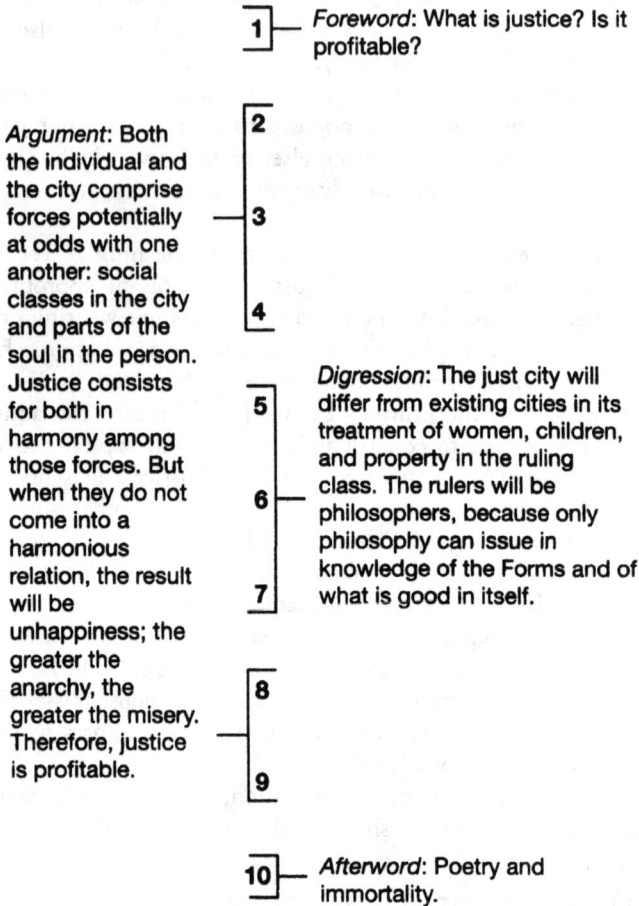

**1** — *Foreword*: What is justice? Is it profitable?

**2**

**3** *Argument*: Both the individual and the city comprise forces potentially at odds with one another: social classes in the city and parts of the soul in the person. Justice consists for both in harmony among those forces. But when they do not come into a harmonious relation, the result will be unhappiness; the greater the anarchy, the greater the misery. Therefore, justice is profitable.

**4**

**5**

**6** *Digression*: The just city will differ from existing cities in its treatment of women, children, and property in the ruling class. The rulers will be philosophers, because only philosophy can issue in knowledge of the Forms and of what is good in itself.

**7**

**8**

**9**

**10** — *Afterword*: Poetry and immortality.

*Figure 1*

*Critics of Popular Rule.* On Themistocles and the fleet, and indeed on the history of an Athenian century of naval power, see Hale, *Lords of the Sea: The Epic Story of the Athenian Navy and the Birth of Democracy.* For additional historical background see Vernant, *Myth and Tragedy in Ancient Greece,* on classical Athens and tragedy; Kagan, *The Peace of Nicias and the Sicilian Expedition,* which is volume 3 of his history of the Peloponnesian War, puts the major political events surrounding Socrates into a compelling narrative.

On the dramatic date of the *Republic,* with extensive citations to the modern debate, see Nails, 'The dramatic date of Plato's *Republic.*'

On the life and thought of Socrates, two anthologies are useful: Vlastos, *The Philosophy of Socrates,* and Benson, *Essays on the Philosophy of Socrates.* On the nature of Platonic dialogue in general, see Hyland, 'Why Plato wrote dialogues,' Nussbaum, 'Plato's anti-tragic theater,' in *The Fragility of Goodness,* and Patterson, 'The Platonic art of comedy and tragedy.' On the thematic structure of the *Republic* see Barney, 'Platonic ring-composition and *Republic* 10.' For more information about Plato's use of dramatic language in his dialogues see Tarrant, 'Plato as dramatist.' On the relationship between the *Republic* and *Ecclesiazusae* see Adam, *The Republic of Plato,* volume I.

# Part II

## THE ARGUMENT
## OF THE *REPUBLIC*

# 2

## WHAT IS JUSTICE? (BOOK 1)

### THE PECULIAR NATURE OF BOOK 1

Plato himself did not divide the *Republic* into the ten parts or 'books' it is always organized into. That was the work of later editors, and many of their divisions (at the beginning of Books 3, 4, 6, and 9) feel arbitrary. But when they separated Book 1 from what came later, the ancient editors were responding to undeniable differences in the writing. Although Book 1 makes an absorbing introduction to the *Republic*, these differences force the question how much Book 1's arguments have to do with Books 2–10.

### DIFFERENCES FROM THE REST OF THE *REPUBLIC*

Book 1 places Socrates in a highly realized setting, with characters who stand out as definite personalities; they sit and get up, sweat and blush, wave their arms. Some speak elliptically and others hyperbolically, but each one seems to say what he really thinks. Socrates in turn treats each one differently, starting with the individual's particular claims about justice and tangling the man in contradictions. He offers very few doctrines of his own (336b–337e), and Book 1 closes with scarcely any satisfying conclusions, except for the ignorance of those Athenians – Sophists and the students of Sophists – who fancy themselves bold and brilliant theorists of morality.

In the liveliness of its characters, and in the way Socrates deflates their pretensions to knowledge, Book 1 resembles those shorter dialogues that the developmentalist view classifies as early and 'Socratic.' The early dialogues tend to finish in *aporia* 'perplexity' and are said to reflect what the historical Socrates did and said in Athens. In his focus on moral issues – as opposed to the metaphysics of the Forms, psychology, and the afterlife – Socrates again resembles the Socrates of those short dialogues, while Books 2–10 will find him speaking to that larger set of topics associated with Plato's middle period. He measures knowledge against the standard set by the professions, though the later books will find him treating mathematics as paradigmatic knowledge. And where Book 1's Socrates reaches mainly negative results – that his contentious interlocutors do not know what they claim to – the Socrates of 2–10 addresses pliant respondents who let him spell out and defend systematic positive doctrines; Socratic questioning becomes, as it generally is in the middle dialogues, no more than pretense.

Remarkable that an author whose works fall into such distinct groups should have written one (and a big one: his second longest) that starts out resembling one of those groups only to change into an example of another. The problem of Book 1 does not depend on the complete truth of the developmentalist thesis, though it is a more dramatic problem if that thesis is true, so that Plato wrote (as I think he did) part of a dialogue in his middle period that resembled one from his early period, in a style he had abandoned. But even without separating the different styles chronologically one can see Plato's dialogues as falling into distinct types, and even in the absence of a developmentalist theory the *Republic* is still a hybrid that joins together two types that Plato otherwise keeps apart.

Beginning with the belief that Plato wrote his different kinds of dialogues at different times, some commentators have proposed that the contrast between Book 1 and the later books shows Book 1 to have been written much earlier, as a freestanding dialogue, sometimes called the *Thrasymachus* after the main opponent faced by Socrates. Later Plato found this short dialogue's treatment of justice inadequate and came back to enlarge upon it; the result – possibly after several returns to the material at several times during the course of decades – is the *Republic*.

The hypothesis of a separate earlier existence for Book 1 acknowledges the reader's frustration at trudging through blind alleys of argumentation. Of course, the hypothesis then becomes a reason not to read Book 1. Since Glaucon and Adeimantus will restate the problems of Book 1 in more philosophical form at the beginning of Book 2, why not skip ahead and begin reading the *Republic* there? Is there no way to recognize the unusual nature of Book 1 without casting it off as a false start?

## BOOK 1 AS A PREFACE

The hypothesis of an earlier existence for Book 1 overlooks the way that it introduces the themes of the *Republic*. Whether in passing or at length, Socrates and Thrasymachus speak of types of human government (338d), the violence of tyrants (344b–c), the onerousness of rule (345e–346a), an ideal city run by good people (347d), the factiousness of injustice (351d–352a), the comparison between a city and an individual (352a), and the possession by each thing of its proper task (352d–353a). All these subjects will find crucial places in the dialogue's argument; taken together, the mentions of these subjects imply that Plato wants Book 1 to foreshadow the coming arguments.

More generally, Book 1 prepares for the *Republic*'s treatment of the virtues. Its conversations draw us away from conceptions of justice that look for that trait in some feature of the *actions* one performs, toward a view of justice as a characteristic of the *person* performing them. Hence ethics will concern itself not with commandments but with accounts of the virtues. This transformation is especially noticeable in Socrates' treatment of Thrasymachus. So Book 1 effects a change in our understanding of justice that must be gone through before the work of the *Republic* can begin in earnest. But in that case we have still more trouble with the hypothesis that

Book 1 had been a separate dialogue; for only the oddest coincidence would permit an independently conceived work to pave the way for precisely the method of inquiry that the rest of the *Republic* will use.

If Book 1 was written together with the rest of the *Republic*, its resemblance to a different group of Platonic dialogues makes it not an example of those works but a deliberate imitation and pastiche of them. Plato began with the themes and topics of the *Republic* in mind and composed a dialogue reminiscent of his Socratic works, into which he embedded those changes.

Why should Plato have wanted to return to another way of writing philosophy only to shift to the style and doctrines of his middle-period writings? Here is a speculation that might illuminate the *Republic*'s reassessment of Socrates (but bear in mind that it is speculation, not proven fact). Plato wrote Book 1 in the manner of his Socratic dialogues to emphasize that it presents the Socrates he had known in life. Inadequacies in Book 1's treatment of justice reveal the limitations of the Socratic method, and the remainder of the *Republic* displays the merits of Plato's new philosophical methods, which will succeed where the others failed.

This account requires Plato to have been a kind of literary mimic, willing to write long stretches of his dialogues in someone else's voice. But he was. The speeches of Agathon and Eryximachus in the *Symposium*, the long Sophistic myth in the *Protagoras*, the Lysian discourse recited in the *Phaedrus*, Socrates' long funeral oration in the *Menexenus*, perhaps even the whole of the *Apology*, are Platonic exercises in authorial ventriloquism. For this writer, with this propensity for mimicry, to imitate his younger self would have taken little effort.

## CEPHALUS (328B–331D)

Cephalus instigates the conversation of the *Republic* inasmuch as he is the speaker who first uses the words 'just' and 'unjust.' Memories of unjust deeds make those on the threshold of death tremble for their fate in the next life. He feels lucky:

> The possession of money contributes a great deal to not having to cheat or lie ... and moreover, to not having to depart for that other

place frightened because one owes some sacrifices to a god or money
to a human being.

(331b)

Socrates takes the old man's remark to be a definition of justice,
as if Cephalus had said, 'Justice is identical with discharging all
obligations.' In reply Socrates offers his counterexample of the
friend gone mad, who returns to reclaim his weapons. Returning
the borrowed weapons does count as delivering what is owed, but
that cannot count as the right or just action to perform. We
would call Cephalus' definition too broad, since it covers more
cases than the thing it purports to define.

As a matter of fact, Cephalus' remark is no definition at all.
It identifies a few kinds of actions as just without saying what
accounts for their justice. Suppose Cephalus had defined rain as
water falling to the earth. Socrates would just as easily have dug
up counterexamples: a waterfall, or laundry water emptied off a
roof. Those counterexamples would have drawn attention to the
crucial feature of rain overlooked by this definition, namely that
rain falls as part of an atmospheric cycle. In the case at hand, the
implicit identification of justice with a couple of specific actions
omits any mention of the character inherent in those actions that
makes for the justice in them.

We could not expect such insights from Cephalus. He has
absorbed his society's rules of good behavior enough to feel happiest
when acting rightly, but without being able to explain why. He
has enjoyed good fortune, reaching an age at which sexual desire
no longer distracts him, and accumulating enough money to guard
him from temptation. His life seems sober and prudent, and his
acceptance of old age has to count as the first stage of wisdom.
But he has no advice to give those who are differently situated, no
hint of how to live virtuously without money or with a virile
young body. And the reader's knowledge that Cephalus' fortune
will soon disappear shows the inadequacy of his complacency. When
we hear him speak of following religious customs as if he were
buying insurance, and quote Sophocles, Themistocles, and Pindar
rather than think for himself, we yearn for something more substantial. No reader misses Cephalus after he goes off to make his

sacrifices (331d); and he would not miss the confusing discussion that follows. Cephalus has kept himself so oblivious to philosophical investigations that, just at that time in his life when he should be evaluating himself and his values, and passing along guidance to his sons, he has nothing to offer but second-hand pieties, and the kinds of anecdotes that seem made to be overrepeated.

Still Cephalus plays a useful prefatory role in the *Republic*. His platitudes about the good life touch on nearly all the ethical themes of the *Republic*:

(a)  bodily pleasures and one's liberation from them;
(b)  the importance of living in the right city;
(c)  fear of punishment in the afterlife;
(d)  the importance of living justly.

Cephalus also initiates the activity of philosophy. Socrates is already at work, eliciting definitions of moral terms and finding counter-examples or inconsistencies that prove them inadequate – work for which he is famous.

## POLEMARCHUS (331E–335E)

Polemarchus takes over his father's definition and improves on it a little, as Cephalus improved on the inheritance his own father had left him. Polemarchus brings greater generality to his conception of justice, so that Socrates cannot demolish the definition with a counterexample. Instead Socrates deploys an extended refutation, showing that the proposed definition of justice, taken together with other premises that Polemarchus accepts, leads to unacceptable conclusions.

### A NEW DEFINITION (331E–332C)

Calling on the poet Simonides, Polemarchus defines justice as the act of giving to each 'what is owed,' which means doing good to friends and harm to enemies. Since doing good and doing harm are broader notions of action than the payment of money and performance of sacrifice that Cephalus spoke of, this definition stands a better chance of revealing something essential about justice. Justice, we might equally well say, consists in adhering to the obligations implicit in social relationships.

It is striking that the Greek of this quote from Simonides may be read more naturally as if the poet had not been defining justice but simply seeking to say something about it. 'It is just to give to each what is owed' does not necessarily identify justice with the discharge of obligations, but may only have named one type of just action. In the same way, 'Rain makes the crops grow' says something true about rain without trying to define it.

The difference matters because a philosophical definition, of the sort that Socrates looked for, is an unusual thing. Unlike definitions found in dictionaries, such a definition does not aim at clarifying the use of a word, but at unearthing new or previously unnoticed information about the concept. In a dictionary, the definition of 'just' might include the word 'right.' To someone like Socrates, who wants the *properties* of justice, this feels like a dodge, as if someone tried defining 'automobile' by 'car,' without talking about engines and wheels.

The difference between philosophical and lexicographical definitions is clearest in the case of ethical terms. Any dictionary can explain how the words 'good,' 'right,' and 'just' are used by speakers of English. The dictionary's information will keep us from linguistic gaffes ('Is the chicken justly done?'), but cannot decide the truth of uses that are linguistically legitimate ('Is the bombing justly done?'). The philosophical definition presupposes the dictionary's information, but it adds necessary and sufficient conditions in the hopes of determining when to use disputable words.

In this century many philosophers have come to shy away from Socratic definitions. Wittgenstein's influence especially has engendered the position that philosophical definitions are neither possible nor necessary. But general critiques of philosophical definitions, for all their importance and power, do not render the *Republic*'s argument irrelevant. First, most of Socrates' arguments could be salvaged against the objection about definitions. In the case of Polemarchus, Socrates' arguments only tangentially depend on this purported misunderstanding between Polemarchus' comment on justice and Socrates' treatment of that comment as a definition.

Secondly, it is far from clear that Wittgensteinian criticisms apply to ethical terms in the direct way they apply to the terms of philosophical metaphysics. The project of clarifying the limits and nature of justice, by virtue of being more concrete than the project of clarifying human perception, say, is not threatened in the same way by critiques of philosophical method.

In what follows, I will treat the problem of defining justice as if it were a legitimate question. As for Polemarchus, changing his definition to a comment about justice will not save him from Socrates' objections.

## THE WORK OF JUSTICE (332C–333E)

The first objection forces Polemarchus to identify what benefits friends and harms enemies in specific contexts. The practitioners of specific skills are more useful than the just man at delivering harms and benefits. Farming is the skill most useful for producing food, and so on. The use of justice must reside in some other sphere of human activity; so Polemarchus tells Socrates that sphere is the making of contracts, or the formation of partnerships.

Even here Socrates finds his answer too broad. Depending on the activity in which one needs cooperation, any number of experts will be more useful than someone who is as it were merely just, or just and nothing else. Finally Polemarchus admits that justice is useful only when money or other goods are lying useless and need to be guarded. Justice has gone from underwriting all social relationships to assisting in one minor task.

Polemarchean justice comes off as badly as it does in this passage because Socrates treats it as a *technê*. This word *technê*, which first appears at 332c, names a number of activities not grouped together in English, from medicine and navigation to horse training, shipbuilding, shoemaking, and sculpture. All these require skill, and 'skill' will do as a translation of *technê*, as long as we bear in mind that a *technê* was typically a person's livelihood. ('Profession' is better, but not a standard translation. Two traditionally used terms 'craft' and 'art' are misleading.) Especially in the short dialogues of Socratic cross-examination, *technê* is a paradigm for knowledge that ethical knowledge must emulate. Socrates compares his interlocutors' clumsy allegations about virtue or poetry with a doctor's skill, or a cobbler's. A *technê* has a clearly defined domain or object (health, shoes), to every member of which it applies. The knowledge of the *technê* can be stated in general terms and taught. Once learned, this knowledge makes someone a practitioner of the skill in question: to know shipbuilding is to be a shipbuilder.

Putative moral knowledge fails all these tests, as Polemarchus' conception of justice does here. As long as Socrates is looking for a unique activity belonging to the just and to no one else, justice will seem to have nothing to do. One wants to object to Socrates that justice, unlike horse-trading, does not exist as a means to some other end, but as a characteristic of all human activities. When it comes to buying a horse, the point is not to distinguish the just person from the one who knows horses, since all the fairness and integrity in the world will not produce good advice if someone knows nothing. We should be comparing two horse experts, one who is just and one not; then it becomes obvious whom one would rather do business with. But this reply is implicitly ruled out by the assumption that justice has to have its own work to do, that it should resemble a specific skill. Just as there is medical practice unmixed with any other art, there should be a just practice also done alone, apart from the practice of any other skill. With this assumption at work in the argument, Polemarchus hardly stands a chance. Justice ends up supervising money when it lies useless.

## THE MORAL AMBIGUITY OF JUSTICE (333E–334B)

Socrates now lures Polemarchus into agreeing that every skill implies the greatest capacity for both good and harm. No one can poison you as effectively as a doctor can; no one leads a ship off course as skilfully as a trained navigator. If justice amounts to the capacity for guarding unused money, the just will also be the best at robbing it.

This argument seems so misguided that we are tempted to throw out any comparison between virtue and an occupational skill, or at least to reconsider the subject matter of which justice may be called a skill. I believe that Plato himself draws this conclusion from Socrates' arguments. However well they silence Polemarchus, they do not lead toward greater understanding of moral knowledge. In the remainder of the *Republic* Socrates will speak much less frequently about *technê*. (The word occurs about .2 times per page in Books 2–10, once per page in Book 1.) When he does propose a model for moral knowledge (Books 5–7), that model is not technical skill but the theoretical knowledge of the mathematician. The assumption behind *technê*, that every activity works toward a goal, prevents the concept from illuminating justice, of which we might say that it is its own goal, or that it has for a goal not some distinct product, but an entire human life. The fruitlessness of this part of Book 1 then reflects Plato's belief that the traditional Socratic method, with its propensity to treat virtues as professions, can only show the inadequacy of purported definitions of those virtues, not produce good definitions of its own.

## FURTHER OBJECTIONS (334B–335E)

Socrates has two additional criticisms of Polemarchus' approach to justice. First is the unclarity of the words 'friend' and 'enemy.' Because one may be mistaken about one's friends, justice might mean helping the wicked and harming the good (334b–335b). The point is well taken but easily answered: Polemarchus amends his definition to speak not simply of friends but of those who both seem to be and really are good, and, instead of enemies, those who are and seem to be bad.

Socrates' last point concerns the role of justice in harming anyone. Having circled around the peripheral flaws in the definition, Socrates goes to its heart – or so it would seem. Unfortunately, his premise that one who is *harmed* becomes *worse* depends on a linguistic ambiguity, almost a play on words. The argument does not work.

Nevertheless the conclusion is worth pausing over. Socrates wants to show that justice never aims at anyone's misfortune. To say such a thing about any other virtue would be bold enough. But justice seems to be about squaring the accounts, settling the score; and one aspect of justice, what is found in the criminal justice system, entails assigning blame and punishing wrongdoers. Isn't punishment a harm? Moreover punishment can blur into revenge, which positively aims at inflicting harm. And that great ancient hero Achilles, the main character in ancient Greece's greatest literary work, spends most of the *Iliad* acting from revenge, hurting the Greeks because Agamemnon mistreated him and then killing Hector after Hector killed Patroclus. The Socratic proposal for a moral code that universally improves people is an extraordinary new idea.

To be sure the proposal is hardly more than an idea here. Other dialogues, most notably the *Gorgias*, develop similar proposals at length and with extensive arguments. And the overarching conclusion of the *Republic*, that justice (as this dialogue reimagines it) amounts to happiness (as that too is reimagined), has its roots in this belief, which appears in the present passage as an optimistic article of faith.

Polemarchus is inadequate in two ways to the task of talking about justice to Socrates. In the first place, his ideas conform too comfortably to his culture's conception of virtue. Despite a sheen of sophistication, Polemarchus is very much his father's son, inheriting the old man's tendency to accept received opinions. Like his father, he appeals to a poet to substantiate his position, as Athenians often did in moral discourse. In Books 2 and 3 we will find Plato ejecting his culture's most highly prized poetry from the well-governed city, because poetry has functioned as a moral authority by dint of its charm, and left its audience adept at quoting nicely turned verses, but hapless at inquiring into the truth or falsehood behind them. Polemarchus shows off his knowledge of Simonides but turns out not to have any arguments to support his sentiments. Under cross-examination he admits, 'I no longer know what I did mean' (334b). Because he has not worked out the implications of his high-sounding but ultimately vacuous apophthegm, Polemarchus really does not know what he is saying. To progress beyond this level of conversation, Socrates will need someone to talk to who can set prevailing wisdom aside.

Polemarchus fails by describing justice in terms of the actions it requires. Socrates' objections, taken as a whole, show how wrongheaded that conception of justice is bound to be. As long as Polemarchus tries to capture justice in a description, however general, of prescribed behavior, it will run the risk of looking like a minor skill or a potentially dangerous one. The rest of Book 1 will change the terms of the discussion from this misdirected approach to a more productive one.

## SUGGESTIONS FOR FURTHER READING

For a detailed treatment of Book 1, see above all Lycos, *Plato on Justice and Power*; Joseph, 'Plato's *Republic*: the argument with Polemarchus'; and Sesonske, 'Plato's Apology: *Republic* I.' Cross and Woozley, *Plato's Republic: A Philosophical Commentary*, and Nettleship, *Lectures on the Republic of Plato*, are helpful here.

For analyses of the historical Socrates' philosophical method, see Roochnik, 'Socrates' use of the techne-analogy,' Santas, *Socrates: Philosophy in Plato's Early Dialogues*, Vlastos (ed.), *The Philosophy of Socrates*, and Vlastos, *Socrates, Ironist and Moral Philosopher*, 'The Socratic elenchus,' and 'Elenchus and mathematics: a turning-point in Plato's philosophical development.' Also (from a more historical perspective) see Blank, 'Socrates versus Sophists on payment for teaching,' and Sellars, 'Simon the shoemaker and the problem of Socrates.'

# 3

## WHAT GOOD IS JUSTICE?
## (BOOKS 1–2)

### THRASYMACHUS (336B–354C)

Thrasymachus violates the conviviality of this conversation and Socrates has to move fast with answering arguments to prevent his respect for justice from looking naive. Thrasymachus ends the fiction of a sociable chat, exactly as his claims about justice try to tear away the self-deceit with which society depicts its moral principles. So it is that Socrates describes Thrasymachus with images of wildness and vulgarity (336b, d; 344d), while Thrasymachus accuses Socrates of mendacity (337a, 340d).

But anyone can be a boor. What sets Thrasymachus apart is the rhetorical skill for which he had already become famous. Like most of the Sophists, Thrasymachus was a non-Athenian who traveled among the major cities of Greece teaching politically useful skills, especially rhetoric. He uses his rhetoric now to produce one of the world's greatest, most abrasive, attacks on principle and moral sentiment.

## THE ADVANTAGE OF THE STRONGER (338C–339B)

Thrasymachus begins with his famous pronouncement that justice is 'nothing other than the advantage of the stronger' (338c). *This is not one more definition.* Thrasymachus does not describe some characteristic of people, actions, or institutions that makes them just. Polemarchus tried to give a definition; but then, Polemarchus thought the adjective 'just' corresponded to a real property of things. 'The advantage of the stronger' differs in using nonmoral language to speak of a moral property. Thrasymachus has warned Socrates not to define the just as 'the needful, or the helpful, or the profitable, or the gainful, or the advantageous' (336c–d), on the grounds that such definitions remain within the conventional view of justice. His account claims to expose the unnoticed origin of justice in the city's power structure: whatever group rules a city passes laws to benefit itself. (Thrasymachus has traveled and observed human societies and evidently takes this to be an empirical claim. This is what he has repeatedly observed.) Since obedience to laws is generally called just, that city's word 'just' comes to refer to whatever behavior benefits its ruling class. Rather than correspond to any actual property of things or people, 'justice' is an attractive word for cloaking the naked exercise of power.

Imagine that Socrates and Polemarchus had been trying to decide whether being in love is the attraction to what one lacks or the desire to possess what one resembles; and that Thrasymachus said, 'Being in love is nothing but a chemical state in the brain.' He would mean that Socrates and Polemarchus had been looking in the wrong place, that there was nothing to be said about being in love beyond its being a brain state. In particular, he would mean that the lover's belief that this feeling is somehow *about* the loved one – the belief that guided those false definitions – is an illusion. In the present case Thrasymachus is claiming that justice, which looks like a characteristic of social relations, amounts to nothing above and beyond whatever suits a given city's rulers. Given the definitions that have been entertained, this means that no definition is possible.

We may call Thrasymachus' definition a naturalistic analysis of the concept of justice. It seeks a factual, nonmoral basis for a phenomenon of morality. The analysis resembles a nihilistic rejection of justice in that it denies that justice exists. But Thrasymachus is not properly speaking a nihilist. To a nihilist, Socrates' talk of justice would be empty talk; our values have no value because nothing corresponds to our ethical language, as no facts about human beings correspond to their astrological signs. By contrast, Thrasymachus grants that Socrates is talking about something, but he insists that it is not what Socrates *thinks* he's talking about.

## THE ART OF RULE (339B–346E)

Socrates presses two objections against Thrasymachus. The first one, in this section, attacks the idea of 'the advantage of the stronger,' exploiting Thrasymachus' comments about an ideal ruler to undercut his cynicism. The second series of objections (348b–354c) more vaguely take on his immoralist contention that injustice pays. I will concentrate my discussion on the latter arguments, because they point ahead to the theory Plato will develop later in the *Republic*.

## RULERS' ERRORS (339B–340C)

The immediate problem with saying that justice is the advantage of the stronger is that the strong can make mistakes about their own advantage. If rulers support a law they believe to serve their purposes, but that as a matter of fact will hurt them, then – on the Thrasymachean view – justice would have to consist in dis-obeying that law. Such an option robs the rulers of any feeling of power, as it commits their subjects to deciding what will most help the rulers. The subjects make the laws.

At this point Thrasymachus may add the qualifier Cleitophon suggests, that justice be the advantage of the stronger *as it appears to the stronger*. Alternatively, he may deny that rulers make mistakes about what helps and harms them. The first option preserves the sensation of power for the strong, since what they really want is obedience. But it leaves open the possibility that justice will benefit the weak. If rulers become mistakenly convinced that lower taxes suited their interests, when they actually served the interests of the citizenry, then lower taxes in the city would be just according to Thrasymachus' own principles, without contradicting the conventional understanding of justice.

So Thrasymachus takes the other option. Distinguishing the true practitioner of a *technê* from the one who is vulgarly called its practitioner, he claims to be speaking only of the former sort of ruler (340d–341a). The doctor who diagnoses incorrectly is not a true doctor in that moment; and rulers, in the moment of erring about their own advantage, are not properly called rulers. Justice is determined by the self-aggrandizing pronouncements of the ideal ruler.

Thrasymachus has slipped out of one trap with this maneuver, but only to find himself in a deadlier one. For by postulating an idealized form of the ruler, he has reintroduced the skill analogy, and with it all the questions about skills that Polemarchus could not answer. If justice or political rule are skills, what are their objects or goals?

## THE OBJECT OF RULE (341C–342E)

Socrates compares the skill of ruling to the skills of medicine, piloting, and horse training. The doctor rules over the human body, for it is the doctor who determines what the body ought to eat and drink and what medical treatment it needs. This sort of rule, in contradistinction to the one Thrasymachus imagined, serves the interests of the thing it governs. Horse trainers, when properly so called, work for the good of the horses they rule. Pilots work for the benefit of sailors.

This point is structural, not psychological. Socrates does not believe that doctors and pilots are altruistic people. He means that medicine, considered as a body of knowledge, makes sense only as a treatment of the sick. To dispense pharmaceuticals with some other purpose is to be a poisoner or a drug dealer. Then if political rule is a skill according to which one person governs others, it must resemble those other skills in *serving* the ones it *rules*. Thrasymachus is in trouble again, for if political rule serves the subjects of rule, the ruler's decrees aim at the advantage of the subjects, and justice will be not the advantage of the politically stronger, but that of the weaker.

It is to Thrasymachus' credit that he still has a reply to make. Against Socrates' appeal to the nature of a skill, Thrasymachus objects that this analogy fails in the case of political rule. Only from a limited perspective does power appear to work on behalf of its subjects. Sheep might imagine that their shepherd cares about their welfare, but the goal of that care is fatter sheep for slaughter. Therefore, political rule diverges critically from other skills, and cannot be illuminated by a comparison to them.

Socrates will try to save his analogy; but he cannot escape the deep significance of Thrasymachus' objection. Skills presuppose a goal: a shoe, bodily health, or music. In every case, a skill or craft directs itself to achieving its goal, not to determining which goal a situation calls for. Should Athens invest in stronger city walls or in more ships for its navy? Depending on the answer, shipbuilders or masons will be the artisans to help the city. But they are exactly the least appropriate ones to ask which goal the city should pursue; and *that* is the political question. So too, while shepherds are ideally suited to tending to sheep's health, their decisions about which sheep to slaughter, and when, will reflect not their skill as shepherds but their own purposes and personal desires. Socrates' analogy misses this point, because his attachment to occupational skills as models of knowledge has blinded him to their unsuitability for discovering *the goals of behavior*.

The question of who is served by justice has begun to seem like a quicksand from which neither Socrates nor Thrasymachus will escape to the solid ground of substantive claims about justice. They have to move on:

> I can in no way agree with Thrasymachus that the just is the advantage of the stronger. But this we shall consider again at another time. What Thrasymachus now says is in my opinion a far bigger thing — he asserts that the life of the unjust man is stronger than that of the just man.

> (347d–e)

## THE PROFITABILITY OF JUSTICE (348B–352B)

In the course of describing the shepherd's true motives, Thrasymachus digressed to remind Socrates of a consequence of his original definition: justice profits not the just, but the unjust who take advantage of them (343c). This point seized his attention, and he directed the rest of his speech to illustrating the profitability of unjust behavior.

Note that this is not the position he began with. In calling justice unprofitable, Thrasymachus is no longer redefining the term, but accepting the traditional *meaning* of justice and denying its *value*. He represents immoralism now – the view that one ought to traduce moral principles – rather than the naturalistic perspective that led him to call justice the advantage of the stronger. This does not mean that Thrasymachus has let himself be confused into misunderstanding his own position. Rather, he has seized on a single implication of his original definition. Assuming one is not in the position of governing, the immoralist view follows from the naturalistic description. (If one *is* the ruler, then by the original definition justice is profitable. Here Thrasymachus has changed his view, since he calls the tyrant unjust at 344a–c. But since the discussion is not focused on rulers, this change does not affect it.) Thrasymachus has decided to clarify and defend one implication of his definition, because that by itself will still let him unseat Socrates' simple-minded faith in the value of justice.

In a series of three arguments, Socrates will now try to show that justice deserves more praise than Thrasymachus has allowed. But not just Book 1. For the rest of the *Republic*, the Socratic question, 'What is justice?,' will be tied to this new Thrasymachean question, 'Is justice profitable?'

## JUSTICE IS KNOWLEDGE (348B–350D)

Socrates first argues that in certain respects justice resembles knowledge and goodness, and therefore stands on the side of virtues, while injustice belongs among the vices.

The argument demonstrates that Thrasymachus still adheres to some traditional values. A real nihilist could shrug when Socrates concluded that the just person is good, since the word 'good' does not have to correspond to real properties of things any more than the word 'just' does. Thrasymachus agrees to Socrates' conclusions only reluctantly; he holds to some values, even if justice is not among them.

Otherwise the argument does not go very far. Because Thrasymachus refuses to group justice with virtues and injustice with the vices, but instead calls the former innocence and the latter 'good counsel' (348c–d), Socrates needs to begin by finding some characteristic of injustice that he and Thrasymachus can agree on. In Greek that characteristic is captured by the word *pleonexia*, the habit or trait of wanting and seizing more than one is entitled to. Justice, by contrast, is marked by the tendency to stay within proper bounds. Justice suppresses the spirit of unchecked competition for personal gain manifested in the unjust person's disregard for law and order. Socrates generalizes these characterizations in this way:

① The unjust try to get the better of all others, the just only to get the better of the unjust.

(349b–c)[1]

Since Thrasymachus accepts ①, the restraint of the just must be a universally recognized characteristic of justice, perhaps a least common denominator of all theories of it. Socrates quickly generalizes from ① to the claim that the unjust try to get the better of both those like and those unlike themselves, while the just restrict themselves to outdoing only those unlike themselves (349c–d). Because the behavior of the just and the unjust resembles that of the knowledgeable and the ignorant, respectively, and because those who know are wise and good, therefore the just resemble the wise and good, the unjust the ignorant and bad (350b–c). So the just are wise and good.

As applied to the unjust, 'getting the better of' means cheating: the unjust get the better of others by taking their money, for instance.

---

1 Certain premises of arguments laid out in this book will be specially marked ①, ②, etc. These premises or assumptions either appear in later arguments, or function as assumptions throughout the *Republic*. They are listed separately at the end of this book, in the Appendix 'Fundamental premises in the *Republic*'s argument.' I identify these assumptions to bring forward, among the welter of claims made in the *Republic*, those to which Plato is particularly attached, and on which he rests his conception of justice.

In other contexts the same phrase refers to competition. The non-musician tries to be better at making music than the musician is. These two senses of the phrase have nothing in common. Competition may be honest. The apparent similarity between the just and the knowledgeable fails to show that the just resemble the good, since the equivocal use of 'getting the better of' someone prevents the two premises from talking about the same thing.

The argument has other problems. The just may share some features with the good and yet not be identical with them. We first have to know how essential those shared features are to the just and the good. Logically savvy readers will also spot ambiguities in the implicit quantifiers of the argument's premises, which must be sorted out before assessing the argument's validity.

But what matters more is the argument's purpose in the larger discussion. It has afforded Socrates the opportunity of presenting a general conception of justice as restraint (①). In the terms of the present argument ① does very little; but once Socrates sets out to define justice in terms of the state of one's soul, the principle will guide him to look for restraint within the soul, the tendency of each human drive to stay in its place.

## JUSTICE IS COOPERATION (350E–352B)

For now that goal still lies far off. Socrates wants to show right away how justice can be profitable, so he spells out one consequence of his last conclusion: justice means cooperation, injustice factiousness. Any human activity that calls for a group to act together requires at least some cooperation, hence at least the minimal justice that is called 'honor among thieves.' So justice benefits the just.

This argument depends on the preceding argument's conclusion (see 351c), and therefore can be no more reliable than that one was. It ignores the obvious objection that while a little justice mixed in with injustice yields better results than unadulterated injustice, that mix of virtue and vice might also prove more efficacious than justice by itself.

In one respect the argument moves Socrates further forward, toward a very new approach. 'When injustice comes into being' in a group, he says, it divides the group's members (351d); then he goes

on: 'If ... injustice should come into being within one man ... '
(351e). Injustice now suddenly sounds like a force abiding within
a group or a person, 'possessing a power' to bring about discord
(351e). Socrates has begun to speak as if he assumed that

> ② Injustice is a force, with the power of promoting disunion,
> that can exist within an individual or a society.

In the remainder of the *Republic* Socrates will spend very little
time looking for a justice or injustice that inheres in the actions
called just or unjust; from now on they will be forces inhering in
persons and societies and giving rise to those acts.

In short, Socrates has already changed the subject of this conversation from just and unjust actions to just and unjust agents.
The ethical system of the *Republic* will not specify which behavior
is right; it will analyze the just person and the just city. The
superiority of justice over injustice will not lie in the profitability
of particular actions, but in the profitability of being a certain
kind of person, or organized in a certain social pattern. Sometimes
this grand change of subject leaves Plato's critics complaining that
he does not address the question of behavior. But whether or not this
complaint has merit, there is no doubt of the revolution in moral
thinking at work in the *Republic*, and first visible in this passage.

## JUSTICE AND HAPPINESS (352D–354C)

We have arrived at the last and best argument of Book 1. Although
it can be broken down into more detail, its outline is simple:

(1)  ③ Everything has a work (*ergon*) that it alone can do, or
     that it does better than anything else can. (352d–353a)
(2)  The excellence or virtue of a thing is that which makes it
     perform its work well. (353b–d)

'Virtue' translates *aretê*, which like many Greek words of praise
and blame combines unexpected connotations. Apparently related
to Ares the war god, *aretê* at first referred to manly prowess in
battle. Its meaning spread to include every sort of excellence: as a
moral term, *aretê* meant 'virtue,' but outside the moral domain it

made sense as a term of praise for animals, property, or anything else. Thus the strangest comment in the argument, that eyes and ears have virtues, is uncontroversial in the original.

(3) The work of the soul is living. (353d)

∴ (4) From (2) and (3), the virtue of the soul makes it live well. (353e)

(5) ④ Justice is the virtue of the soul. (353e)

∴ (6) From (4) and (5), the just live well. (353e)

∴ (7) The just are happy. (354a)

There is a sense of prestidigitation in this argument, as if it moved to its conclusion by an unexpected path. The biggest surprise may be Socrates' sudden introduction of the soul, which appeared only incidentally before now. The premises that speak of the soul are too vague to call true or false. In what sense is life the work of the soul? Because dead things have no souls? But then the soul might be an effect of life, not its cause.

As for premise (5), Socrates may have shown justice to be a virtue; but for (5) to work in this argument, justice must be not only *one* virtue of the soul among many but its characteristic or defining virtue. For a virtue to make a thing do its work well, it must correspond to that thing's function, as sharpness does to cutting and keen-sightedness to seeing. If a thing possesses more than a single function, it may have more than one virtue, each one making different work possible. Think of a fork as performing two tasks: it spears food on the plate, and also carries it to the mouth. To spear well the fork must possess the excellence or virtue of sharp tines, and to carry food well it needs a sturdy handle. The two virtues cannot make up for one another. Likewise, even if one thing the soul does is live, and even if justice is one of its virtues, we have no grounds for attributing good living to that virtue. Here again the argument suffers from remaining silent where the context calls for explanation.

Other crucial terms have been left unexplained. 'Happy' and 'living well' are as vague in Plato's Greek as in modern English, and depending on how they are defined the step from (6) to (7) can be obvious or incoherent. Either happiness means the same thing as living well, in which case (7) merely restates (6) and therefore goes without saying; or else living well describes one's able performance at the tasks of being alive, a thing quite different from happiness understood as a subjective joyous condition, in which case (7) lies a long way off from (6).

But I called this Book 1's best argument, and it is time to see its merits. First, ③ brings to the fore an assumption that will prove important later in the *Republic*. The word *ergon* can be indeterminate. Literally 'work' or 'deed,' it applies to anything that requires work – my business, the fruits of my labor – or even, very broadly, any act. But one's *ergon* often refers to the occupation *proper* to the person, and Plato will rely on this sense of the word, first specified in ③, when he says that each inhabitant of his city will perform a single task (⑥, 370a–b). In that context it will mean the person's essential and defining function: the soldier's fighting, the baker's bread making.

Secondly, this argument anticipates the strategy of Books 2–4 in tying morality to happiness. Rather than link the two directly, Plato will argue that both moral behavior and genuine happiness issue from a single source, namely the soul's being in a certain state. Once in that state, which Plato conceives as a balance or harmony, the soul will automatically produce just behavior; because that state is enjoyable to possess, the one whose soul is in the state will be happy.

Redirecting attention to the soul will let Plato answer radical attacks on morality. Whether they take the nihilistic form that there is no moral truth at all, or the cynical form that the moral truth that exists is not worth paying attention to (because it does not pay), such attacks say that morality corresponds to nothing natural. These attacks on morality are heard today, but they already existed in Plato's time and were known to Plato. He will reply that morality and its effects are truths of human psychology (or perhaps, that a world might come to be in which they are truths of human psychology), therefore truths we can call scientific. The closing argument of Book 1 fails to establish any such natural grounds for morality, not because its approach is misguided (by Plato's lights, at least), but because the pivotal term it introduces, 'soul,' shows up in the argument without definition or elucidation. Before proving that justice is profitable Plato will have to say what the soul is. We might say of Book 1's last argument, then, that it goes as far toward proving the profitability of justice as Plato can go without any ancillary investigation.

How did these flawed arguments silence Thrasymachus? Assuming we do not want to accuse Plato of either blindness to his arguments' flaws, or dishonesty in making them victorious, we must conclude that he takes them as sketches for a successful defense of justice. Because they are no more than sketches, they slide past crucial points with equivocal words and *ad hoc* premises. But because the arguments point the way to a better account, those very equivocations and assumptions offer opportunities for discovering deeper philosophical ideas. The arguments work against Thrasymachus, despite their obvious faults, precisely because those faults betray the over-compression of deep truths. The remaining nine books will correct the faults of this one, not by turning the discussion in a new direction, but by doing with a political, metaphysical, and educational theory what the Socrates of Book 1 has been content to accomplish with scattered intuitions.

## GLAUCON AND ADEIMANTUS

### THE BROTHERS

Thrasymachus represented an advance over Socrates' other interlocutors. He detached himself from received wisdom enough to propose a genuine analysis of justice. He displayed his argumentative skill by keeping Socrates from scoring easy victories. But in the remaining nine books of the *Republic* he will say almost nothing: Glaucon and Adeimantus speak up at the start of Book 2, and continue talking to Socrates until the dialogue's conclusion. What makes them better than Thrasymachus?

One sign of the limitation of Thrasymachus as an interlocutor is that Socrates takes their discussion to be done when he has silenced him, even though the originating question about justice dropped out of their conversation unanswered, and even though justice's profitability received only a hasty treatment. Faced with such a belligerent opponent, Socrates can only refute his particular position or let it stand, not develop it into a constructive analysis of justice. He wins when Thrasymachus loses: they cannot both win together by arriving at truth about justice. Thrasymachus lacks the flexibility to see where their argument might lead, precisely because he believes his cynical critique of justice.

In that case, the ideal person for Socrates to talk to would share Thrasymachus' independence from popular opinion but not his immoralism. It would be still better if that interlocutor resembled Cephalus in behaving appropriately even without a theory of justice. The best interlocutor would also retain some of Polemarchus' respect for received opinion – not enough to obey traditional society unthinkingly, but enough to recognize that any proposal of a new society must speak to those who live in the old one.

When Glaucon and Adeimantus open Book 2 with their elaboration of the Thrasymachean position, they show that they possess all the qualities of ideal interlocutors. They want a defense of the just life (358c, 361e, 367b, 368a), but they have enough intellectual integrity to know that Socrates has not provided one (357a, 358b, 358d). They question or reject many details of traditional Greek morality (362e ff.); at the same time, they expect a satisfactory answer to Thrasymachus to preserve some version of the values they have grown up believing in.

But the most noticeable difference between Thrasymachus and Plato's brothers is their docility toward Socrates. With the transition to Book 2 the *Republic* settles into a long Socratic speech sometimes interspersed with questions from Glaucon and Adeimantus, more often broken only by the sounds of their agreement ('Yes, Socrates'; 'Certainly'; 'How could it be otherwise?'). Glaucon and Adeimantus can remain as restrained as they do because they do not believe their own speeches against justice: they have given up the partisanship that often characterizes Socrates' interlocutors. Most of the dialogues classified as Plato's middle and later works contain such agreeable interlocutors, as if Plato feared that the pricklier type – despite their ability to inspire an exciting conversation – lacked the curiosity and discipline needed for following sustained exposition.

The two types of interlocutor correspond to different visions of philosophical practice. In Book 1 Socrates exposes the errors in other people's views; in the rest of the *Republic* he lays out a theory that he treats as his own view. Socrates the gadfly breaks into people's lives to ask what they mean by a word they used, e.g. Cephalus when he spoke of justice. To learn from Socrates the lecturer, people step aside from their lives and hear what he means by justice. Both ways of philosophizing can teach the interlocutor, but in one case Socrates teaches by responding (*strategically*) to an interlocutor's particularity; in the other case by developing (*systematically*) a general account that has not been tailored to this or that interlocutor. In the process philosophy starts to turn into something more like a body of knowledge and an institution that imparts this knowledge, something more like a *school*.

## THE CHALLENGE TO SOCRATES (357A–367E): THE ARGUMENT

Socrates must show that justice considered by itself is preferable to injustice. 'Justice by itself' will be justice understood apart from its social effects; for if its benefits lie in those effects, justice might be a merely conventional social relation.

Glaucon distinguishes three ways of valuing an object, activity, or experience (357b–d). It may be valued and pursued for its own sake, as pleasure is, or merely for its consequences, or for both the intrinsic experience of it and for its consequences. Glaucon and Socrates rank valued things:

(i) Good in itself and for its consequences
(ii) Good in itself
(iii) Good only for its consequences.

The second category will not enter into the discussion, since everyone agrees that if justice is good at all it is at least good also because of its consequences; so it must fall under either (i) or (iii). Glaucon fears, and he argues to Socrates, that justice belongs to the lowest class of good things, because

(1) The rules of justice arise in social situations, out of agreements made by people pursuing their own interests. (358e–359b)

WHAT GOOD IS JUSTICE? (BOOKS 1–2)

   (2)  No one who could get away with cheating would abide by the rules of justice – i.e. people value justice only for its consequences. (359b–360d)

   (3)  When actions are separated from their usual social consequences, the life of the unjust is better than the life of the just. (360e–362c)

Glaucon's speech builds rhetorically from the most neutral claim, the account of the social origin of justice, to (3), which most criticizes the worth of justice. Their *logical* order, though, is (1) → (3) → (2). *Because* justice originates in convention, its pursuit disadvantages the just when they are deprived of the social rewards for their behavior. And *because* everyone has come to realize this fact about consequences, people ignore the demands of justice when they can. From the point of view of its logical importance to the argument, therefore, (2) is secondary. People's reluctance to obey the rule of justice is only a symptom of the deeper problem, that there is in fact no good reason to obey those rules. People are only responding to this truth. The core argument that Socrates has to answer may be stripped down to this:

   (1')  The rules of justice have arisen only within organized society, as a means of preserving that society's members.

∴ (3')  When the society's sanctions are left out of consideration, injustice pays better than justice does.

If Socrates wants to deny (3'), he will have to argue either that (1') is false, or that (3') does not follow from (1'). He has no need to address (2).

   Hence Glaucon's story about Gyges and the ring does not logically advance the brothers' argument. Since most people would exploit a ring of invisibility, they must already believe that they have no reason to act justly in the absence of social sanctions. Their actions prove that they agree with Glaucon.

   Why include the story, then? The tale of the ring is memorable, and it shows how much Plato can do with images and parables when he chooses to deploy them, despite usually restricting himself and his reader to the plainer diet of premises and logical inference. But calling it a lively tale misses the ways it hints at the *Republic*'s greater statements about human psychology. Working through his unwitting character Glaucon, Plato begins the constructive argument of the *Republic* with a revision of the story that the historian Herodotus used (in the previous century) to begin his monumental *Histories*. Both versions tell of a man usurping power, though where Herodotus puts a decent man into extraordinary circumstances to make a tyrant of him, Plato's tale implies that all of us, to the extent that we would be inclined to abuse a ring of invisibility, already carry tyranny latent in our souls. Herodotus sees tyranny and warfare as intrusions into human culture; for Plato it is justice that has to intrude as the exception to the human norm.

The tale even points ahead to the argument in Books 8 and 9 that vicious lives are their own punishment. Why was the ring on the hand of a naked corpse inside a bronze horse? Greek myth contains one image close to this one, the story of the Cretan queen Pasiphaë hiding in a wooden cow to satisfy her pathological love for a bull. (Crete's Minotaur was their child.) In Book 9, describing the worst kind of soul, Socrates puts it under the influence of a desire so wild that it even seeks to copulate with animals (571d). That perversion already appears in the story Glaucon tells, even if Glaucon has not yet seen that he is answering his own question. Why act morally? Because the alternative is a steadily worsening disease of the soul, until the perfectly unjust person exists in an unenviable, sickened condition.

## THE ORIGINS OF JUSTICE (358E–359C)

Not yet seeing justice and injustice as psychological phenomena, Glaucon imagines their historical origin. What we call by the name of justice, as if it were a natural force in the world, actually describes an arrangement made within human society. Everyone would like to enjoy the fruits of domination over everyone else, but no one wants to end up dominated and exploited. So everyone agrees to ban the behavior that is called unjust, giving up the benefits of exploitation in order to avoid being victimized. The result is the social contract or convention we call justice; so goes an argument that has been credited to Sophists antedating Plato (though Plato may be misrepresenting their view).

On this view, every legal or moral principle has the status of those laws we recognize as conventional. We accept the conventions of traffic law, not as embodiments of moral goodness, but as necessary rules of the game called driving in traffic. According to Glaucon's story of justice, our prescriptions against murder, burglary, and contract violation carry no weight above and beyond the weight of such rules. Thus justice is a convenience, not an intrinsically valuable state of character.

Glaucon's speculative history of morality invokes the distinction between *nomos* and *physis* (359c) that was used in Plato's Athens as a critique of all moral standards. The latter term denoted nature and the former anything that developed out of human social organizations, hence anything not natural. ('The natural' was not contrasted with 'the artificial,' as it is today, i.e. with anything touched by human hands, but more narrowly with the customs of human communities. For other uses of this distinction in Plato, see *Gorgias* 482e and 492a–c, *Theaetetus* 172b, and *Laws* 888e–890a.) If justice is a social arrangement, its desirable consequences cannot exceed whatever benefits the society is able to grant to the just.

The appeal to convention reveals what Glaucon meant by opposing 'good in itself and for its consequences' to 'good only for its consequences.' These phrases may be misunderstood if we take the consequences of an activity to include *all* possible effects. For then Glaucon would be seen as taking sides in the modern debate between deontological and consequentialist conceptions of value. For the deontologist, consequences are irrelevant to the evaluation of an action. Telling the truth is right and lying is wrong not because of their effects, but because of the kinds of actions they are. Consequentialism claims, on the contrary, that an action is right if and only if it produces good consequences. In this debate, Glaucon would seem to be a deontologist. He asks Socrates to dismiss the 'wages' of justice and injustice, and 'whatever comes of' them (358b). The remaining constituent of the value of justice would then have to be evaluated deontologically.

But the deontological reading does not fit many things that Glaucon acually says. In the first place, he asks Socrates to defend justice by revealing the 'power' (*dunamis*) that it has in the human soul (358b). *Dunamis* refers to the capacity to perform in a certain way, so justice must be in the soul to *do* something, and its doing that thing, its effects, must be what makes justice worth possessing. Secondly, when Glaucon describes the three kinds of good, his language refers to the acts of liking, welcoming, and choosing those things. To value them is not to esteem them in an impersonal manner, but to want the things for oneself, to *profit* from having them. Finally, Glaucon's examples of things that are good in themselves include pleasure, joy, good health, and eyesight. Whatever these states have in common, it is no abstractly conceived value. One *enjoys* them.

So the distinction between deontological and consequential value misses Glaucon's point. The consequences he sets aside do not include all effects. In his story of the social nature of justice, Glaucon has in mind only those consequences it produces *in a society*. Since Glaucon has opposed society to nature, he must be distinguishing those social consequences from the consequences of justice we acknowledge as natural. Then a thing is both good in itself and productive of good consequences if both its natural and social effects are good.

## LIVES OF THE JUST AND UNJUST (360E–362C)

This reading is borne out by the last part of Glaucon's argument, which contrasts the life of the just man who is universally considered unjust with that of an unjust man with a reputation for justice (360e–362c). Glaucon spells out the penalties that fall upon the misunderstood just man, and he lavishes every benefit on the cunningly unjust. Any advantages that we may think belong to one who lives justly are merely the advantages of a just reputation.

The social consequences of justice and injustice need to be set aside because they follow less reliably than the natural effects of the two states. The natural effect of physical strength would be an enhanced sense of vigor, while its social consequence might be steady work at heavy labor. Because employment requires more than strength alone (jobs have to exist), that social consequence is an indirect effect of the strength. But vigor always comes with bodily strength. Glaucon wants Socrates to identify a natural effect of justice that similarly follows straight from a person's just disposition without the aid of social sanctions.

## ADEIMANTUS (362D–367E)

Where Glaucon bemoaned the bad reputation that justice has gotten, Adeimantus speaks despairingly of the praise that people give it. He is not contradicting his brother but rather describing the same disrespect for morality. As a society grows aware that its prescriptions are artificial, its moral rhetoric makes people cynical about virtuous behavior. When fathers try to persuade their sons to be just, they praise not justice itself but the good reputation it leads to (363a). Even promises of otherworldly rewards for justice implicitly call it a burden, by suggesting that in the next life no one bothers to practice virtue (363c). Moreover, once the just life has been made a mere intermediary to something else, people will look for a shortcut to that other goal. Look at religious rituals: if the gods mete out rewards and punishments after death, then supplications, sacrifices, and initiations into mystery cults can bring bliss after death without the bother of virtuous living (365e–366b).

Adeimantus focuses on existing society. As the more pedestrian brother, he lacks Glaucon's capacity to imagine the origins of justice in a time before all human societies. But his speech does underscore two important points. First, Adeimantus makes clear – as Glaucon did with his tale of Gyges' ring – why purely conventional justice is bad for a society. Eventually everyone realizes that the only advantages of just behavior inhere in the rewards that society bestows on the just. Respectability becomes the basis for morality; once this fact becomes widely known, people turn cynical about respectability and evade the call of justice whenever they can.

Secondly, Adeimantus echoes one of Glaucon's assumptions when he complains that no moral teacher has yet argued 'what each [justice and injustice] itself does with its own power when it is in the soul of a man who possesses it' (366e). Glaucon already expressed the wish to know 'what each is and what power it has all alone by itself when it is in the soul' (358b). In using this language, both brothers are accepting ② and ④, assumptions that Socrates slipped into his arguments against Thrasymachus. ② spoke of injustice (hence justice too) as something in a person that exercised certain powers; ④ specifically located justice within the soul. Socrates has already succeeded in changing the subject of their conversation from justice as a characteristic of human actions to justice conceived as a trait of the human soul.

It is not yet clear what this distinction amounts to. When we attribute honesty to someone's character, we mean that the person tells the truth. Character traits could be seen as shorthand for telling what a person has done. Glaucon and Adeimantus want more. By 'justice by itself in the soul' they mean some features of the soul that cause one to act justly, as depression may cause me to lose my temper, though depression is not the same thing as anger. The brothers want Socrates to show that the features of the soul that produce just behavior also lead, by some natural process, to more happiness than do the features that produce unjust behavior. The argument from here to the end of Book 4, which then continues in Books 8 and 9, will aim at establishing this conclusion.

## SUGGESTIONS FOR FURTHER READING

For information about the historical figure of Thrasymachus, see Gotoff, 'Thrasymachus of Calchedon and Ciceronian style.' Lycos, *Plato on Justice and Power*, and Santas, *Understanding Plato's Republic*, are particularly helpful on this last part of Book 1, as are Bambrough, 'Plato's political analogies,' and especially Barney, 'Socrates' refutation of Thrasymachus.'

Annas, *An Introduction to Plato's Republic*, and Nettleship, *Lectures on the Republic of Plato*, help to explain the challenge posed by Glaucon and Adeimantus; also see Weiss, 'Wise guys and smart alecks in *Republic* 1 and 2.' On the transition from Book 1 to 2 see especially Ferrari, 'Socrates in the *Republic*,' which speaks to the negative methods Socrates employs against Thrasymachus as well as the new way of philosophizing he turns to later.

# 4

## JUSTICE IN THE CITY
## (BOOKS 2–4)

To show how justice naturally produces good effects, Socrates sets himself an even more ambitious task than the one the brothers defined. He will make his subject not merely justice in the soul, but also the justice of an entire city. Whether Plato conceives this larger project as a pretext for addressing political issues, or he genuinely thinks he needs the discussion of justice in the city to prove the worth of psychological justice, from this point on the *Republic* concerns itself with politics. At times the individual's justice is even eclipsed by the question of how to produce and sustain a just city.

### THE CITY AND THE SOUL (368B–369B)

Since justice exists in both souls and cities, Socrates says, it should prove easier to study in the latter. Hence he will begin by asking how justice arises in a city, and only then apply what he has learned to the smaller matter of the soul.

Socrates asserts without argument that because a city and a soul can both be just, there must exist a single property, justice, possessed by the just soul and the just city. When it comes time to derive results from the analogy, though – when the subject turns back to the soul – he argues at length that what his inquiries have revealed about cities will hold true of individuals. Despite the surprising sound of this assumption, then, we should not regard it as a surreptitious move in the argument, but as a hypothesis. Plato will work out his picture of the city and then look to see how well it applies to the soul.

Still it is already clear that the analogy predisposes the *Republic* toward the conception of individual justice that Book 1 introduced. In a just city, justice takes the form of just institutions and laws, and just relations among residents. Its legal systems will not discriminate unfairly among citizens. In a word, the justice of the city consists in *internal relations*, whether between two individuals or between one individual and the city taken as a whole. So Socrates will say only a little about a city's relations toward other communities, almost none of it concerned with just behavior (422e–423a, 469b–471b).

So, for the analogy between soul and city to work, the just soul will have to be not the soul of one who behaves justly toward other people, but the soul that is internally constituted in some particular way. This will mean, among other things, that the soul contains internal divisions corresponding either to the city's individual citizens or to collections of them.

Socrates' picture of the soul (Book 4) will follow out these implications of the city–soul comparison. The *Republic*'s political theory will also be shaped by the comparison; for if a city resembles a soul, it should be thought of as a unity. The good of the citizenry ought to yield to the good of the city taken as a whole, since in the case of the soul only the good of the whole matters. Furthermore, in the case of the soul, unanimity benefits the individual so much more than discord does that the comparison predisposes us to prefer unanimity in the city over any manner of dissent. As we investigate the theory of souls and the theory of cities, we shall have to remain on our guard to distinguish between those claims that follow from explicit arguments and those that creep into the theory – unjustified and often unstated – thanks to the work of the analogy on Plato's imagination.

## THE FIRST AND SECOND CITIES (369B–373E)

### THE PRIMITIVE PARADISE (369B–372E)

Beginning with the needs for food, shelter, and clothing, Socrates describes the growth of a minimal community. Justice and injustice reside somewhere in the relations among its members, for if it is a real community it will contain both just and unjust behavior. Since this first city has been conjured up in the simplest terms, it will contain none of the institutions, bureaucracies, and power relations that complicate our study of existing political organizations. The seat of justice and injustice will come more readily into view.

It is hard to imagine a plainer community than this first city Socrates describes, although he is practical enough not to make the city *too* stark (369b–372e). It will have farmers, builders, and weavers, every variety of craftworker, even merchants and a currency. The city owes its simplicity to its having been derived, as if mathematically, from two principles:

(1)  ⑤ Humans taken individually are not self-sufficient. (369b)
(2)  ⑥ People are naturally disposed to perform different tasks. (370a–b)

The city comes into existence in the first place because of ⑤; it takes the form it has because of ⑥. To ⑤ the city owes its characteristic of being a unity formed out of the multiplicity of its inhabitants: if it were not a unity it could not truly represent the joining of its citizens. Plato repeatedly emphasizes the preservation of civic unity; when he does, he believes himself to be returning to one of the guiding principles of all human society.

Given that a city must exist, and that it exists to satisfy human needs, the remaining question is how those needs might be met most efficiently. Plato introduces ⑥, the principle of the division of labor, to explain why societies tend to be heterogeneous rather than homogeneous. Nothing could guarantee efficiency better than a social arrangement in which all work is done by those best suited to it.

Three comments about ⑥. First, the division of labor has a natural origin. Socrates uses words for 'nature' and 'natural' in defending ⑥ (370a, b; 374e). Secondly, the principle should not be mistaken for praise of individuality. Plato wants nothing to do with a society that encourages experimentation in ways of life – see his disapproving description of democracy (557c–558c). On the contrary, ⑥ defends a political organization with the power to impose social roles on its citizens. Finally, ⑥ has far-reaching implications. In this chapter alone, it underwrites both a standing army and the censorship of dramatic poetry. Plato has been preparing for this principle's appearance with the proposition (③) that everything has its special work. ⑥ merely applies that principle to human beings.

The first city complete, Socrates asks where its justice and injustice may be found. Adeimantus suggests that they arose 'somewhere in some need these men have of one another' (372a). ⑤ and ⑥ together entail that every city requires cooperation. People have to come together but also have to perform different tasks. Since justice is the essential social virtue, it must amount to cooperation. (① and especially ② are also reflected in Adeimantus' suggestion.) Plato cannot rest with this analysis, since he is about to turn to complex societies whose justice and injustice call for complex definitions. But the definition he finally reaches (433a) will resemble this initial account in finding justice in the cooperation among social groups with different functions.

Aside from wanting a first sketch of the city, Plato has an ulterior motive in describing this primitive community. In mounting his challenge, Glaucon looked back to the birth of human society as evidence for a conventionalist interpretation of justice. The history of an institution often makes a feature of it that had been taken for granted look arbitrary. If the concept of justice arose at a particular time in human societies, it is not an inevitable fact about such societies.

Plato counters this skeptical use of history with his own story of the origins of society. By basing his first city entirely on ⑤ and ⑥, both of which he claims to be natural facts, he is arguing that human society is natural. Because justice arises in that one social relationship that is essential to every city, justice in turn becomes a natural possibility for every society. The social contract that constitutes the ground for morality was not invented by human beings but reflects necessary truths about their natures.

The dismissive way to put this point is by saying Plato wants to help his argument move forward smoothly. He would be hard-pressed to prove the natural value of moral behavior if he has to start with morality understood as social. Modern philosophical tastes, shaped by Hobbes and other philosophers, incline toward what feel like tougher truths about human beings' selfishness and drive to dominate. Social scientists sometimes call this the debate between functionalist visions of society and those that read society as conflicted. Is Plato the innocent unaware of such rival explanations of communal life, or is he merely playing the innocent as he advances premises very close to the conclusion he wants to prove?

The question whether people are really selfish or really cooperative is notoriously intractable. Humans have never been observed in a natural condition prior to the emergence of society. But two considerations might support Plato's conception of society. For one thing, Glaucon's argument, like Thrasymachus' 'advantage of the stronger,' gives short shrift to nonhuman threats and challenges: scarcity, cold, accident, and predatory animals. Cooperation looks like a reaction to the more basic fact of human aggressiveness, only assuming a scenario that conveniently omits those challenges. Cooperating may be the second thing people do if they start by attacking one another, but if they start out under attack by large predators and hungry for the food they can't hunt alone, then cooperation looks more like the first order of business, and there is nothing idealistic about saying so.

Glaucon and his modern sympathizers also misrepresent nature by imagining human beings as inherently unsociable. Soon Socrates will compare the city's soldiers to dogs, and dogs ought to call to mind social animals in general. The natural world contains beasts that prowl alone, but also plenty of others for whom collective life is the norm. No question, social life for humans is fragile – it is compromised almost as soon as it begins – but a healthy community does not have to rest on denying human nature.

## THE SECOND CITY (372E–373E)

Glaucon objects that Socrates has described 'a city of pigs' (372d). The hardy hamlet strikes Glaucon as too much unlike any civilized community he'd want to live in. To keep his society close to the demands of nature, Socrates permitted its inhabitants only the desires required by nature; Glaucon, who is accustomed to more rarefied tastes, wants a city to provide for those tastes as well. So Socrates agrees to expand his initial account to produce what he calls a 'feverish' and 'luxurious' city, as opposed to the true or healthy city of his own fantasy (372e).

If the point of the political discussion had been to describe the best city possible, why look at a worse variety? Since Socrates never returns to his first city, the entire *Republic* might seem to betray the political organization that Plato really wants.

One explanation is that Plato does not really endorse the city of pigs, but only inserts it into this passage as a first draft for the true city. After all, this will be an unphilosophical city. It does not promise to foster the self-awareness needed for cultivating genuine virtue. Maybe Cephalus could live in the city of pigs, but not Socrates. If the virtuous life calls for an understanding of what makes virtuous behavior right (and certainly Plato thinks it does), a city this simple could never achieve the highest virtue. Socrates never rejects the name of 'city of pigs' for this town: so he may be conceding that life here falls short of the fullest possibilities open to humans.

If the city without philosophy is perforce something less than the best city, Plato's abandonment of it hints at the role that philosophy will play in his city. Modern readers find antecedents of totalitarianism in the way Plato's philosopher-rulers impose their superior theoretical understanding on the citizens (see Books 5–7). The very idea of rule by philosophers, solely on the grounds that they are philosophers, *can* smell of totalitarianism. But with the move beyond the city of pigs, Plato might be saying that the only workable alternative is too unreflective to contain virtue.

This explanation may go too far. Socrates does not challenge Glaucon's moniker for the simple city, but he also does not stop calling it the true or healthy city. The first city's limitation might consist, not in its inability to foster justice, but in our inability to see the justice in it. In that case it is the wrong entity to study from the point of view of developing a political philosophy. The very perfection of the first city, which leaves it lacking any irrational or expansive elements that call for social constraint, makes it an unilluminating case study for a theory that will see justice as a network of restrictions. Perhaps justice will not appear as clearly unless it has the opportunity to contrast itself with the injustice possible in a more complex city. However desirable in itself, the city of pigs is not an apt subject for philosophical inquiry.

Likewise, the human soul that resembles this first city would be a harmonious soul untouched by inner conflict. Some interpreters read the *Republic*'s psychological theory as allowing for some souls, the best ones, that are perfectly simple, always agreeing with the dictates of reason (see 443c–e). But while this is the best soul to possess it is not an instructive one to study, precisely because it is so different from existing souls.

The more plausible reading is this second account, in which the city of pigs gets passed over not as a political option but only as the object of inquiry. For one thing, Plato often speaks fondly of rural life (see *Statesman* 271d–272b, *Laws* 739). More significantly, this reading makes the passage a warning not to mistake the *Republic* for a fantasy. To the extent that utopias describe the best communities possible, the *Republic* acknowledges and resists the temptation to utopia. It would be sweet to daydream about the perfect community, but Glaucon's grumble shows that such daydreams would never bear fruit. Plato wants to produce a political philosophy not only rigorous in its theory, but also imaginable in practice. He will compromise enough with the world as he has found it to make his theory desirable to more than just a few ascetics.

This does not mean that Plato concedes everything to popular tastes. Even though Socrates begins by listing every luxury an Athenian of his time could have wanted, from perfume to poetry, he eventually purges this city of its excesses (399c). Not every taste will find satisfaction in the city. Some (especially the taste for poetry) are by their natures corrupting, while others (e.g. for jewelry) are tolerable only in moderation. But Socrates never again suggests trimming the city back down to its first incarnation.

## THE GUARDIANS (373E–412B)

## A STANDING ARMY (373E–376C)

A luxurious city will go to war (373d–e). ⑥ comes into play again: just as a city functions more efficiently when the cobbler and the merchant perform their tasks and no others, it will also function better if its warring is conducted by specialists – if it has a standing army (374), which Plato calls an army of guardians.

Plato finds himself in a difficult position. Without ⑥ he would have no organizing principle to justify his city's politics, and ⑥ forces him to accept the existence of a permanent professional army. At the same time, he has seen enough of politics to fear that a permanent class of warriors might impose a self-serving dictatorship on the defenseless citizenry. In such a city there could be no justice.

The army of Plato's city evokes Sparta, which Plato admired in spite of his own city's war against it. Following Socrates, one of Athens' foremost sympathizers with Sparta, Plato appreciated the discipline and stability of Spartan society. He respected a society that won so many wars, as every Athenian did in that time before underdogs became attractive. But he knew that Sparta's class structure meant tyranny and bursts of civil war. The Spartans had settled their city by conquering a native population, whom they forced into servitude as landed slaves or serfs, performing all their productive labor. The Spartans had to keep these Helots docile with constant threats of force; even so they rose up in protracted rebellions. One revolt early in the fifth century had lasted for years. And when the subject populations did finally win some measure of independence (as they did when Plato was writing the *Republic*) they made clear how little attachment they felt for the old, stratified Sparta. Rule by force was distasteful and also, in the long run, inexpedient.

Thus keeping the guardians loyal to the other citizens' best interests becomes Plato's next challenge. He specifies that challenge as the difficulty of ensuring that an armed class is both ferocious and gentle. Gentleness and rage seem unlikely to live together in one soul, so the city appears to be an impossible project (375c).

This passage deserves close attention for several reasons. It is the *Republic*'s first expression of the fear that the well-designed city will be impossible – or more precisely, the first acknowledgment that when planning a good city one must constantly ask how to make it possible. Anyone can invent utopias. The political philosopher has to invent a way to live in one. Even if a human community is a naturally occurring object, a good community might not be.

The second point to pause over is that Plato's response to the city's threatened impossibility (as it will be again at 473d) appeals to the nature of philosophical souls. In this passage, being philosophical only means loving knowledge (376b). Perhaps for this reason the discussion is unsatisfying. Later Plato will have much to say about philosophers' natures (e.g. 475d–480a, 485d), and when he does say more his claim of something philosophical about rulers will not sound as gratuitous as it does here. But the grain of his idea is present: philosophy makes the impossible happen.

In any case, Plato's call for a special nature suited to military duty shows how deep he takes the problem to run. The *Republic* persists in the faith that a single character exists that displays both ideal rage and ideal quiescence; later, as in the *Statesman*, Plato will give up his hope for a soul that perfectly harmonizes all good motives. With that hope he will also give up the hope for an ideal city.

The third significant feature of this passage is its comparison of guardians to dogs, a sign of the role that nature will play in his city's government. Though Plato speaks of noble dogs' 'natures' as both fierce and mild, he understood that a dog's nature does not exist in the wild, that as the longest-domesticated animal it possesses a nature shaped by human interventions. (See 459a–b on dog breeding.) It would be good if the city's guardians likewise represented a mix between vigorous natural endowments and patient, foresightful acculturation.

In short, Plato trusts the guardians' education to complete the process of making them good rulers. Like other radical reformers, he is a pessimist about the possibility of a good society, given human nature as it exists, and an optimist about the power of education to change human nature. But education as he imagines it will not much resemble what it had been in ancient Athens, and transforming the system goes far beyond tinkering with reading lists or overhauling systems of formal schooling. Plato's educational reform will transform the entire society. From here to nearly the end of Book 3, he details what activities the young guardians may engage in, what poetry they read, even what music they listen to, in order that they might be simultaneously fierce in war and gentle at home (375b–c).

## THE GUARDIANS' EDUCATION (375B–412B)

Socrates calls music and gymnastics the elements of the guardians' education. 'Music' (*mousikê*) means all the activities sponsored by the Muses: poetry of every stripe, dance, astronomy, and history. Of these, Socrates enters into the greatest detail regarding poetry; only in this case do his remarks about education become part of a larger critique of Greek culture.

### Poetry (376c–398b)

From his earliest dialogues to the last one, Plato returns to the subject of poetry, almost always distinguishing between one's irrational experience of poetry and the saner participation in philosophy. Philosophy defines itself against poetry even more than it does against sophistry or rhetoric. Book 10 of the *Republic* refers to an 'ancient' quarrel between philosophy and poetry (607b) that in Plato's philosophical city must result in poetry's expulsion. In the *Ion* and (more ambiguously) the *Phaedrus*, poetry becomes a species of madness; elsewhere (*Apology*, *Laws*, *Protagoras*, *Sophist*) Plato identifies poetry with ignorance, fraud, and cognitive confusion.

In Books 2 and 3 of the *Republic* Plato's attack focuses on the role of poetry in the guardians' education. First Socrates forbids the young guardians' exposure to tales that depict the gods initiating evil, promoting unwarranted suffering, changing their shapes, or lying. Such myths misrepresent the gods and set bad examples for the young. Nor should stories about gods or heroes show them as weak or undignified, for the guardians ought to have no share in such traits. The protagonists especially should not fear death or lament it, and should master their ignoble appetites rather than yield to them.

It is too early in the game to legislate the content of stories about human beings. That will have to wait until we have shown what sort of life is in fact best (392c). Socrates seems to be saying that the regulation of poetry brings it into agreement with what we know to be true. This principle echoes Socrates' first criticism of tales about the gods, that they are lies that do not resemble what we can demonstrate to be true about gods (377d–e, 379a). Since the poems of Homer and Hesiod accounted for nearly all of a young Athenian's reading, Plato wants to correct their errors. His censorship seems to work only against falsehood, and only with an eye to audiences too young and impressionable to read these pieces critically.

Justified in such terms, Plato's censorship may sound inoffensive, as if he only wanted to weed outdated textbooks out from local schools, as we routinely discard books on genetics and astronomy that contain superseded theories. Of course, Plato is speaking of falsehoods about the gods rather than about the motions of the planets. But even overlooking the important differences between these subjects, we cannot excuse this section so easily. How pernicious Plato's censorship is depends on the answers to two questions: To what extent does the censorship in fact trim poetry in accord with the truth of the matter? And how far into the community will Plato reach to suppress false or insidious poetry?

In the beginning, Plato's goal seems to be to avoid falsehood at all costs. But a few lines after the beginning of his critique, Socrates expresses his willingness to ban stories about Cronus 'even if they were true' (378a). By the time he has gone on to Homeric heroes, Socrates' references to what must be true dwindle beside his concern over what effect the stories might have on the guardians (386c; 387b, c; 388a, d; 391e). Any history book can supply stories of tyrants who live into hearty old age: Plato would never accept such tales merely on account of their truth. Nor does he object to his rulers lying to the young (382c–d). When a lie would benefit the city it is positively called for (389b–c; also 414–15, 458b–460b).

This greater importance of psychological effect over factual truth implies that the truth of Plato's sanitized myths is not an integral part of his argument. If he had reason to believe the gods to be deceptive and malicious, he would still advocate censoring stories about them. His educational plan aims above all else at inculcating the right behavior in his young soldiers.

The fact that this is a plan for education might still make the charge of censorship sound premature. School libraries today don't stock their shelves with pornography or manuals for making bombs. They have to care what children are exposed to.

Still, Plato's position is more radical than any advocated today. Contemporary book bannings at their worst concentrate on books written for juveniles. Plato wants to bowdlerize Homer's *Iliad* and *Odyssey* and the works of Hesiod and Aeschylus. Homer's poems stood at the heart of a cultural education, and together with Hesiod's poetry they transmitted the essential elements of Greek religion. The tragedians were considered moral teachers. In subjecting his civilization's morally most prestigious poetry to such stern scrutiny, Plato is advocating censorship more extensive than anything familiar to contemporary democracies.

One more apology is possible. Children can be easily confused, especially by exciting stories. Near the end of the film *Birth of a Nation*, a mob of emancipated slaves besieges the cabin that holds a family of former slave owners. The little cabin shakes before the crazed and bloodthirsty mob. At last the brave warriors of the Ku Klux Klan ride over the hill to preserve justice. The artistic elements combine so powerfully to depict the Klansmen as heroes as to mislead young viewers into a despicable moral belief. It would be simpler not to let children watch the film until they are old enough to resist its narrative strategies. Why not let Plato do the same for the young guardians and Homer?

The problem, often overlooked, is that everyone in the city is affected by the censorship. As long as anyone at all has heard the objectionable tales, eventually the children will hear them as well. Socrates specifies that 'as few as possible' should know that Cronus castrated his father (378a); that no one, 'younger or older,' may hear it said that a god causes evil (380b-c); that mothers will remain ignorant of stories about the gods changing shape, so that they do not pass them along to their children (381e). To protect the young guardians, the entire city will have to change its uses of poetry.

In Book 10 Plato will make clear that even virtuous adults risk moral corruption from the poets. For now this implication remains latent, given that his topic is the education of the young. But he tips his hand when Socrates says the city will 'not provide a chorus' (not arrange the funding on which performances depended) to any tragedy that slanders the gods (383c), or when he says that certain things 'should not be heard, from childhood on' (386a; see 387b). '[W]e'll not let our men believe' that Achilles was illiberal with money or disdainful of the gods (391b). It is worth bearing this greater implication in mind, to lessen the shock of Book 10 when it comes. The plain fact is that this first criticism of poetry already goes beyond care for children's minds and into the realm of state control over the arts. One might agree with Plato's recommendations; one may not believe them to be mild.

From the content of poetry Socrates turns to its formal characteristics (392c–398b). Stories can be cast in either narrative or dramatic form, depending on whether the author makes the characters speak for themselves. Drama tells its stories exclusively through dialogue; most historical narrative contains none; the Homeric epics combine dialogue and narrative. With few exceptions, Socrates proposes purging poetry of its dialogue. Direct speech is inauthenticity and deception on the poet's part, the path to vice for a play's actor. The *Iliad* and *Odyssey* will become plot synopses of their former selves, while tragedy and comedy disappear altogether.

This passage contains the *Republic*'s first discussion of *mimêsis*. Sometimes translated 'imitation,' *mimêsis* began to function as a technical term of aesthetics just before Plato's time. Plato built from earlier mentions of the term, constructing a theory of art around the relationship between a thing and its representation in poetry and painting. In Book 3 his attention is restricted to the representation of character. Since the Platonic city was founded on the assumption that each citizen would perform a single task (⑥), writing and performing a character's part become perversions of citizenship, as they give a single person more than one nature to live out (397d–398a).

Then the argument sets the division of labor aside to look at the commonsense problem with imitating vicious behavior. Mimicry leads the young into bad habits, coarse language, and inappropriate responses to crises (395c–d). At most the young guardians should dramatize the lives of their most virtuous role models (396b–e).

This last complaint reveals Plato's sensitivity to the power of drama. Good acting feels so magical that we can forget how common it is – forget that children act when they play house and war and feign courage, devotion, indignation (but also play at smoking and cursing), and that children's performances enter into their characters. Even professional actors might be changed by their roles: on this point we're tempted to smirk at Plato's simplemindedness, but the contrary assumption – that people simulate passions toward strangers and then return to feeling nothing – is at least as naive.

Still, apart from its ambiguous use of the word *mimêsis* – Socrates sometimes seems to be thinking about acting, sometimes about playwriting – this stretch of argument is prosaic. It works only against the practice of reciting parts in a play, or the dialogue from an epic, and it understands recitation in the crudest way. Finally, the implications of the argument are limited by Socrates' focus on the one who is acting out a part. Since only a fraction of any city would write for or perform in a dramatic festival, the argument blames mimetic literature for damage to what could only be a few citizens. In Book 10 Socrates will expand *mimêsis* into a more complex phenomenon, and overtly bar all poetry from the city.

## Music and gymnastics (398b–412b)

Most of the remainder of Book 3 prescribes more details of the guardians' education. The modes and rhythms of music, and the guardians' physical training, all aim at producing tough soldiers, sufficiently immersed in the fine arts not to treat the unarmed citizens savagely, but not so softened by sweet food and music as to become incapable of fighting the city's enemies. Education unites their aesthetic taste with their conscience.

This last point is worth noting. For Plato, education begins with the inculcation of good habits (even if it must go beyond habit in the end). He may insist that drama corrupts the city by multiplying citizens' tasks, but he seems more moved by the claim that mimicry establishes 'habits and nature' (395d) in the mimic. Plato's reader must not neglect this side of the pedagogical theory, for it underwrites an important aspect of his moral psychology. Perfect virtue might work from the inside out, with intellectual understanding of the good coordinating one's actions in service to the good; but virtue also works from the outside in, which is to say that copying fine habits helps to produce a fine nature. Indeed this process by which behavior shapes the soul helps to ensure that the good-souled people who end up being the happiest of all are identical with the people who act according to the principles of justice. The next chapter will show how much this matters.

The *Republic*'s discussion of early education even finds a moral benefit in purely aesthetic experiences (400d–402a). Painting, furniture making, architecture, and the other crafts can issue in either graceful or malformed productions (401a). The beautiful productions dispose a soul toward virtue – reason and the virtues themselves being beautiful – before that soul even has the capacity to follow an argument on virtue's behalf (402a–d). If Plato is a moralist about the arts, he is one with sensitivity to the purely aesthetic features of art. He is a moralist not by virtue of rejecting grace and charm, but inasmuch as he justifies such properties of a work on moral grounds.

By now Plato's attention has drifted from the inhabitants of his city as a whole to the army that defends them. After introducing the guardians he hardly goes back to the huge class of merchants, farmers, artisans, and wage laborers, except occasionally to say that they should know their place. *Their* children's education remains unexamined; the pattern of their daily life apparently deserves no comment, though Plato will specify the dining and sexual practices of his guardians. It has become a commonplace to accuse Plato the aristocrat of keeping himself unaware of ordinary people's lives. But that accusation suggests that the large productive class consists of thuggish, unskilled workers. In fact, Plato conceives of this class as equivalent to an entire Athens: some of its members make shoes, but others are doctors, and others wealthy traders. Plato says little about them because their lives remain unchanged.

More importantly, Plato addresses only the class of guardians because only they *need* special attention. The members of the productive class find sufficient incentive for their labors in the profit they earn. Their motives are purely economic. This is why they gladly live in the *Republic*'s good city, where inexpensive public servants take over all the chores and risks of warfare and administration, leaving money lovers free to make money. The army cannot act from the same kinds of economic motives, for then the soldiers would loot the citizens. The good city only exists if political power remains divorced from economic power. Plato saw as clearly as Marx later would that in the usual course of events all power rests on wealth. Without the chance to share in the city's riches, the guardians need another incentive; their education provides that incentive by molding them into obedient patriots.

## CLASS RELATIONS AND THE JUSTICE OF A CITY (412B–434C)

### THE COMPLETE POLITICAL PLAN (412B–427C)

With two of the city's classes specified, Plato turns to the question of who 'will rule and who be ruled' (412b). Socrates selects the best and oldest guardians to rule. In one sense his act does not define a third class, given that the rulers come from the ranks of the guardians. But because the work of the two groups will differ, Socrates gives them two different titles, 'complete guardian' for the ruler and 'auxiliary' for the one ruled (414b).

This analysis of social roles, now complete, marks the total break between the *Republic* and the conception of citizenship that informed politics in most Greek cities. The Athenians (and many others) combined in their persons the functions that the *Republic* separates. The typical male citizen farmed or did other productive work for money, fought in his city's army, voted on legislation or to elect public officials, and often participated in public office. He was ruler, soldier, and producer rolled into one, and most cities of the classical era besides Sparta saw this coordination of functions as the defining virtue of their citizenry. Thus the proposal to divide up these three social functions is not just one more bright idea about making the city efficient, but a repudiation of classical Greek civic life. If Plato has his way, classical Greek civilization must come to an end.

If the triply engaged man of Athens was its paradigmatic citizen and the face of the democracy, the exemplary member of the *Republic*'s body politic, now fully visible, is the ruling guardian, not the commonest citizen – probably the rarest – but nonetheless the figure Plato chooses to embody his political ideal. In place of the yeoman hoplite (as the armed infantryman was called) comes this new model for Greek youths to emulate, and the closest thing in the *Republic* to a complete human being.

Accordingly, just as he stopped referring to the city's productive class after introducing the standing army, so too Socrates will increasingly ignore the army as he examines the nature and nurture of the city's administrators. We see as soon as the rulers are named how much of their lives will be marked by tests above and beyond the military discipline they grew up with (412e–414a). If the concentration of arms into the class of soldiers made Socrates eager to provide for their civic loyalty, the more dangerous concentration of legislative, executive, and judicial power in the hands of the guardians makes him double his efforts to exclude unfit citizens from this rank. His stress on the subject betrays Plato's worry that the good city will never work *without* a concentration of power, but that *given* a concentration of power it will be kept only by superhuman effort from sliding into corruption. Again, the opposed pressures on the guardians – to wield power freely and yet never abuse it – threaten to render their existence impossible; but at the same time (again) the city's existence is only possible if theirs is.

We come upon one of Plato's superhuman efforts in the *noble lie* that Socrates proposes to tell the citizens (414b–415d). Their memories of childhood and education had been a dream, for in fact, the story will go, all the citizens sprang fully grown out of the earth. As they are children of the earth, it is not surprising that some (the guardians) have gold mixed into their souls, others (the auxiliaries) silver, the rest bronze and iron. Hence their place in the city reflects their true nature as crafted by gods, not the historical accident that separates the citizens of other societies.

Again we find Socrates seeking a natural basis for social phenomena. He takes his story to be an allegory of ⑥; the lie is 'noble' because it resembles the truth, as poets' lies about the gods do not (see 382d). As any effective propagandist has to, he fashions this myth of the state out of elements that his audience would have found familiar. Thus his positive mythmaking resembles the negative arguments in Book 2, against poets' treatments of the same material. The tale is 'Phoenician' (414c) because it recalls the mythical birth of Thebans out of the earth in which Cadmus, a Phoenician, sowed a serpent's teeth. The differentiation of people by metal, meanwhile, recalls Hesiod's five ages of humanity.

Closer to home is Athenian autochthony, some form of which was long-standing and common in Athens. Sometimes the first kings of Athens were called earthborn, sometimes the city's entire original populace; tragedy, comedy, and funeral rhetoric all cited this hometown belief, which appears explicitly in Plato's dialogues (*Critias*, *Menexenus*, *Timaeus*). The Athenians prized this supernatural guarantee of their belonging in Attica, which for them was something very much *not* merely for Thebes and Phoenicia.

The *Republic* is ultimately conservative about religion. Socrates defers to the Delphic oracle as the highest authority (427b–c, 461e, 540c), no matter what he has said about stories of the gods. So the noble lie is the strongest possible way to justify allegiance among the people at large, but it is also supposed to show that the political order is true. Plato does not use religion cynically. As told, the noble lie is meant to generate two kinds of loyalty. It implies that the city is its citizens' mother (414e), and that nothing matters more than each citizen's assignment to the right class (415b–c). By this point ⑥, the principle of the division of labor has outweighed any question of how the citizens want to live. For that matter, the citizens' unity as children of one mother reinforces ⑤, and the so-called lie actually states, the two basic principles of society; in practice, however, Socrates uses the noble lie to refer to the differences between citizens more than to their common origin. In any case, both principles feel alien to modern open democracy, especially as Plato draws ever-stronger conclusions from them, and this might be the first point at which the reader accuses Plato of totalitarian politics. Not only has he separated a society into castes, but he wants the people to accept a myth of the state that justifies their own positions.

Although Plato is no democrat, one might defend him from the harshest criticisms by pointing out how his classes are supposed to function. Since the class differences in his city separate economic from political power, higher status does not translate into wealth or enjoyment. Indeed, Adeimantus will complain about the rulers' unhappiness (419a; also 519d–521a), because ruling this city promises no advantage to the stronger.

But on a more adventurous reading of the noble lie, the *Republic* does not even need this much defending; for rather than propagandizing to young citizens, the lie may be said to initiate the lifelong process of their philosophical enlightenment. Other stories might communicate deep truths and hidden meanings, but their exciting surface story (a god chains his mother to her throne, etc.) distracts the youthful mind from digging for those truths (378d). The noble lie tells the young citizens their life has been a dream, a thing Socrates will say about nonphilosophers at large (476c). This surface meaning inspires young minds to seek out deeper truth. The shrewdest ones will think: If what felt like vivid waking life was really a dream, what opinions of today might turn out to have been illusory too? As a redescription of the life that we naively trust, the noble lie valorizes philosophical awakening; it warns you not to trust the beliefs and values haphazardly taken in during childhood. If the noble lie is a useful fiction describing political relations in the city, it is the kind of fiction that overtly proclaims the fictionality of such descriptions.

A final line of defense is often made at this point, but it does not work as well as the others. Plato bases class distinction on ability. An undeserving child of guardians will pass to the lower class, and the talented child of farmers or laborers can become a guardian (415b–c). Socrates makes this promise explicit at 423c–d, and at 468a he provides for the demotion of cowardly guardians. It is a nice intention, but barely more than that. Plato expects gold and silver children to turn up only rarely among bronze parents, so the *Republic* identifies no mechanism for examining children of the productive class for signs of talent. Without some such examinations, they can never be moved up. Plato means what he says, but he does not care enough about social mobility. It would be such an injustice, on his terms as well as ours, to deny gifted children the place they are most suited to, that anyone who seems to be establishing a caste system but promises that mobility is possible had better say exactly *how* it will be possible. Anything vaguer is an insult to the people in question, however sincere Plato may have been, in the same way that modern politicians' slogans about poverty, however heartfelt, demean the poor if the slogans do not turn into programs.

With the social structure of his city in place, Plato begins to describe its workings. As before, the greatest issue is the potential corruption of the guardians. Although the radical proposals for avoiding that corruption will wait until Book 5, we already see how unusually the guardians will live. The rulers and auxiliaries share their meals. No one among them owns more than essential personal property; no one has a private room (416d–e). No guardian or soldier may touch gold or silver, or even be under the same roof with it (417a). In a sense the soldiers' education never ends, for this discipline is intended to stave off any temptation they might feel to seize worldly power.

Socrates will expand on the guardians' lives later, and especially on one comment made in passing here, about the community of women and children (423e). He says enough already to make clear why the auxiliaries and rulers are permitted nothing we would recognize as private. Even to consider private benefits for this class would be to give its members an allegiance distinct from their allegiance to the city. The rulers would divide into factions, and the city would lose its opportunity for happiness.

One characteristic version of Plato's emphasis on the whole city comes at 420b–421c, when Socrates answers Adeimantus' complaint that the guardians will not be happy. Another occurs in a discussion of war. Every city but the ideal one, Socrates says, 'is very many cities but not a city ... There are two, in any case, warring with each other, one of the poor, the other of the rich' (422e–423a). This passage, both revealing and typical, names Plato's greatest fear, civil unrest, and identifies its cause in competition over money. Plato imagines a solution not in terms of achieving an equitable balance among competing interests, but one that comes with the elimination of competition. For Plato all civil discord is a sign of political failure, not because he venerates order for its own sake, but because he refuses to see discord as the clash between genuinely opposed philosophical views. Like Marx, Plato locates all conflict in economic conflict; hence it always means that members of the city are putting their needs above the good of all. Civil unrest represents an abandonment of the enterprise that the city makes possible.

## JUSTICE AND THE OTHER VIRTUES (427C–434C)

Finally Socrates returns to one of the two originating questions of the *Republic*'s conversation, 'What is justice?' The participants have characterized a city in enough detail to assure themselves of its goodness; now they can use it as the large-scale model of justice they needed. Socrates lays out the strategy for finding justice:

(1)   The city as described is perfectly good.
∴ (2) It is wise, courageous, moderate, and just.
∴ (3) If we set aside those defining characteristics of the city responsible for its wisdom, courage, and moderation, whatever characteristics remain will define its justice. (427e–428a)

Although this argument may point to a fruitful *strategy* for identifying justice, we should not expect too much from it as a *proof*. Even granting the truth of (1), the argument cannot reach (3) without two unstated assumptions. First, (2) will not follow from (1) unless we assume

(1')  If a thing is good, then it is wise, courageous, moderate, and just.

Goodness must include at least these virtues for (2) to follow. All four were indeed accepted by most of Plato's contemporaries as virtues, though not in any systematic way. But even if we accept (1'), we also need

(2')  If a thing is good, then it is wise, courageous, moderate, and just, *and nothing besides*.

For Plato to know that once moderation, wisdom, and courage have been accounted for, 'what's left over' must be justice, he first needs to demonstrate that no other virtues exist. These four may indeed add up to a moral life. Together they allow for action and reflection, both self-regarding constraint and consideration of others. The problem is that, as Plato lays out this section, he makes the site of justice appear to depend on its being the only virtue not accounted for when the other three have been assigned to their places in the city. He turns a casual belief into a technical claim, as if an astronomer were to pronounce the cause of supernovas to be a mineral, on the grounds that it is neither animal nor vegetable.

Counterexamples of other virtues come to mind. The suppressed premise (2') will seem all the more unconvincing to modern readers who might want to include humility or love in the list. But even someone of Plato's time and place might object that the list is incomplete. In other dialogues Plato treats piety as a virtue (*Laches* 199d, *Meno* 78d, *Protagoras* 329c, *Gorgias* 507b); by the time he writes the *Republic* it has disappeared from his list. Has justice absorbed piety, at least inasmuch as that is understood to be law-abiding behavior? Or perhaps the *Republic*'s psychological definitions of the virtues cannot accommodate the virtue that is oriented toward the gods outside. In any case the disappearance of piety weakens the argument that depends on an exhaustive list of virtues.

Suppose we do name three features of the city. Where will its leftover features appear? The argument can dissolve into metaphors. Its main value lies in outlining a method of inquiry for someone who wants to identify a community's virtues.

Using this method, Socrates and Glaucon can conclude that the city owes its wisdom to the rulers (428d). They are not the only citizens with knowledge of their work, but they are the only ones whose wisdom makes the city wise. A city's wisdom manifests itself in the city's treatment of its citizens and of other cities (428c–d). But that wisdom is nothing but wise rule, and rule is the work of the guardians. To be a wise city is therefore to have wise guardians (428a–429a).

Why does Plato rule out the expertise of other citizens? He would answer that only the guardians' knowledge concerns benefits to the city *as a whole* (428d). This is not a matter of the producers' motives but of the kind of work they do. A farmer may know best how to maximize the city's production of wheat. But political questions about farming, which the city will answer either wisely or unwisely, concern tariffs on imported food, embargoes on exports, and state support for foods that are otherwise too expensive to produce. In such cases the benefit of food production needs to be weighed against other benefits to the city. Even supposing farmers look beyond their interests, the narrowness of their expertise would leave them incapable of subsuming their farming knowledge under a more general question about the city. Farming knowledge is the only expertise they have.

Modern proponents of free enterprise may object that a society functions best when all producers aim at their own profit. But even if that is true, the decision to make enterprise free in the city can only be made by its rulers. Even advocates of the free market would not call a society wise just because it contains profitable businesses, but only if its government permits those businesses to seek profit without hindrance.

Plato's point is not to glorify the guardians, but to analyze the concept of 'a wise city' in a way that will yield him a strategy for defining justice. A city's virtues can seem like vague entities. Plato points a way out of the vagueness by locating wisdom in the individual wisdom of the members of a class.

Next, courage means the army's courage, as only that constitutes the 'political' bravery belonging to a whole city (429a–430c). The auxiliaries' courage, however, unlike the rulers' wisdom, might not amount to a fully developed human virtue (as Socrates hints at 430c), for the city is courageous even if its soldiers do not fully understand what they should and shouldn't fear, but only persist in true opinions about danger that they were taught (429c–430b).

Courage does reside in the military class (431e). And the 'right opinion' about what is terrible need not pass from rulers to soldiers – Socrates' language rather implies that the content of this education comes from the city's founders. Nevertheless it is worth bearing in mind that the army's courage amounts to something different from complete courage in its individual members, for complete courage in a human being requires that the person know (not just believe rightly) what is worth fearing.

This is one of the points at which it becomes difficult to conceive of the classes in the *Republic*'s city containing full-fledged human beings.

Moderation resides in the city's classes, too, but now the analysis of virtue gets complicated (430d–432b). *Sophrosunê* means a habit of restrained, even deferential behavior – self-control that expresses itself as modesty. It also implies self-knowledge: one becomes gentle by virtue of being conscious of one's shortcomings. Now that the simpler virtues have brought Socrates to look for virtues in the city's class structure, he can define self-mastery in terms of the same structure, as the harmonious domination of one class over the rest. Because their domination is harmoniously achieved, the classes ruled by the guardians accept their rule willingly.

Only justice remains to be defined. But rather than look for some social structure his analysis omitted, Socrates announces that justice in the finished city is the principle according to which he and his interlocutors constructed the city, namely the principle that everyone has a single job to do and ought to do only that one job (432e–433a). As a principle of justice this definition deviates from ⑥, for Socrates is no longer interested in the division of occupations into farming, shoemaking, and so on. The effect of carpenters making shoes poses no threat to a city's well-being, compared to what happens if either carpenters or shoemakers govern (434a–b). The city's three classes correspond to the three major kinds of work a person may do for one's society, and it is these three labors that must remain distinct for a city to be just.

Socrates defends his definition with a mix of common sense and theoretical arguments. He identifies his definition with the proverbial injunction 'not to be a busybody' (433a). Then he claims that it satisfies the argument with which he began the search for virtues. Justice is 'left over' after the other three virtues are defined, presumably by being a virtue not identical with any of those three. Its status is higher than the others' because when the members of each class do what they ought to, the rulers will rule (wisely), the soldiers will preserve the city (bravely), and the farmers and laborers will get their private work done and leave the rest to the guardians. In short, if everyone in the city is politically just, the city as a whole will be wise, courageous, and moderate.

Justice includes all the other virtues; it is not *identical* to the sum of the others, because it has a distinct description.

Plato has not relied illegitimately on the argument that introduced this section. The virtues other than justice can be assigned to their classes of the city whether or not they add up to goodness. As for justice, Plato's essential point about it may be lifted off the argument: justice cannot be accounted for by the operations of any one class, institution, or social body in a community. Analytical approaches to justice will always fail to explain its origins, as long as the inquirer looks at something less than the whole community, i.e. looks at some social action that is less than the cooperation of all parts of the community. The point works equally well if there are three virtues or thirty.

But now it seems as if the irreducibility of justice to any one class in the city makes the whole class structure irrelevant. Why build a picture of the stratified society if its stratifications are unrelated to the city's most important virtue? Why introduce multiplicity – diversity of roles – into the citizenry only to dissolve that multiplicity in the unanimity of their agreement? Here Plato has a plain answer. Justice may not reduce to the functioning of any single part of the city, but its cooperative work requires parts of the city if it is to be defined. The cooperation occurs among discretely identified groups in the city. So the purpose behind Plato's theoretical division of the city had been all along to show how the classes come harmoniously back together.

A similar question will arise about the divisions within a person's soul, and there too the *Republic*'s argument can specify the agreement that is justice only after distinguishing potentially disagreeable elements.

Socrates concludes this passage with two more arguments for his definition of the city's justice, trying to accommodate his theoretical account to ordinary conceptions of justice. First he points out that justly decided court cases are those that assign the appropriate reward to each person. Appropriateness of reward is nothing but an example of his definition (433e–434a). He argues that since the movement between classes destroys a city, and since the greatest evil one can commit against a city is injustice, social mobility must constitute injustice. Social stability is the essence of justice (434a–c).

A crucial premise of this brisk argument is the assumption that injustice is the greatest evil one can commit against a city. This assumption is presented as common sense, and common sense remains a touchstone for Plato's political theory. This does not mean he is out to justify the prejudices of his fellow Athenians. His very separation of the city into functional classes denies the grounding principle of Athenian culture. But a philosopher bent on examining ethical and political concepts is not free to redefine them out of existence. However alien justice might first appear when Plato has defined it, it must bear some relationship to justice as commonly conceived. Otherwise Socrates' interlocutors will rightly complain that this condition of the city may be useful and stable, but not in any way *just*.

Plato continues the balancing act that he began in Book 1. He wants to challenge and change his readers' *conception* of justice in order to produce a better world, but he also wants to preserve their *allegiance* to justice enough not to destroy the world as it stands. His readers should resemble Glaucon and Adeimantus, open to new proposals about morality while retaining their soundly moral characters. In this sense Plato's political and ethical theories need to be both radical and conservative.

## SUGGESTIONS FOR FURTHER READING

This chapter covers a variety of questions and there is a variety of additional readings to consult. On the parallel structure of city and soul see Blössner, 'The city–soul analogy' and above all Ferrari, *City and Soul in Plato's Republic*. On the critique of poetry see Belfiore, '"Lies unlike the truth": Plato on Hesiod, Theogony 27,' Havelock, 'Plato on poetry,' and the relevant parts of Halliwell, *The Aesthetics of Mimesis: Ancient Texts and Modern Problems*. On music in the guardians' education see Schofield, 'Music all pow'rful' and Fitzpatrick, 'Soul music in Plato's *Republic*.' Lear, 'Allegory and myth in Plato's *Republic*,' develops the alternative reading of the noble lie sketched in this chapter. Santas, *Understanding Plato's Republic*, illuminates the idea of a city's virtue; regarding the specific virtue of piety in the *Republic* see McPherran 'The gods and piety of Plato's *Republic*.'

Some historical background has been presupposed in this chapter. For more about those Greek citizens – farmer, soldier, voter – see Hanson, *The Other Greeks: The Family Farm and the Agrarian Roots of Western Civilization*. On Spartan society oriented around its repression of Helots see Paul Cartledge; his introductory works on Sparta include *The Spartans: The World of the Warrior-Heroes of Ancient Greece*, and advanced studies may be found in *Spartan Reflections*.

The reader who begins (around this point) to wonder about Plato's dictatorial tendencies should consult Popper, *The Open Society and Its Enemies*, which calls Plato the predecessor to modern totalitarianism. Responses to Popper are gathered in Bambrough, *Plato, Popper, and Politics*.

# 5

## JUSTICE IN THE SOUL
## (BOOK 4)

The closing pages of Book 4 (434d–445e) bring Socrates back to the subject that Glaucon and Adeimantus had challenged him to explain, justice as it arises in the soul. This section begins to deliver answers to the *Republic*'s initiating questions, though often with hints of further, unanticipated questions.

### JUSTICE IN THE SOUL (434D–445E)

Here, as elsewhere in the *Republic*, its double argument can be disorienting. At times Socrates' language suggests that justice in the city serves only as an analogy to illuminate justice in the individual soul; elsewhere he speaks as though the city had been his subject all along. The argument's divided loyalty is in fact one of the *Republic*'s virtues, proof that Plato takes both subjects seriously. If the dialogue were only an extended analogy, then at this point we would find Plato mechanically transferring what he says about the city to the individual soul. Instead he emphasizes that the political analysis will have to be shown to apply to the soul on independent psychological grounds. If it does not, they will go back to the city and revise their account of *its* virtues (434d–435a). The analogy to the city works only to suggest how to look for justice in the soul.

Because the city's virtues were analyzed in terms of political classes, the *Republic*'s guiding analogy requires that something about the soul correspond to those classes. The stretch of argument that follows (436b–441c) will aim at showing that the soul is complex enough to support the analogy.

## PARTS OF THE SOUL (436B–441C)

The core argument of this section lays out a psychological theory according to which the soul has three parts or agencies. Any word would be imprecise here, and the first subsection of 'Further Discussion' ('Question 1 How does a Soul Have Parts,' pp. 112–15) will address just what Socrates finds three *of.* In any case the soul is a hazy entity, especially in modern secular societies, and imprecision might be the best approach. It may help to replace 'soul' by 'personality' or 'character,' which despite unwanted connotations are broad enough to serve. 'Mind' as the psychoanalysts use it may do; or you can sidestep the problem of translation by bringing the Greek word into English: 'psyche.'

These renditions all have the advantage of not making the entity immortal. Although Plato believes that it is, he does not need immortality for his psychological theory.

The argument begins with internal conflict:

(1) Conflict in the soul implies different parts opposed to one another. (436b–438a)

(2) Desire is opposed by the calculating part of the soul. (438a–439d)

(3) Spirit is different from both desire and the calculating part. (439e–441c)

∴ (4) From (1), (2), and (3), the parts of the soul are identical in number and function with the parts of the city. (441c)

∴ (5) Virtue in the individual person will be structured the same way as virtue in the city. (441c–442d)

As Freud also will, Plato sees inner conflict as both the most important fact about human existence and the phenomenon that most reveals the structure of the personality. They both begin with the misery that people generate in themselves that consists in simultaneous inclinations to accept and refuse, to love and to reject (437b). And both Plato and Freud look at malfunctioning souls to learn how the mechanism ought to work. Biologists cut a plant or animal open to find its internal structure; this breed of psychologist finds the structure of the soul most perspicuous when as it were the soul's conflicts cut it open.

Plato's first premise says that when one thing performs two different acts at once, the thing must contain more than one part (436b–437a). The soul performs two different acts when it moves toward an object and yet keeps itself from the object (437a–438a). Socrates argues at length (438a–439a) that desires by themselves are impulsive, not the sorts of motives that can regulate themselves. A thirsty person's urge not to drink, for instance when the water supply needs to be rationed, cannot be another desire like the desire to drink. Because that urge is a motive to self-regulation, it must be the faculty of reason that counsels against drink when one's thirst is clamoring for it (439c–d). The dieter's debate over whether to take another helping, the night guard's battle to stay awake, and the celibate's struggle with lust, all illustrate the conflict between reason and desire. Reason sometimes holds back desire on moral grounds (as perhaps in the case of the celibate), sometimes (as in the dieter's case) on prudential ones. But always, reason is that part of the soul best suited to look after the welfare of the entire person. It is not one more impulse among many, but the part of the soul by virtue of which I *decide* between desires instead of being simply *buffeted about* by them. Plato is not looking at cases of just accepting and rejecting an object, but at cases in which the two opposed motivations are qualitatively different.

Into this simplified conflict, Plato introduces *thumos* 'spirit,' distinct from both reason and desire, though more sympathetic to the former. Socrates' examples of *thumos* (440a, c) make good sense if we construe it as anger – the most literal meaning of the word – as long as we stretch anger to encompass such complicated manifestations of it as driving ambition and competitiveness, and also such morally tinged emotions as indignation and the thirst for revenge. These emotions entail judgments. I cannot feel indignant without believing that someone has gotten away with doing something wrong: being angry means doing some thinking. But these emotions are also feelings that cause action. So spirit shows traits of both the other parts of the soul. It can therefore support reason, because anger and competitiveness can make one more likely to act as reason commands. My abstract judgment that someone is being mistreated will not always make me intervene, especially if I worry about the risk. But if I get angry, I might forget the danger and butt in.

Some variety of shame also has its roots in this part of the soul. Indeed, and with allowances for all the important differences between Plato and Freud, the closest thing to *thumos* in contemporary culture is the superego of psychoanalysis. If Platonic reason corresponds to the ego – seat of the self, arbiter among impulses, the motivation to face reality – and desire shares the id's disorderly demands for satisfaction, then spirit fits in the superego's place. Both are irrational agencies that have learned to desire a best version of the self, and that punish any failure to reach that best self. The inclination toward anger, when properly trained, serves as a powerful motivational force in the ethical life. In today's terms, ethical behavior requires superego development.

By introducing spirit into what would otherwise be the simple dualism of reason and desire, Plato offers the rational impulse a strategy for good behavior. Once anger has been trained, it can enforce the moral law within the individual's soul, because it matches the appetites in strength.

## PLATONIC JUSTICE AND ORDINARY JUSTICE (441C–445E)

Given this much similarity between the class structure of an ideal city and the motivational structure of a soul, Socrates claims to be justified in translating definitions of virtue from one domain to the other. A soul is wise when its reason rules, courageous when its spirited part acts bravely (441c–e), and moderate when all three parts accept the rule of reason (442c–d). Justice, as the all-inclusive virtue, therefore consists in each part's performing its appropriate task (441d–e). Its essence is unity: justice makes a person '[become] entirely one from many' (443e).

Socrates was right to have called justice *the* virtue of the soul (④) in his battle with Thrasymachus. He was right to have seen in justice the spirit of restraint (①) and cooperation (②), though Thrasymachus mocked the very ideas.

If the soul is as Plato describes it, it will function smoothly only through governance by its calculating function and the well-trained expression of its spirit. Anyone who has experienced inner conflict will agree that existence is more desirable without it. And since it is the calculating part that understands the demands of morality, rule by that part produces actions most in accord with the strictures of ethics. Thus the soul that functions best by nature will also be the best behaved. The just soul is the happy soul. Human psychology is the foundation for morality.

To this point (442d) Socrates has argued that the well-organized soul, which he calls just by analogy with the just city, is the healthy soul. But when Glaucon and Adeimantus challenged Socrates to show that the just man could be happy despite his misfortunes, they meant one who was just in the ordinary sense of the word, meaning one who performed actions that are conventionally regarded as just. The justice that has emerged from Socrates' process of definition consists in coordination among motives. Even supposing that someone with a soul in that condition enjoys life more than anyone in psychic disarray, what good does that do for the one who obeys legal and moral rules?

Socrates first plays up the similarities between the justice he defined and the one the brothers asked about, to assure them he has answered their challenge. Then he turns around and emphasizes the *difference* between justice in its everyday description and this new justice. Merely because existing society has stumbled over some truths about how to live, does not mean it has understood the significance of those truths, any more than the traditional practice of cooking food to make it safe bespeaks knowledge of bacteria.

Socrates first brings the two conceptions of justice closer together, testing the new definition 'in the light of the vulgar standards' (442e). The just-souled will be the least likely people to embezzle

JUSTICE IN THE SOUL (BOOK 4)  111

money, rob temples, betray friends, break oaths, or commit impiety
or adultery (442e–443a). Such deeds are committed by those with
their souls in some less orderly pattern (442e, 443a). Therefore, the
cause of conventionally just behavior is the arrangement in the soul
(443b). Socrates has not changed the subject.

It does not follow that he left things as they were. Justice in
the good city now appears in its true light as 'a phantom of justice'
(443c), an approximation to the genuine article. True justice
applies the injunction to stay in place to 'what is within,' to
the parts of the soul (443c–e). Those with just souls, when they
behave according to conventional rules of behavior, do so not out
of blind obedience, but because that behavior helps to preserve
the order in their souls.

Socrates insists on this last claim (444a–e) and the reader needs
to acknowledge its place in the argument. Just actions are both
*symptoms* and contributing *causes* of justice in the soul, unjust ones
both symptoms and causes of injustice. Someone with the riotous
internal constitution of the unjust will give in to every impulse
and carry out every shameful misdeed, and those misdeeds will,
through force of habit, encourage the unruly elements of the soul
and leave reason still more powerless. The just and unjust actions
that Glaucon and Adeimantus asked about are therefore still
relevant to this discussion of justice, but in the secondary way
that symptoms are relevant to the discussion of a disease. They
betray the existence of a deeper problem, and they can exacerbate
that problem, but they are not identical with it.

Having defined justice and injustice, Socrates needs to address
the second part of the brothers' challenge, to show that justice by
itself, even without social rewards, will benefit the just (444e–445a).
He will examine the notable species of injustice available to souls
and cities, and argue in each case that the vices lead naturally to
misery, or at least to less happiness than virtue does (445a–c).
The end of Book 4 (445c–e) finds Socrates poised to go through
his list of five political regimes and the five corresponding souls,
from the best form of each through the categories of badness,
down to the worst souls and cities.

Of course, even if justice is preferable in the soul to every kind
of injustice, it does not follow that justice brings happiness no

matter what. The comparative argument supports the more modest conclusion that, under any given circumstances, the just are happier than the unjust would be *in those same circumstances*. Accordingly most scholars today take the argument to be aiming at the more restricted point. But Plato's language does often imply the stronger, absolute conclusion; and his ancient readers, like the many philosophers who studied Plato's works in the Roman Empire, read the *Republic* as an argument for the happiness of the just come what may.

## FURTHER DISCUSSION

Plato's psychology gains familiarity from its resemblance to Freud's; it is also the picture of the soul we expect from Plato, with reason, philosophers' favorite faculty, disciplining the more pedestrian impulses. But because this section contains the heart of Socrates' answer to Glaucon and Adeimantus, it is worth pausing over a few of the steps in these pages that have most exercised scholars and students.

## QUESTION (1) HOW DOES A SOUL HAVE PARTS?

This chapter presented the traditional interpretation of Plato's tripartite soul, sometimes called the 'realist' view because it takes Plato to argue for a real division in the soul, and distinct parts, real agencies, within every person. But traditional or not, the realist reading has been contested. The 'deflationist' view proposes that the argument in Book 4 does not justify this full psychological structure. According to deflationists, the realist reading goes beyond what Book 4 says, contradicts other dialogues that make the soul essentially simple, and in general risks incoherence as a description of human motives.

Many scholars have advanced the deflationist view in recent decades (though prominent scholars have defended the realist position too). Deflationism includes the claims that (1) whatever motives the theory does recognize do not have to be complete agents within the larger soul; (2) when a multiplicity is present, it can number more than three parts; and (3) the Platonic soul does not have to be essentially multiple, but might only possess internal complexity in vicious souls.

Depending on how robustly they interpret their own reading, realists can accept some deflationist claims. For example, the text clearly indicates that more than three elements might exist in a soul – on this see Question (2) below. But on other topics the debate will probably not resolve in a compromise.

## Other Platonic passages

Plato's *Phaedo* contains his most sustained treatment of the soul, and never suggests dividing it. The virtuous soul is single and simple. An essentially simple soul in the *Republic* would render the two dialogues compatible with one another. And later in the *Republic* itself, Socrates promises Glaucon that the soul looks very different when freed from the body (611b–d). Bodily existence taints and cripples the soul; in its pure state it might have many parts or only one (612a).

But the statement of bare possibility that the soul has no parts is more than matched by passages in Books 8 and 9 that support the realist reading, with the soul's parts politicking against one another (550b, 553c, 560b–c; see especially the image of the soul at 588c–589b). Deflationist interpreters concede that these later books appear to conflict with Book 4 as they read it. Some explain the conflict away by saying the later passages are metaphorical; others leave this as a standing interpretive problem about the *Republic*.

Outside the *Republic* are discussions of the soul in the *Phaedrus* and *Timaeus*, not as extensive as the *Phaedo*'s but still substantive, that depict the human soul as tripartite. The Platonic corpus will not settle this debate.

## Intrinsic incoherence

Another way of arguing from outside Book 4 is by asking which view makes more sense on its own. This approach favors the deflationist, not because human beings act with unified characters, but because some descriptions of their disunity – like Plato's description on the realist reading – build each conflicting voice into a whole little soul-within-the-soul. It makes sense to expect each part to issue its own *commands*. But if each part also possesses its own *desires* and even its own special *beliefs*, then the part resembles a little person. Now the deliberation that a complex soul was supposed to explain takes place inside the smaller soul. The explanatory questions have been pushed into the separate parts, not answered.

Where is the person, on such a view? Is it one of the interior agencies? Socrates speaks of the parts as those things with which the person as a whole acts (436a), which suggests that no single part can be the person. If the person is some being above and beyond these parts and choosing among them, the argument never implies such a thing.

You can attribute a false view to Plato, of course. The realist might point out the inherent demands that the *Republic's* governing analogy place on a psychological theory. When the argument calls for the soul to resemble a city, with parts corresponding to people in that city, it is hard *not* to envision those parts as complete agents. Rigorous logic may reject such fairy tales of mental life, but then most analogies fail the test of rigorous logic.

## Arguments in Book 4

The most productive deflationist arguments focus on specific passages in Book 4, which – like Plato's arguments in general – often contain more nuance than the popularizations of them. It has been pointed out that Socrates' principle about inner conflict (436b–438a) does not require the soul to contain independent parts and that, although Socrates does use the word *meros* 'part,' he does so only now and then, not systematically.

Furthermore, Socrates says the desirous impulses arise from disease (439c–d). A boil is not part of a leg, and appetites produced by disease should not be called parts of your soul. Indeed the condition called justice is a harmony among three notes, turning the person who had been many things into one (443c–e).

Equally briefly, here are some replies. First, the word 'part' does appear in this passage – sparingly, but then Plato tends not to use his vocabulary with the consistency of technical terms. And if the conflicting impulses are not parts, what are they? Viable alternatives have been hard to find. And while it can sound logically silly to describe a person as containing three little persons within, that picture fits the experience of psychological conflict, when one can feel as though one's actions are not one's own – as though some stranger is inside your soul.

As for desire as pathology, partly this raises the question of how Plato sees human desire (Question 2 below). Realists should be open-minded about whether every human soul must contain divisions, or only those souls rendered imperfect by bodily existence. But then that group of souls rendered imperfect includes nearly all existing souls. The divided souls may be diseased, but so is the divided city. Maybe the best soul resembles that true simple city that Socrates began with, something fine but also something irrelevant to most people.

Mentioning the city analogous to the soul returns us to the broadest consideration that favors the realist reading: the *Republic*'s analogy requires it. The city says nothing about individual people's justice without some entities in the soul that are substantial enough to correspond to the city's classes. Socrates may get elusive about what those entities are, but he very plainly begins the psychology by looking for what in the soul are *ta auta* 'the same things' as what is in the city (435b–c).

## QUESTION (2) WHAT IS DESIRE?

This part of the soul probably strikes the reader as familiar. Everyone has experienced desire. The problem is that once we leave the examples of hunger and lust, which crowd out their competitors in philosophical discussions, we become less sure which other motives to include. And then it gets harder to spot the defining characteristics of desire. If Plato makes this part of the soul too complex, he cannot draw the sharp distinction he needs between a desire and the calculation that it should be curbed. If he makes the third part of the soul too simple, and desire looks bestial, then the word 'desire' will only work to describe hunger and thirst, not also all the other impulses that need to fit into that commodious category.

The problem arises in the first place because of Plato's use of inner conflict to demonstrate the complexity of the soul. Suppose Socrates described someone who was simultaneously thirsty and libidinous. In such a person the appetites would reach in two directions at once. Since pursuing cool water is ordinarily incompatible with pursuing sexual gratification, we have a conflict in this sexually excited thirsty person between wanting and not-wanting, embracing and denying, just the sort of ambivalence that Socrates takes to characterize ethically relevant conflicts.

But if the conflict between thirst and sexual desire is a legitimate conflict, it calls for a further division within the conflicted person's soul. In that case the grab bag of 'desire' divides up into a mob of more specific appetites, each corresponding to a part of the soul, and the soul looks something like this:

reason
spirit
hunger
thirst
sexual desire
sleepiness
greed.
    (580e)

'Desire' begins to look like a an umbrella term for several motivations, any two of which may come into conflict.

Plato recognizes the multiplicity of desires. He will call the appetites a 'crowd' and a 'swarm' (see 573e–575a). He hints that the full theory may be more complicated, when Socrates mentions that there might be 'some other parts in between' the three he has unearthed (443d; see 580e–581c). But proliferating psychic entities confuses the analogy between city and soul and jeopardizes the primary conclusion of this section. For if all these conflicts occur at once, there is nothing special about the conflict between reason and any appetite. The demands of reason take their place alongside the demands of hunger.

To show that the soul's desires share some essential property, and to distinguish their demands from the voice of reason, Socrates

argues that they lack any means to qualify themselves, aside from
their choice of object:

> [T]hirsting itself will never be a desire for anything other than that of
> which it naturally is a desire – for drink alone – and similarly, hungering
> will be a desire for food ...

> (437e)

So a particular sort of thirst is for a particular kind of drink, but
thirst itself is neither for much nor little, good nor bad, nor, in a
word, for any particular kind, but thirst itself is naturally only for
drink. (439a)

If thirst could discriminate between the drinks that quench it
and those that bring the thirst back with a vengeance, or between a
quantity of drink that satisfies the body and a quantity that sends it
into cramps, then thirst could curb itself. Reason would have no
work to do; we would lose the conflict between reason and thirst.
To make that conflict clear, Socrates strips thirst of any powers of
judgment or deliberation. Then reason conflicts with an appetite
in a way that two appetites cannot conflict with one another. If
I have to choose between the contingently incompatible desires
for eating and sleeping, I follow my stronger wish. The philosophical example of Buridan's ass, equipoised between its water and
hay and paralyzed by indecision, describes a case of incompatible
desires, but not two desires that directly attack each other.

But if I choose between eating and sticking to my diet, I am
caught between two kinds of motivation, one of which considers
factors that the other, because of its nondeliberative nature,
can't understand. Desire impels me to move while reason forbids
the movement (439c). Desire can do many things but it lacks the
capacity to *forbid.*

The city offers a helpful comparison. Although the rulers and
auxiliaries each have a single job to do, the large class that
Socrates calls 'the ruled' accounts for a multiplicity of skills. We
can only specify the nature of this class's work by identifying what it
does *not* do. The members of this class work toward nonpolitical
goals. So too in the soul: disparate though the appetites may be,
they resemble one another in their unconcern for the person as a

whole. They are not more stupid than reason so much as heedless of reason's concerns. Reason deserves to rule because 'it is wise and has forethought about all of the soul' (441e); as such, only reason ever entertains the question how a given desire, or its satisfaction, will affect the person. Appetites no more know how to rule the soul than doctors know how to set public policy. All desires, therefore, however blunt or specific, natural or perverse, join together in their unconcern for the good of the person.

This picture of the 'lower' drives is familiar enough. Too familiar, in fact. For if Plato's account of the soul opens itself up to an interpretation of desire too contemptuous toward that kind of motivation, the account threatens to fail. Normally Plato does not think of all appetite as dirty, bad, and bodily. Sometimes he comes close to it, though. And oversimplifying desire in this way has two bad consequences. It makes a mystery of Plato's preference for harmony in the soul, a preference on which his ethical theory relies; and it excludes too many other motives, which find themselves without a place in the soul.

At 431a–b, examining the virtues of the city, Socrates speaks of moderation as self-mastery: 'The phrase "stronger than himself" is used when that which is better by nature is master over that which is worse.' This 'something worse' refers to one's desires (431c–d), even though Socrates has not yet mapped out his psychological theory. Now, it is striking that on the whole, Book 4 refrains from calling the appetites a worse part of the soul. They form the *lowest* part (443d), the part that ought to be the reason's slave (444b), but not a part with intrinsically immoral aims. Immorality arises not from the existence of desires, since many of them are necessary to life, but from their usurping the authority that belongs to reason (443d, 444b).

Nevertheless the *Republic*'s language sometimes betrays a more pejorative view of the appetites. In the passage just quoted Socrates calls them *worse* than the other parts. In that case, the good life would require not that the three parts of the soul harmonize with one another, as individually valuable impulses coordinated to produce a greater good (443d–e; cf. 589a–b), but that the worst part suffer constant suppression.

A bestial interpretation of desire also threatens the plausibility of Plato's theory. Consider conflicts that Socrates never describes.

Pity is repeatedly recognized in the *Republic*: sometimes Socrates speaks of it as of an appropriate motive with good effects (516c, 518b, 589e), but at other times he calls for its suppression (415c, 606b–c). Pity can conflict with reason, as when one pities the suffering patient who has to undergo painful treatment; it can conflict with spirit on the battlefield. Thus pity must belong among the desires.

In itself this is no criticism. Plato has called desire a mix of different motives. But recall how brutish desire had to become to stand apart from reason and spirit. An appetite gropes after its object. How well does such a description characterize pity, even leaving aside a more complex case like friendship? The mechanisms of thirst and drowsiness hardly accommodate pity.

It is telling that for Plato compassion has to join the grubby ranks of hunger and lechery. It would be a greater criticism of his theory if there were no room for such motives at all. Without pity the theory fails as a description of human behavior; with pity included, the meaning of 'desire' is stretched to the point of vacuity.

## QUESTION (3) DOES PLATONIC JUSTICE HAVE ETHICAL CONTENT, OR IS IT MERELY A FORMAL CHARACTERISTIC OF SOULS?

Does the ethical view developed in this passage give its readers guides for living?

We have learned from Socrates' argument that justice means the cooperative functioning of all the parts of the soul. This has an almost amoral sound; to say that reason rules is to say barely more than that the person decides what to do and then does it. Plenty of people are incapable of that much. But even if Socrates' definition of justice leaves us with a small number of 'just' people, it says next to nothing about how they will behave. Does Plato's system end up incapable of distinguishing between right and wrong?

The answer will depend on what exactly reason does when it rules in a just soul. How does the calculating part of the soul deliberate about what is just? If it faces no constraints besides the definition of justice already seen, we seem to face an absurd conclusion. If I am Platonically just by virtue of my soul's non-rational parts serving my reason, then anything I decide to do will be a just action. What makes it just is the way my spirit and appetites fall into place and do as they are told, *no matter what my deliberations lead me to do*. Justice seems to be a function of what happens *after* I have deliberated.

But this way of putting the problem already shows there is some content to Platonic justice. The soul not only has to remain orderly after reason hands down its commands, but must remain orderly *by virtue of* those commands. The commands must contribute to the soul's continuing orderliness. Because reason is the part that thinks on behalf of the entire soul, and because it wants to maintain its authority, it must weigh possible actions with an eye to determining which ones best preserve the soul's balance. Although indulging once in tobacco is not wrong, I would want to abstain if I suspected that one indulgence would make me crave more. The just act would be the act of denial, on the grounds that denial best maintains the soul's order.

Similarly, if my temper is provoked, my calculating faculty has to decide whether expressing anger is the wisest course of action. If I always suppress my anger, I run the risk of dampening that emotion until it no longer serves me. If I lose my temper at the slightest provocation, I run the risk of coming unduly under its influence. My reason has the task of deciding how much anger, and when, best suits my soul's orderliness.

Therefore, not anything that reason decides to do will be a just decision. Platonic justice requires self-regulation – not a condition of having no emotions or appetites, but one in which they are kept from overpowering your future capacity to reach sane decisions.

But reason still lacks a mandate that might narrow down its choices of action further. As gatekeeper to the other motivations, reason may give a bigger role to the appetites, or deny them altogether, as long as it maintains control over the soul. The just life pins all the work of ethics on the soul's administrator without giving that administrator any other goal but administration. Intrinsically empty, reason conducts the traffic of the other motivations in the soul, but lacks aims of its own that it will privilege above all other claims on its attention.

This is not the only view of reason put forward in the *Republic*. It soon emerges that reason has its own desires, which will turn out to be directed toward philosophical truth. Just as the city's guardians turn out in Book 5 to be philosophers, their time divided between governance and metaphysical inquiry, so too reason will play two different roles in the good person's life. On the view offered in Book 4, reason evaluates and ranks the options available to a person. On the view still to make its appearance, reason contemplates the truth, and organizes the soul in such a way as to make contemplation available to the person. Plato is holding his full plan for living in abeyance, until he can explain in greater detail what reason does. The ethics of Book 4 look empty not by accident, but because the dialogue has not yet reached the point at which it can reveal the work of reason.

## QUESTION (4) HOW CLOSELY DOES PLATONIC JUSTICE RESEMBLE JUSTICE AS IT IS COMMONLY CONCEIVED?

The *Republic*'s argument to this point yields a definition of justice – or rather a definition of what we may call 'P-justice,' as a reminder that Plato has not yet shown that the state *he* calls justice produces the behavior commonly called just:

(1)   P-justice is the good organization of the soul.

If Socrates can show that

(2)   The well-organized soul is the happiest possible soul,

he will be able to conclude that

(3)   ⑧ The P-just soul is the happiest possible soul,

thereby answering the challenge posed in Book 2.

The argument for (2) will have to wait until Books 8 and 9, when Socrates compares the just life to all varieties of unjust lives. But already we can see that ⑧, as welcome as it may be, will not answer Glaucon and Adeimantus, who wanted Socrates to show that

(4) Justice, by itself in the soul, makes the just happier than the unjust.

For in this challenge we identify just people through the acts they perform (360b–362c). Glaucon wants Socrates to show that

(5) The soul of one who performs O-just deeds is happy,

where 'O-justice' refers to an ordinary conception of justice. For (5) to follow from ⑧, it must be the case that

(6) ⑦ The P-just soul = the soul of one who is most likely to perform O-just deeds.

⑦ requires the P-just soul to appear in a person who regularly does O-just deeds.

Why should this be a problem? The 'vulgar standards' to which Socrates subjects his nascent definition are intended to connect P-justice to O-justice (442e–443b). He lists cases in which the person with a P-just soul refrains from acts of O-injustice. Examples are not arguments, but Socrates has a compelling reason for his claims. P-justice entails self-control, and the more self-control that people enjoy, the less likely they are to surrender to their desires. Most ordinary misdeeds may be traced back to such temptations, so the P-just soul will probably find itself suited to avoiding them.

The problems begin, as modern critics stress, when we look back to Glaucon's performer of O-just acts. Socrates has argued that

(7) P-justice in the soul brings about regular, predictable, habitual O-just action.

This is indeed a comforting thought. If P-just souls ever come into existence, they will serve as inspirational examples of

O-just-act-performers who also — assuming Socrates can prove (2) — enjoy happiness. But this will not quite satisfy Glaucon's request, which was that Socrates show not that *some*, but *all* performers of O-just acts lead happy lives. To reach that, Socrates needs the additional premise

(8) The regular practice of O-just action implies a P-just soul.

The identity stated in ⑦ is the conjunction of (7) and (8). According to some of Plato's critics, he not only never shows (8) to be true, but seems not even to realize that he needs it. Without (8) Socrates never answers Glaucon's challenge; for what drives Glaucon to anxiety about justice is precisely that justice, *as he conceives it*, the performance of just actions, might not benefit the well-behaved person. If Socrates does not speak to that anxiety, he will have committed the fallacy of irrelevance.

(8) is hard to prove. What is worse, it sounds un-Platonic. It asserts that all diligent servants of society's laws will have, even without knowing it, the arrangement of their souls' parts that the philosopher labored through four books of the *Republic* to discover. It would make more sense, given Plato's aloofness from ordinary practices, to deny his interest in (8). He may be better off claiming, not that everyone popularly considered just is just, but that those normally considered just have made substantial though incomplete progress toward genuine justice. If Glaucon remains depressed after learning this, too bad for him. He needs to get better at accepting revaluations of his moral values.

Some interpreters understand the *Republic* this way, as a repudiation of ordinary morality rather than a justification of it. But some evidence suggests that any person who predominantly performs O-just acts — a more reliable Cephalus, who did not have to wait until old age before reforming — does have a P-just soul. Socrates has not yet suggested that P-justice belongs only to philosophers. And if anyone is to enjoy the benefits of P-justice, why shouldn't it be the steady workers of O-just deeds?

Indeed, Socrates says that they do. When applying vulgar standards to his definition of justice, Socrates concentrates on the question of what the P-just man will or will not do. But he also attributes to the P-*un*just some of the O-unjust acts from which the P-just will refrain:

> [In the case of embezzlement,] do you suppose anyone would suppose that he would be the man to do it *and not rather those who are not such as he is?*
>
> (442e–443a; emphasis added)

> Further, adultery, neglect of parents, and failure to care for the gods *are more characteristic of every other kind of man* than this one.
>
> (443a; emphasis added)

Socrates is saying that

(9) If one does not have a P-just soul, one is more likely to do O-unjust acts.

Let us identify being unjust with not being just, as Plato does. Then we infer from (9) that

(10) If one does not have a P-just soul, one is not the most likely person to do O-just acts,

which implies that

(11) If one is the most likely to do O-just acts, one has a P-just soul.

(11) is only a restatement of (8). So Socrates has indirectly argued that the performer of O-just acts does possess a P-just soul.

Socrates asserts (8) outright only a page later:

> Doesn't doing just things also produce justice and unjust ones injustice? ... Isn't to produce justice to establish the parts of the soul in a relation of mastering, and being mastered by, one another that is according to nature?
>
> (444c–d)

The guardians' early education, which let them mimic only good characters and filled their souls with images of beauty, implies a similar model of soul formation. The regular practice of O-just action *does* imply that one's soul is P-just, because dutiful adherence to just behavior, even if one obeys the laws unphilosophically, promotes the rule of reason (see 518d–e).

Far from despising the common conception of justice, Plato wants to show its close relationship to true justice. If what he says about P-justice baffles his readers, that is because we are unaccustomed to a philosophical analysis of justice, not because the justice of daily life is a fraud. Naturally, without the philosophical analysis we are doomed to misunderstand justice, and likely to deliberate about it in clumsy language. Let no one accuse Plato of congratulating nonphilosophers on their grasp of moral issues. But none of his praise of philosophy means that a conscientious moral life is aimed in the wrong direction.

Plato never explains *how* O-just actions could affect the deep structure of the personality. He does not analyze virtue into cognitive and habitual components, as Aristotle will, to show what acculturation accomplishes in the soul. Without a more specific causal story to tell, Plato can't demonstrate that the justice defined in Book 4 is identical with the conception of justice with which Socrates' interlocutors began the conversation. He has only begun responding to this problem. But he has not ignored it.

## SUGGESTIONS FOR FURTHER READING

On the two readings of justice as happiness (comparative or absolute) see Annas, *Platonic Ethics Old and New*.

On the very lively contemporary debate over 'parts' in the soul (Question 1) see especially Cooper, 'Plato's theory of human motivation,' along with Shields, 'Plato's divided soul,' and Whiting, 'Psychic contingency in the *Republic*'; on the other side of that debate, the relevant sections of Bobonich, *Plato's Utopia Recast*, and Lorenz, *The Brute Within: Appetitive Desire in Plato and Aristotle*. On the nature of desire (Question 2) see the discussion in White, *A Companion to Plato's Republic*. On the formal conception of justice (Question 3) see Irwin, *Plato's Moral Theory*, and Nussbaum, 'The *Republic*: true value and the standpoint of perfection.' For the relationship between Platonic justice and just actions as ordinarily conceived (Question 4) see Sachs, 'A fallacy in Plato's *Republic*,' which inspired the debate; a powerful recent reply appears in Singpurwalla, 'Plato's defense of justice in the *Republic*,' but Santas, *Understanding Plato's Republic*, puts in a spirited defense of Sachs.

# 6

---

# RADICAL POLITICS
# (BOOKS 5–7)

Once the argument has defined justice and injustice in the city and the soul, it should proceed directly to show how both city and soul are better off virtuous than vicious. And indeed, when Socrates takes up the thread of this master argument again in Books 8 and 9, it goes where the reader expects it to, using the dynamic definition of justice to make every decline in virtue a less stable and less desirable political or psychological condition.

The surprise is that Socrates takes as long as he does to return to the argument. Between defining justice and proving its desirability he digresses through Books 5–7, during which he barely acknowledges his analysis of justice or the need to find justice's benefits. The *Republic* would cohere much better without this digression, which confuses many readers.

But argumentative tightness is not all that matters in philosophy, and without Books 5–7 the *Republic* would lose much of its richness. In these books Plato outlines both his most revolutionary political proposals and the defining version of his metaphysical theory, which comprises both a method (dialectic) and the entities this method discovers (the Forms). This is one detour that covers more vital territory than the trail it leads away from.

(Plato's dialogues frequently digress from their main point to explore a more abstract or metaphysical topic. Part of the dialogues' charm comes from the sense of freedom that results. Philosophy might reach its greatest treasures when it lets itself drift off topic.)

This chapter will address the politics of Books 5–7, leaving metaphysical issues for Chapter 7. This is not to say that Plato would have conceived the subjects as separate, only to recognize that these three books make more sense if the reader takes up one of their topics at a time.

## THE DIGRESSION

Book 5 signals its new beginning with dramatic cues, all the more remarkable for the undramatic style that the dialogue has settled into. Socrates prepares to itemize the four types of vice in the individual and in the city. Then we learn that Polemarchus, silent since Book 1, has been listening from his seat close to Adeimantus (449b). He grabs Adeimantus by the cloak (449b) and asks, 'Shall we let it go' – meaning the communistic life of the guardians, which Socrates only mentioned in passing (423e–424a). At the beginning of the *Republic*, Polemarchus sent a slave to grab Socrates by the cloak (327b) and refused to *let him go* back up to Athens (327c). Now he wants to initiate the discussion all over. No wonder Socrates speaks of moving back to 'the beginning' (450a).

Socrates' interlocutors want him to suspend the analogy between city and soul. The city may have come into their conversation to illuminate justice in the individual, but in Books 5–7 Socrates drops the pretext of erecting a city parallel to the soul. Plato wants the freedom to talk about the good city without the encumbrance of its analogy to the soul. He also sees the figure of the philosopher within that city, a figure who will emerge in Book 5, as an opportunity to pursue more abstract metaphysics.

Note that Socrates had no intention of going into these details except at his companions' prodding. In other places he might move strategically, subverting his interlocutors' opinions. Here he speaks as one caught off guard and exploring the subject naively, more interested in getting the good city and first philosophy right than in exposing anyone's ignorance.

## TWO WAVES OF PARADOX (451C–471B)

Glaucon charges Socrates with describing the community of women and children among the guardians. Socrates demurs. The city he describes might prove either impossible or bad (450c). Glaucon eggs him on as if those questions didn't matter (450c–451c), though soon (471c) he will be pressing Socrates to answer them. The good city's possibility will begin to nag at Socrates' friends as soon as they talk about the city without regard for the city–soul analogy: for if the city is worth discussing as a political being, it must be a political possibility.

## WOMEN (451C–457C)

Socrates begins with the equality of the sexes. Women differ from men in degree, not in kind, so they should share in men's work and education. Everything Socrates said about the young guardians' training will apply equally to those guardians who happen to be girls. And when the guardians go to war, they will fight as a mixed group of men and women (452a). In short, the two sexes should do everything together, without regard for unenlightened public opinion. The sight of naked old women wrestling with naked old men would 'look ridiculous in the present state of things' (452a–b), but Socrates maintains his scorn for 'what is habitual' (452a). In the matter of gender relations, he ignores how people live and what they value. Indeed, Socrates hardly shows greater contempt for public opinion in the *Republic* than here.

What does give him pause is the political principle that underlay his description of the good city, that each citizen is naturally best suited to a single task. ⑥ would ostensibly define a separate civic role for women. Since they bear children and men do not, their natures must be different from men's, hence also their jobs (453b–c). This is a familiar argument, even today, against women's participation in government or the professions. 'How can you run a company when you have children to take care of?'

It is a threatening argument for Plato because, while respectful of women's abilities, he cannot abandon ⑥.

Socrates responds by distinguishing (454b–c) between those characteristics that define a person's nature and those that do not. Only traits that affect the performance of a task should determine what tasks the citizens are set to (454c–d). So women's child-bearing should have nothing to do with the political question of their civic duties.

Socrates' analogy to bald and hairy-headed cobblers is astonishing. Does the difference between the sexes amount to no more than the difference between a bald man and one with a full head of hair? Even if women's reproductive organs have no effect on their physical or intellectual abilities, still one might argue that child-bearing links women naturally to the care of children, whereas men's hair commits them to no extra work besides combing it. If those who bear children also take responsibility for rearing them, this difference between male and female natures implies great differences in their activities.

In reply, Socrates specifies what 'nature' means (454c–456b).

(1) 'Nature,' as used politically, means the aptitude for one kind of work rather than another. (455b)

(2) Aptitudes are distributed without regard for sex, as shown by men's ability to do everything that women do. (455c–e)

∴ (3) There are no differences in nature between men and women relevant to the role each should play in the city. (456a)

Many readers raise an eyebrow at (2), a most unfeminist claim. What is the point of giving women responsibility and power while also positing men's superiority at every task? But Plato is shrewdly using male contempt for 'women's work' to dissolve the old assumption of an absolute difference between the sexes. Precisely because men are better than women at everything (on average), there is no such thing as men's work or women's work.

Premise (2) *is* vital to the *Republic*, however, though for another reason. It is true only if you exclude childbearing, the undeniably female task. Plato cannot dismiss childbearing as unimportant to the city, so omitting it must imply that having children takes too little time and effort to count as true work. On traditional conceptions of the family, that assumption is unreasonable. Depending on how many pregnancies a woman guardian goes through and what complications she encounters, we *might* discount pregnancy alone as a full-time job. But if the one who gives birth to children also cares for them, childbearing turns into a demanding occupation. Socrates must be assuming that women do not take responsibility for child care. His argument assumes a division between bearing and rearing children, therefore a very different system of child care.

This is why Socrates moves quickly to his next point. The additional premise he needs to justify women's participation in government, namely that childbearing may be separated from child care and so does not affect the division of labor, requires the abolition of the family.

## MARRIAGE AND CHILDREN (457C–461E)

Children and parents will not know one another in the upper classes (457d). But even that change is more imaginable than the next one, that wives and husbands will not know each other – or rather, that men and women will not share any relation comparable to the one now known between husbands and wives.

The cohabitation of men and women in the guardians' camp will lead to sexual activity. Sex needs to be regulated (458d). Therefore the rulers should use sex to benefit the city, arranging marriages so that the best young male and female guardians breed together. When Socrates speaks of these 'marriages' among the guardians, he means temporary procreative couplings. At special times of the year the rulers announce which pairs may mate. To ward off the soldiers' resentment at this control over their lives, the rulers will use a fraudulent lottery that makes the pairings seem random (460a). The children born to the best couples will be reared as a group by specialists, while their parents return to their own communal lives. Infants born to unheroic guardians will not be reared; nor will other children born outside approved 'marriages.'

Plato is elusive about what happens to inappropriate children. For those born to older guardians he recommends abortion (461c), while babies of the worse guardians, and those born deformed, apparently are to be exposed in a cave (460c). At other times he speaks of not rearing certain children (459d–e, 461c), which probably means demoting them to a lower class. It is becoming clear that the rulers will exercise more power over the guardians than Books 2–4 indicated. They 'will have to use a throng of lies and deceptions for the benefit of the ruled,' Socrates says calmly (459c–d). But at least now he can claim that women's reproductive capacities have been severed from the usual work of motherhood (460d); and now it makes sense that he shrugged off childbearing as incidental to women's natures.

## PLATO'S FEMINISM

Book 5 argues for a remarkable degree of sexual equality. Conscious of women's potential, Plato calls for their participation in the governance of his city, and insists that they be educated alongside his most talented young men.

The *Republic* even contains the first call for gender-neutral language. In Book 7 Glaucon compliments Socrates, 'You have produced ruling men who are wholly fair' (540c). Glaucon uses the word *archôn*, the masculine participle of *archô* 'to rule.' Socrates corrects him by adding the feminine participle: 'And ruling women [*archousas*], too, Glaucon … Don't suppose that what I have said applies any more to men than to women' (540c). With his insistence on including the feminine participle, Socrates is warning Glaucon, with modern scrupulousness, that applying masculine language to all people may lead one to forget the place of women among men.

Plato deserves still more credit for his proposals given the misogyny of his world. Women of the Athenian middle class were married off in their early teens to men twice their age. When they did not die in childbirth, they could look forward to a life enclosed in the house, supervising the kitchen and spinning or weaving cloth. As a practical matter women left their homes for numerous reasons, but the idealized wife never went out in public. Respectable women's names were not stated in public, not even in the Attic comedies that permit themselves every obscenity. Plato recognizes the waste of human resources in this social system and opposes it pitilessly.

Still, the worry about his feminism persists, and the thought that these congratulatory remarks are simplistic. Some interpreters claim that Plato's apparent empowerment of women has nothing to do with genuine feminism. On a variant of this criticism, Plato continued to share in the misogyny of his time despite his best intentions.

Feminism today is too varied and self-critical to be reduced to one definition. But we can say that if modern feminism does not recognize itself in Plato's proposal, this is because modern feminists want to uphold women's rights or help women fulfill their desires, while Plato gives no thought to either purpose. It has struck him that a more efficient city would make its women fight in wars and write laws. Women might feel more fulfilled under such a political arrangement, but the argument works just as well if they do not. Such thorough disregard for what women want, or how they might benefit, seems to exclude Plato from consideration as a feminist.

The objection to Book 5 on the grounds of women's rights is too strong, because it rules out every political utterance in the *Republic*. The guardians get no right to happiness in their work (420b, 421b), nor any right to privacy (416d). The other citizens have no right to govern themselves (432a, 434a–b). And no one has rights in the sense of enjoying personal liberties (557b). Since no one's rights matter to Plato, his inattention to women's rights is no sign of his failure as a feminist. If we only take as a necessary principle of feminist theories the proposition that women have been wrongly denied equality of opportunity, then Plato counts as a feminist, as long as 'equality of opportunity' refers to the society's right to exploit its citizens' talents, rather than the citizens' rights to pursue their dreams.

Then there is the problem of misogyny, and it is not a trivial one. Several of Plato's dialogues speak disparagingly of women. In the *Apology* Socrates calls those who plead for their lives in court 'no better than women' (35b); in the *Phaedo* he speaks of the distractions of womanly lamentations (117d). The *Timaeus* warns men that if they live immorally they will be reincarnated as women (42b–c; cf. 76d–e). The *Republic* contains comments in the same spirit (387e, 395d–e, 398e, 431b–c, 469d), evidence of nothing so much as of contempt toward women. Even Socrates' words for his bold new proposal about marriage, 'the community (*koinônia*) of women' (e.g. 464a), suggest that the women are to be 'held in common' by the men. He never says that the men might be held in common by the women, even after we realize that a woman could have as many as twenty breeding-relations with different men. Plato cannot shake the idea that women belong to men: Socrates twice refers to the *ktêsis* 'possession' of women by men (423e, 451c). And there is no mention of an expanded role for women in the city's large lower class.

We also have to acknowledge Socrates' insistence that men surpass women at any task that both sexes attempt (455c, 456a), and his remark in Book 8 that one sign of democracy's moral failure is the sexual equality it promotes (563b). We cannot blame these statements on carelessness; they follow from a deep-seated belief that women are not equal to men. To say this is not to reject Plato's recommendations, but to recognize his vulnerability to the prejudices of his age. He becomes less of a feminist by virtue of these persistently misogynistic beliefs, even though his considered proposals remain as revolutionary as when they first appeared.

## THE BIG FAMILY AT HOME AND AT WAR (462A–471B)

With the dissolution of the family, Socrates completes his picture of the good city. The present section, which furnishes the most vivid glimpse at the good city in action, also shows how different Plato's city will look from any society that his readers ever inhabited.

First Socrates defends his proposals about the family, arguing that unity offers the greatest good a city can possess (462a–464b), then identifying the immediately appreciable benefits to the city. The double strategy should be familiar by now. After every significant political or ethical claim in the *Republic*, Plato first puts forward the theoretical defense for his position, then renews his acknowledgment of conventional morality with a defense that requires no theory.

By abolishing families, Socrates has turned the city, or rather its governing class, into a single family. That 'or' glides over an important question, hard to answer on the basis of the textual evidence: Is Plato imagining unanimity and fraternity to arise among all the citizens of his town, or only among the guardians, given that the family reforms apply only to them? His language sometimes implies the former (462b, e; 463e; cf. 432a) and sometimes the latter (463c; 464a, b). In all likelihood he is forgetting the productive class, thinking of unity among the guardians as sufficient for unity among the citizens at large. In any case, he argues that the unity improves the city:

(1) The greatest good for a city is that which unifies it; the greatest evil, that which divides it. (462a–b)
(2) When all citizens share in the same pleasures and pains, the city is unified; when they have private pleasures and pains, it is divided. (462b)
(3) The city in which women and children are held in common enjoys the greatest unanimity about pain and pleasure. (463e)
∴ (4) The community of women and children among the auxiliaries brings the greatest good to the city. (464b)

The argument is valid; but are its premises true? It is hard to say about (3). That the Platonic city will contain total harmony is unlikely, for people split into groups even without families or property to fight over. Plato barely considers the possibility of intellectual disagreement among the rulers and auxiliaries, but that disagreement can divide a community. And even though the guardians have no money or land, they enjoy lesser and greater honor within the city. Surely a desire to be the city's bravest warrior could make two guardians rivals.

Nevertheless Plato is right to place special blame for civil unrest on the family. More than any other institution, the family engenders loyalties of the same sort and the same intensity as loyalty to the state. Aristotle observes that families are microcosms of the state, with their own rule and their own economies (*Politics* II.7, 13). But whereas Aristotle will use this parallel between family and city to justify government, Plato interprets it as a threat to organized society, since loyalty to the family may undermine one's loyalty to the state. Moreover, Plato seems to think that the feelings produced within a family possess an irrationality unmatched by the feelings that the guardians will share with the members of their class. Among the ills to be found in traditional cities, Socrates includes 'private pleasures and griefs of things that are private' (464d). Although any guardian's death in the good city will pain all the others (462b), that pain will not reach the level felt in private mourning. Within a family the relationships are simply more intense.

Plato's reorganization of the family might reduce civil unrest, as he says. But if the guardians' sentiments are so diffused they will simply not be present in any form, as Aristotle observed: intense feelings may be replaced by no feelings, so that the guardians lack personal loyalties altogether.

Aside from these worries, it is premise (1) of this argument that really sounds an alarm, because it shows how far Plato takes the implications of his fundamental assumptions. As his definitions of civic and psychic justice in Book 4 showed, Plato identifies the greatest threats to the good life as internal conflict, whether civil war in the city or ambivalence in the soul. Book 1 prepared for this position by identifying injustice first with unbridled competition (①), then with whatever force dissolves the unity of a social group (②). The present premise (1) replaces 'injustice' with 'the greatest evil that can befall a society,' and hence follows from those premises. Again, the establishment of a city in Book 2 began with the assumption (⑤) that human beings require a community in order to lead recognizably human lives. That principle implies that whatever erodes the bonds of the community will threaten its citizens' capacity to lead acceptable lives; therefore, (1) may also be said to follow from ⑤.

If premise (1) builds on assumptions about justice that have so deeply informed the *Republic*'s argument to this point, it can be discarded only at risk to the greater argument. It does not matter if Plato's quest for unanimity grows out of his experience with civil war, his interpretation of philosophical reasoning, or some psychological quirk. The value may begin as an idiosyncratic bias, but Plato weaves it through the argument so thoroughly that the *Republic* cannot exist without it. And the discussion at 462–64 makes clear that (1) leads to extremes in social control. As long as unity outweighs every other value, Plato's city may justify any concentration of power, any violation of what the modern world considers rights of free speech and religion and due process for the accused. The present argument warns that unity demands sacrifices from the individual.

Again appeals to mundane benefits follow the theoretical argument (464c–466d). The city in which women and children are held in common will escape lawsuits, assault, and the ignominies that accompany household poverty. If anything Socrates is belaboring the point, when he should face the question of whether such a city could ever exist. Since the matter of the city's possibility has already arisen twice in Book 5 (450c, 457d), this would be the time for Socrates to address it. Instead he postpones the discussion a third time, until Glaucon's protest at 471c–472b. Seldom does Plato build his reader's anticipation so deliberately: this delay tips us off to the importance and difficulty of that remaining issue.

In the meantime, Socrates describes the city at war (466d–471b). The passage from 469b to 471b deserves special notice. Socrates distinguishes between the city's practices in wars against barbarians and in wars against other Greek cities. The limitations he prescribes in the latter case are an early recognition that some constraints may hold even in the state of war. And this is the lone case of 'externalist justice' for the city, i.e. rightness or wrongness in its behavior toward other cities.

But even as he asks his guardians, and implicitly his contemporaries, to transcend their traditional allegiances to the home city, Plato reveals his own attachment to the attitudes of his time and place. Like most Greeks, he draws a sharp line between those who share his language and culture and everyone else (see 452c). Later Socrates will hint that the good city might be born in a barbarian land (499c), but the hint comes and goes far more quickly than the present condemnation of barbarians does. We may take Plato's inconsistency here, as in his treatment of women, as an example of the extent to which even thinkers determined to escape popular opinion can slip into accepting its pettiest beliefs.

It is noteworthy, on the other hand, that Plato's *Statesman* – often thought to have been written years later – rejects the arbitrary division of humanity into Greeks and barbarians (262c–e). See also Plato's acknowledgment of the non-Greek origins of many Greek words in the *Cratylus* (409d–e, 425e), and his respect for Egypt in the *Laws* (e.g. 656d–657b, 819b–d) and *Timaeus* (22b–23b).

## PHILOSOPHER-RULERS (471C–502C)

### THE POSSIBILITY OF THE CITY (471C–473C)

Socrates tries every maneuver to escape saying whether this fine city will be possible. He resorts to the disclaimer that he only talked about the just city in order to discover the nature of justice in the soul (472c; cf. 592a–b). But the city has come to life too much to have its existence ignored. It is no mere analogue to the soul any more but an object of inquiry in its own right. The very fact that Plato wrote the pages to come proves that the *Republic*'s politics do not reduce to its psychological theory.

What follows is the statement and defense of the *Republic*'s most radical political idea, that either philosophers become kings or kings learn philosophy. Since a defense of this proposal presupposes a conception of philosophy, much of the ensuing discussion covers metaphysical and epistemological topics to be addressed in the next chapter; the rest of this chapter will take up the explicitly political issues from here to the end of Book 7, which amount to a two-part defense of rule by philosophers:

(1) Why philosophers make good rulers, and why rule by philosophers is possible (473c–502c).
(2) How to prepare the guardians for rule as philosophers, given their existence in the city; or, how a city we recognize as good may be maintained in existence (502c–541b).

### KNOWLEDGE, BELIEF, AND THE PHILOSOPHER (473C–487A)

Once he agrees to speak to the city's practicability, Socrates proposes that philosophy and political power 'coincide in the same place, while the many natures now making their way to [the practice of] either apart from the other are by necessity excluded' (473d). Though neither small nor easily accomplished, this political change *is* possible, he says (473c). It follows that the good city is possible as well, rule by philosophers functioning as a strategic first move that paves the way for all subsequent reforms. The tradition of revolutionary politics will follow the *Republic* in identifying a change in governance that leads to systemic change; in fact Socrates will soon even name the revolutionary act that first creates the philosophical constitution, when the revolutionaries drive all adults out of the city and teach the new order to the children (540e–541a).

For now though he reasons as if philosophers could be seated on the throne, and from this first statement of the plan until 502c, Socrates argues that the good city might come to exist. Broadly stated, the argument ascribes every excellence to philosophers and thereby justifies their dominance:

(1)   The good city is possible if and only if virtuous and expert rule by its leaders is possible. (484d)
(2)   ⑨ Virtuous and expert rule is possible if and only if the rulers may be philosophers.
(3)   Rule by philosophers is possible. (502a–b)
∴ (4)   The good city is possible.


It is ⑨ that most occupies Socrates' attention, as he tries to show that *the defining characteristics of philosophers also make for virtuous and effective political rule.* He will separate ⑨ into claims about virtue and knowledge, then claim that both of these are found in philosophers and in no one else. Thus the present passage (474c–487a) argues for the truth of ⑨, on the basis of philosophers' attachment to learning:

(1)   Philosophers love every kind of learning. (474c–475c)
(2)   No one else loves every kind of learning. (475c–480a)
(3)   ⑩ The love of every kind of learning produces knowledge of ethical matters.

(4) The love of every kind of learning produces virtue. (485a–486e)

∴ (5) By (3) and (4), the love of every kind of learning makes one a virtuous and expert ruler.

∴ (6) ⑨ By (1), (2), and (5), one is a virtuous and expert ruler if and only if one is a philosopher.

If this argument works, it will defend Plato's political theory. It will also turn politics into an intellectual pursuit instead of the practical pursuit we are accustomed to – or rather, it will force us to reevaluate what we mean by 'intellectual pursuits.'

Premise (2), ruling out governance by nonphilosophers, comes into this argument for a concrete reason, as we realize when Glaucon warns Socrates that a mob will seize and punish him for his proposal (473e–474a). Plato's dialogues often foreshadow the trial and execution of Socrates – the *Republic* alludes to his fate at 494d–e, 516e–517a, and 539a–d – but *this* foreshadowing especially resonates, because the discussion of philosopher-kings would have reminded every Athenian of the contempt with which Socrates' associates had treated democracy. The decisive Athenian loss during the Peloponnesian War took place in the botched Sicilian Expedition, which could not have been executed without the influence of Socrates' young friend Alcibiades; after the war, Critias and Charmides instigated the worst antidemocratic excesses of the Thirty Tyrants. And here is a conversation, set before all those events, during which Socrates proposes rule by philosophers. The challenge for Plato is to distinguish these philosophers from their imitators, the dictators who seize power armed only with false confidence in their own wisdom.

So Socrates defines the philosopher, lest that figure be mistaken for a Critias or Charmides. He calls the philosopher a lover of every kind of learning, but Glaucon points out that lovers of sights and sounds (including especially the sound of political speeches) also want to learn (475d–e). Socrates therefore draws a sharp line between the philosophers and their rivals.

Two arguments follow, a quick one to explain this distinction to Glaucon (475e–476d), and a more elaborate one to explain to nonphilosophers why their 'knowledge' really only amounts to opinion by comparison with the genuine knowledge of philosophers (476d–480a). The details of this argument belong in the next chapter; for the moment, suppose that Socrates' conclusion is true. The question remains: What has he shown of relevance to political rule by philosophers? If the argument justifies their rule, it must demonstrate not only that philosophers alone know something, but also that what they know will make them the best rulers. They must possess knowledge of ethical matters (⑩), and knowledge of a sort that can lead a city.

Among the objects of a philosopher's knowledge, both parts of the argument include justice (476a; 479a, e). Nor is that a trick on Plato's part. Moral terms, as the next chapter will show, fit especially well into this critique of the dilettante's opinions. Still the critique remains inconclusive because it directs itself to saying why the dilettante *lacks* knowledge, not to why the philosopher *possesses* it. As a strategy for excluding pretenders to political expertise it works much better than as a justification for ⑩. This passage is vague about what these Forms are that philosophers know, and how they can be said to know them. In this sense the argument is a promissory note on arguments to come, beginning at 502d and continuing into Book 7. So far Plato has not shown that the theoretical knowledge associated with philosophy can promise practical knowledge of the kind that rulers need.

If it seems impossible to imagine practical and theoretical knowledge going together, ethical insight and abstract understanding, that is no accident, nor any minor issue, but probably the most important problem facing the *Republic*. Plato wants to take philosophers, whom he values for their independent minds, and move them into the center of society hoping they will retain that power to think freely.

On the *Republic*'s own terms the problem is even more specific. Remember that ⑥ asserts, and the *Republic* keeps repeating, that every person is best suited to a single task. Now Socrates proposes yoking together political rule, which depends on practical expertise, and philosophy, whose expertise is highly abstract. How can this proposal fail to violate the division of labor? If Plato gives up ⑥ his political system collapses. If ⑥ stands, the conjunction of philosophy and rule is unnatural; but since the good city depends on that conjunction, the city is unnatural too, and can never exist.

Plato must surrender his hopes for a good city, unless he can show that philosophy inherently entails ethical knowledge.

For the moment, Socrates leaves that issue aside and turns to the remaining necessary premise of this section's argument:

(4) The love of every kind of learning produces virtue.

If he can show that philosophers 'will be able to possess these two distinct sets of qualities' (485a), knowledge and virtue, then his argument will be complete.

Socrates argues (485a–487a) that virtue always accompanies the practice of philosophy, thanks to the passion for wisdom found in every philosopher, a passion that reduces one's other passions (485d). Freed from mundane concerns by their love for wisdom, philosophers grow moderate (485e), courageous (486b), and just (486b).

This argument is too brief to persuade its readers of such an implausible claim. In another sense it goes on too long: if intellectual curiosity really did guarantee good character, people would have noticed that fact ages ago, in light of its obvious value to society. The point would have needed no proof at all, as Socrates needs no proof when he talks about breeding fast dogs to produce fast puppies.

What people might *not* have noticed before Plato, that does need a proof, is the mechanism by which he accounts for philosophers' virtue. The soul seems to be fueled by a certain quantity of energy, and channeling that energy into cerebral pursuits causes it to withdraw from others. This idea, which Socrates states explicitly in Plato's *Symposium*, anticipates the process that Freud would call sublimation. One directs one's desires away from antisocial ends and toward the activities associated with intellect and culture.

But to speak of sublimation raises a further question that leads us to what is most significant about this argument; it is one of the most consequential claims in the *Republic*, certainly the most consequential one to slip by, as this does, without fanfare. For if philosophers are redirecting energy or desire away from thoughts of sex and power when they pursue philosophical knowledge, the motives in all cases must be commensurable. In some relevant respect the drive to learn resembles the drive for bodily pleasure, for money, or for fame. Otherwise it wouldn't make sense to speak of 'the same energy' moving from one to the other.

So Socrates calls the philosopher's fondness for learning erotic. Philosophers *erôsin* 'are in love with' a kind of learning (485b) and their attachment to it is *epithumia* 'desire,' the word that the *Republic* originally reserves for the soul's least rational drives (485d; cf. 475b, 499b). In short:

⑪ The rational part of the soul has desires of its own.

To begin with such a claim revises the *Republic*'s psychological theory. As originally defined, the calculating faculty adjudicated among the soul's other impulses, determining how well those impulses worked with one another and whether they served the good of the person. Ethical reasoning seemed formal as a result. Now suddenly it has content, for if reason has desires, justice will consist in more than a balancing of passions. The good life now includes intellectual activity – as the final assessment in Book 9 makes clear, the just soul is the philosophizing soul.

Whom do we call wise? From this point on the *Republic* represents the wise person ambiguously, sometimes as a decent thoughtful person possessed of moral sense, increasingly as a professionally trained thinker. If these two kinds of wisdom do coexist, if reason equally tends to the whole soul and inquires into metaphysics, then the philosopher is both a practical master of the city and a theoretician looking for abstract truth. These become a single job; the division of labor positively demands that the philosopher rule, because the one great way of being intelligent makes that personage the most able leader.

Plato only has to take care not to let any tension between the two conceptions of reason enter his argument. For then the philosophical ruler does after all render the good city unnatural.

## PHILOSOPHERS IN EXISTING SOCIETY (487B–502C)

Before completing his theory of philosophocracy, as we may call rule by philosophers, Socrates has to face the untheoretical person of Adeimantus. This flattering portrait of the philosopher is all well and good, Adeimantus says, and Socrates has drawn Glaucon into it with his famously tendentious questions, but no one could believe it (487a–d). Experience shows that most adults who pursue philosophy become eccentric – 'not to say completely vicious' – while the few decent ones are useless to the community (487c–d).

Plato needs to confront this accusation if his political philosophy is to speak to political realities. Again he follows the abstract argument with one that acknowledges popular perceptions. This time it is a parable: the city is like a ship and its public like the ship's owner, a powerful but deaf and myopic man with scant knowledge of seafaring. Politicians resemble sailors who vie for the captaincy, scheming against their competitors for the owner's approval, all of them hostile toward anyone with real knowledge of navigation. They call the true captain's study of the stars and wind 'stargazing'; for them, every attempt at navigation is useless (488a–489a).

This image is indebted to Aristophanes' *Knights*, a political allegory in which a befuddled old man Demos ('the people' or 'the commons') has to be protected from wily merchants; Plato transports the comic situation to a ship. The parable does not quite work as an argument, because it presumes some knowledge about statecraft that the philosopher possesses, and Plato has not yet shown that any such knowledge exists. Navigators possess (or fail to possess) a definable skill: the ship's owner chooses a destination and they steer toward it. But political leaders identify the goal toward which they aim their community, be that equality or imperial strength or economic self-sufficiency. Ranking one of those aims above the others does not obviously call for knowledge or skill in the way that reaching an identified goal does, whether in a ship or in a city.

When Socrates turns to the subject of vicious philosophers, he agrees again with Adeimantus, and again turns the criticism back against the society that corrupted the philosophers. The public ruins young intellectuals by forcing them to court popular favor rather than pursue the truth (489d–495b). It persecutes anyone who tries to educate them, thus diverting that teacher's talents to the undignified practice of political intrigue. (At 494c–495b especially, Plato wants the reader to think of Socrates and Alcibiades.) As for the perversion of philosophy that Adeimantus overlooked, the pretend wisdom of fake philosophers (495c–496a), that too happens only because human society has refused to honor the insights of philosophy. In this world an uncorrupted philosopher can hope only to lead a virtuous private life – not a bad goal, but far from the best (496a–497a). (Here too Plato is thinking of the historical Socrates, regretting the political realities that stopped him from doing the true philosopher's work.) Philosophers belong in the good city, where their talents can improve everyone's life. In every other city Adeimantus' objections will be true (497a–c).

Adeimantus has seen something important about the volatile relationship between philosophers and politics. Even in the good city, its rulers will have to mind the potential for corruption that is latent in talented intellects (497c–498c). It is not only that philosophers, being human, remain vulnerable to corruption. Instead something about their natures leaves them *unusually* susceptible to the blandishments of wealth and glory. This passage marks the first overt statement in the *Republic* of the need to preserve and test philosopher-rulers in the light of their fragility.

Still, despite these concessions to Adeimantus, Socrates has not answered him. He has offered an alternative account of the phenomena Adeimantus describes: rather than proving the intrinsic badness of philosophers, their failure in society condemns the society's separation of power from knowledge. But an alternative account has to have its own plausibility if it is to come closer to the truth than the usual story, and the plausibility of Socrates' account rests on his claim that philosophers have knowledge that would make them the better rulers. They know what one needs to know to set goals for a society. Plato must show that what philosophers naturally do is directed toward politically valuable insight; he needs to prove the truth of ⑩.

## PHILOSOPHERS IN THE GOOD CITY (502C–541B)

Here is the heart of the *Republic*. First Socrates defines the purpose of this section narrowly: Assuming the birth of the good city, how can it maintain itself? What education will protect the philosophers from corruption? But the answer to this question also has to explain how a philosophical education prepares a guardian for political power. To solve *that* problem Socrates will have to investigate the ultimate purpose of philosophical activity. So he digresses again to sketch the highest goal of philosophy. We may therefore divide this section into two, the sketch of the Form or Idea[1] of the Good (502c–521b) and the pedagogical system of the city (521c–541b).

## THE FORM OF THE GOOD (502C–521B)

Still purportedly speaking only about the philosophers' education, Socrates mentions exposing them to 'the greatest study' (503e, 504d). Pressed to explain that phrase, he uses a series of images to suggest the Form of the Good, the pinnacle of philosophical inquiry. The Form of the Good is like the sun (507c–509c); the relations among the Form of the Good, all other Forms, and the objects of the visible world may be mapped out along a divided line (509d–511e); human beings' relationship to the Form of the Good resembles the relationship of prisoners in a cave to the sun (514a–517c).

As the highest principle for both ethics and metaphysics – both the best thing in the world and the most real – the Form of the Good promises to justify rule by philosophers (506a). One who masters the philosophical practice of looking for the most general principles behind a phenomenon will eventually come to this entity, which explains what the goodness of everything else consists in. Without knowledge of this Form one can never think coherently about moral issues, and certainly not plan a moral pattern for human life (505a–b).

The cost of this all-inclusive theory of reality and the good life is that it diminishes the value of ethical behavior that is practiced without philosophy. In terms of the *Republic*'s argument, this means that the Form of the Good replaces justice as the object of ethical inquiry. It also means that ⑦, which equates Platonic justice with ordinary just behavior, and which Socrates worked to demonstrate in Book 4, will prove not to be the last word. Book

---

1 This is one of the very few points at which I depart from the terminology of Bloom's translation. Bloom uses 'idea' to translate the Greek *idea*; I will use the more customary 'Form.'

4 defined justice as the preeminent virtue. Now all eyes turn to the Form of the Good. Socrates not only calls that Form 'greater than justice' (504d), but claims that 'it's by availing oneself of [the Form of the Good] along with just things and the rest, that they become useful and beneficial' (505a). In Book 4 he warned that their definition of justice would be a second-best accomplishment, inferior to the true understanding of moral principles (430c, 435d). We have now glimpsed that understanding. From this vantage point, 'the other virtues of a soul' lose their luster, amounting to no more than 'habits and exercises' (518d–e).

Does this new account falsify the theory of Book 4? It would be more accurate to call that theory *partial* in light of the greater theory. The definition from Book 4 fails to analyze reason; a complete ethical theory will add a more active role for philosophical reason.

The Allegory of the Cave brings politics back into this discussion of the Form of the Good. Human life, says Socrates, may be depicted as the condition of prisoners in a cave, shackled in rows with their backs to the cave's opening, unable to do so much as turn their heads away from the shadow theater that plays on the cave wall in front of them (514a–b). These are not the shadows of real objects, nor are they cast by the light of the sun, for sunlight cannot penetrate into the cave. Instead, there is a fire behind the prisoners, with men walking back and forth holding up models of real objects. The prisoners watch the shadows of those objects and take themselves to be viewing reality (515b).

In this allegory, learning philosophy becomes the process of being unshackled and turned around and forcibly brought to see first the fire, then the mouth of the cave, and at last the sunlit world outside. Once out in that world, the initiates accustom themselves to the brighter light by first looking at the shadows and reflections of humans and other things, then at those objects themselves, and finally at the source of all light, the sun (515c–516b). It is no wonder that anyone who returns to the cave and tries to disabuse the remaining prisoners of their misguided opinions about reality should be scoffed at. The prisoners, ignorant of the greater light behind them, mistake the disorientation of one who comes from light into darkness for the confusion of someone going from darkness into light (516e–517a, 518a–b).

Although the prisoners' derision for the philosopher brings Socrates to mind, Plato wants to do more than defend his friend's memory. The focus of the allegory shifts from the society to the philosopher, from the mistreatment philosophers face in the world as we have found it to the duty they shoulder in a well-run world. Anyone who reaches the Form of the Good will prefer not to return to the petty affairs of humans (517d–e, 519c), but in the Platonic city philosophers will be compelled to enter politics (519d).

Glaucon protests that this compulsion would do the philosophers an injustice (519d). The answer from Socrates, recalling what he told Adeimantus about the guardians' happiness (420b–421c), is that the city does not exist to benefit any one class of its citizens (519e–520a). Furthermore, the guardians have already profited from their city: unlike philosophers who manage to spring up on the stony places that are existing cities, these owe their contemplative happiness to the city's institutions (520a–c). And only rule by these philosophers benefits the city more than any other rule would, for it is the only example of power wielded reluctantly. Only philosophers know a happier life than that of ruling; hence only they will rule without falling into factions (520d–521b; cf. 345e).

The *Republic*'s relentless denial of individuals' rights to run their lives should bother any reader. But the argument threatens Plato's political theory on its own terms, in that it implies that the philosophers have something better to do than rule the city. If the philosophical activities of ruling and contemplating are different enough for Socrates to deny that the former is 'fine' (540b), then the unity of philosophy and politics becomes questionable. Though not denying philosophers' aptitude for rule, this passage gives them two distinct tasks to perform. So ⑥, which the Form of the Good was supposed to accommodate to philosophocracy, appears still at odds with the political organization of the city. The union of theoretical and practical knowledge remains a problem for Plato.

Denying the guardians their right to happiness also violates the *Republic*'s argument another way. These are just people given a just command; but in that case they should be happy to do what is just, happy by virtue of doing what is just. Otherwise the *Republic* has broken its promise that justice is profitable to the just. Plato needs his rulers *unwilling* to take office so that political power does not benefit the powerful. (On any alternative, justice is indeed the advantage of those who rule, as Thrasymachus said.) He also needs them *willing* to rule as proof that justice benefits the just.

What makes the predicament harder is that every theoretical consideration calls for the philosophers' happiness, while the value of their unhappiness follows from the plain shrewd observation that desiring power leads to trouble. It is to Plato's credit that he does not give up this commonsense observation about power even when it is a stumbling block to his political theory. But his recognizing the problem does not stop it from being a stumbling block.

## THE EDUCATION OF THE BEST GUARDIANS (521C–541B)

Socrates returns to the originating question of this digression within a digression. What steps will turn the city's governors into philosophers, attentive not to the changeable sights of the world but to the eternal truths of the intelligible realm? The remainder of Book 7 outlines a curriculum. To the music and gymnastics that made up the guardians' education in Books 2 and 3, Socrates adds arithmetic, plane and solid geometry, astronomy, and harmonics (522c–e, 525b–526c). After the end of that period of education the guardians undergo two or three years of gymnastics (537b). From twenty to thirty they pass through a synoptic study of all subjects (537b–c), after which, from the ages of thirty to thirty-five, they receive their first introduction to dialectic (537c–d; see 532d–534c on education in dialectic). They next serve the city for fifteen years in military and civil posts, as soldiers, police, and lower administrators (539e–540a). Only at fifty are they brought to a vision of the Form of the Good, and once they see *that* they divide their time between philosophy of the highest order and government at the highest rank (540a–c).

## PLATO'S EDUCATIONAL THEORY

As an educator, Plato combines progressive recommendations with repressive and militaristic ones. His most general proposal here has grown into an attitude so common that the reader might overlook its significance. Plato denies that schooling consists in packing knowledge into the soul (518b); it is more like a conversion in which the soul 'turns around' (518c, d) and directs its attention to new objects (521c–d). Book 3's list of books to ban may have suited the earlier education of the guardians, which aimed only at moral training; the production of philosophers calls for the development of a particular kind of ability. Pure and applied mathematics enhance that ability, providing the city's educators keep their approach to those subjects philosophical (526e, 529a, 531c).

Such comments make it abundantly clear that Plato (probably the first to do so in European history) is advocating an education centered on methods of analysis rather than on facts. He envisions the process as a natural growth, at least for talented students (535c): this is why their learning can begin as games (536d–537a).

These visionary comments come together with reactionary ones. Though Plato wants mathematical studies to draw the soul upward to being, he also recommends them to military strategists (522d–e, 525b, 526d). He is motivated by the desire to show that a single curriculum serves both warriors and philosophers (525b), hence that the guardians can naturally fulfill both roles at once. But this motive does not make up for the objectionable sound of Socrates' arguments. He repeats his earlier point about children watching battles (537a), stressing that war and philosophy are on a par in the guardians' lives. If we should not generalize glibly that Plato was a militarist, we equally should not forget that the guardian class began as the city's standing army, that for all his hopes about the perfectibility of human beings Plato is always prepared to exercise force on those who remain unperfected.

## THE THREAT OF DIALECTIC

The education described here scarcely resembles the process by which the historical Socrates brought his friends into philosophy. According to certain Platonic dialogues, Socrates took to his investigations after realizing that his fellow Athenians had only inconsistent and anecdotal things to say about vital issues (*Apology* 21c–22d). The dialogues that are thought to reflect Socrates' practice (*Charmides*, *Euthyphro*, *Gorgias*, *Laches*, *Lysis*) show him making his interlocutors aware that their high-sounding pronouncements fail to cover even the most obvious phenomena, and that their talk of ethical matters is meaningless.

Plato has substituted a formal curriculum in mathematics for his teacher's cross-examination of Athenians' moral claims. He mistrusts Socratic teaching. Here, Socrates warns Glaucon that the philosophical examination of moral principles must not be revealed to young men (537c–539d). Young students of dialectic are 'filled full with lawlessness' (537e), sharp at refuting tradition (539b) but not stable enough to remain virtuous in the face of moral uncertainty (539d). These warnings against exposing the young to dialectic suggest that Plato has come to share – however qualifiedly, however provisionally – the Athenians' judgment that Socrates corrupted the youth. Plato would rather populate his ideal city with obedient citizens who never interrogate the received wisdom as Socrates had; at the same time, he cannot gainsay the value of that interrogation for anyone who wants to develop moral theories. He hopes that his propaedeutic of arithmetic and geometry will inspire the same fervor toward abstraction that Socrates had wakened, without inspiring the same skepticism in these future rulers that Socrates did in the loose cannons of Athenian aristocracy.

The young guardians' weakness before the corrosive power of dialectic recalls Socrates' explanation to Adeimantus that the philosophical nature is especially open to corruption (491d–492a; cf. 518e–519a). The warning against dialectic intensifies our sense of the philosophers' vulnerability. Even what makes them can unmake them, for those character traits that produce philosophical ability – quick intellect, love of argument – may also produce a cunning demagogue or a tyrant's apologist. As at 373–76, when Socrates first mentioned the guardians, the existence of a good society is linked to the possibility of these good rulers; and *their* possibility again sounds like a contradiction. Then, the joint wildness and mildness needed in a standing army seemed unable to coexist; here it is the philosopher's theoretical bent, hence also agility of mind, and the governor's practicality – which means: steadfastness of mind (503c–d). No wonder Books 6 and 7 harp on the need to test the city's guardians (503a, e; 539e), to make them labor in their education (504d), to watch for the bad ones (536a). The philosophers' sureness of knowledge is matched by their corruptibility.

The weakness of the philosophical temperament becomes a worse problem when we remember how much power these rulers wield. They make the laws and set policies for enforcing them; they keep the army in houses where no one escapes a master's scrutiny; they move their citizens' children up and down across class lines. Such power finds its warrant in the infallibility of the philosophers' knowledge. But now one must ask how firm that knowledge can be, when it is held by people so susceptible to moral decay. Perhaps such a nature can be trained into incorruptibility; but then that degree of perfection, on which Plato's investment of power in his guardians depends, makes a mystery of the inevitable decay of the city in Book 8, a decay that Plato blames on the guardians' fallibility (546a–547a).

One wonders why Plato's awareness of human fallibility did not bring him to see the virtues of democracy, whose ideological confusion and endless horse-trading, though they make democracy the government least likely to pursue systematic policies, also help it to resist tyranny. Given that we live in a world in which the best people err both morally and intellectually, perhaps we should provide for a system that offers not the best way of life imaginable, but the best at avoiding some worse state. In the *Statesman* Plato will reason this way, concluding that when human society cannot depend on the stable rule of fixed laws, democracy is the most desirable constitution (303a–b). In the *Republic* he only selectively acknowledges, and cannot seem to bear in mind, that we live in what Christians call a fallen world.

## SUGGESTIONS FOR FURTHER READING

Ferrari 'Socrates in the *Republic*' is invaluable for elucidating the form and nature of Socrates' narration and the loss of control exemplified at the beginning of Book 5.

On Plato's proposals for the city, see first of all Aristotle, *Politics* II.1–6; also Barker, 'Communism in Plato's *Republic*.'

Bambrough, 'Plato's political analogies,' is invaluable. For a very recent synopsis of the scholarly debates over the *Republic*'s politics see Fronterotta, 'Plato's *Republic* in the recent debate.'

On the guardians' education and the Form of the Good see especially Cooper, 'The psychology of justice in Plato.' On forcing philosophers to rule, see most recently Smith, 'Return to the cave': besides advancing the debate Smith contains references to much of the preceding discussion.

On the perennially provocative topic of women in the *Republic*'s city begin with Santas, *Understanding Plato's Republic*. Then see Bluestone, *Women and the Ideal Society: Plato's Republic and Modern Myths of Gender*, which addresses both the reforms proposed in Book 5 and the history of their reception; also Lesser, 'Plato's feminism,' Smith, 'Plato and Aristotle on the nature of women,' and above all Vlastos, 'Was Plato a feminist?' On women in Athens see Keuls, *The Reign of the Phallus: Sexual Politics in Ancient Athens*.

# 7

## METAPHYSICS AND
## EPISTEMOLOGY (BOOKS 5-7)

Metaphysics, very generally considered, asks: What things are real, and what gives them their reality? Epistemology asks: What can we know, and how do we know it? The two questions may be kept distinct from one another, but in the *Republic* Plato interweaves questions of reality with questions of knowledge, on the grounds that the kind of reality or being an object has corresponds to the mode of cognition one can have of it. This grand unification of all philosophical inquiries is typical of the middle section of the *Republic*, and it is one reason for the dialogue's philosophical importance, though the ambitiousness of this project also produces the *Republic*'s greatest difficulties.

### THE PROBLEM WITH PARTICULARS (475E–480A)

We have seen Glaucon object that philosophers resemble dilettantes (475d). Socrates uses this opportunity to distinguish philosophers by the superior objects of their inquiry, and to begin separating those objects from the less perfect ones that the lover of spectacles pursues. His argument approaches the distinction from both sides, first appealing to the superiority of the Forms (475e–476d), then demeaning everything else (476e–480a).

## THE FORMS (475E–476D)

Socrates begins by speaking of 'justice and injustice, good and bad' (476a). Then he refers to 'the fair itself' (476b), as if that were the same manner of thing. Glaucon expresses no surprise at the new terminology: Socrates seems to be referring to a theory that he has already heard and been convinced of. Indeed, whenever Socrates introduces such language, it meets with Glaucon's immediate agreement (507b, 596a–b). In Plato's other principal discussion of '(the) X itself' in the *Phaedo*, Socrates again finds his combative interlocutors assenting without resistance to the existence of entities they somehow already know (100b; cf. 74a).

These passages introduce what are called Plato's Forms. Plato uses different words to speak of a Form of X, but most commonly calls it 'X itself,' to express the perfect way in which a Form holds its property X. Sometimes he calls the Form simply 'X,' sometimes *eidos*, sometimes *idea* (though the Greek word *idea* does not refer to thoughts in people's minds as its English cognate does). 'Form' has become the commonest English word for the entity; it captures two senses of the Greek, both the sense of 'species' (a pistol is a form of gun), and that of 'shape' or 'pattern' (form letter, dressmaker's form).

Whatever he calls them, Plato tends to introduce Forms with no argument for their existence. Perhaps his first readers knew the theory already; perhaps Plato wanted to keep his theory available only to initiates; perhaps he had no argument, and posited the existence of Forms in order to get on with the rest of the theory. Whatever the explanation, Plato's dialogues offer no proper introduction to the Forms, and we can understand them only by determining what Plato expects them to accomplish.

In the passage at hand, Socrates defines Forms by contrast with non-Forms. Each of these qualities – justice and injustice, good and bad – is 'itself' a single object; 'but, by showing themselves everywhere in a community with actions, bodies, and one another, each looks like many' (476a). These 'many' are the beautiful sounds and colors through which the beautiful itself shows itself (476b); they 'participate' in the beautiful itself but are not identical to it (476d).

This passage implies three features of Forms:

(1)  Uniqueness: The Form of $X$ is the only one of its kind.
(2)  Self-predication: The Form of $X$ is the exemplar of the property $X$.
(3)  Nonidentity: Individual $X$ things – actions, bodies, shapes, manufactured objects – might have a share in the Form of $X$, but none of them *is* the Form.

Whatever other details about Forms we may argue about (see Chapter 11), their uniqueness, self-predication, and nonidentity with individual $X$ things constitute their core properties.

Even this simplest statement contains vague language. What does it take to exemplify a property? What makes individual things fall short? What can it mean to say that an $X$ thing 'participates' in the Form of $X$? As Books 5–7 progress, Plato will work to clarify his theory, though the answers to these questions remain open to further elucidation. For example, Plato hints by way of explaining participation that the $X$ thing is 'like' the $X$ itself (476c); but what this likeness means will not become clear until later.

The Forms do not prove that philosophers stand above the lovers of sensory experience, because the lovers of experience occupy a lower state only if we grant that the beautiful things they admire are mere likenesses of beauty itself. To grant *that*, we would have to agree that Forms exist, and that $X$ things owe their property of being $X$ to the Form of $X$.

Oddly, Socrates does not fill in these missing steps. But he does concede what follows from his failure to fill them in, that the argument will not convince the person who holds opinions without knowledge. '[C]onsider what we'll say to him' (476e). The rest of Book 5 sets philosophers apart from their rivals not by proving the existence of Forms, but by criticizing non-Forms on separate grounds. In other words, when it comes time to defending his metaphysical theory, Plato begins in the realm of ordinary experience and tries to prove its inadequacies. Nonphilosophers might not understand the abstract theory or even entertain it, as long as they remain rooted in their experience. Demonstrating the truth of a theory like Plato's, so opposed to ordinary experience, requires demonstrating the need for it, by showing that ordinary experience fails on its own terms.

Thus, although Socrates scarcely mentions the Forms in the next argument, he is indirectly arguing for their existence. The argument directed against the nonphilosophers concludes that ordinary experience cannot lead to knowledge. If there is to be any knowledge at all, it must have Forms for its objects.

## KNOWLEDGE AND OPINION (476E-480A)

The argument says:

(1) Knowledge is knowledge of what is, while ignorance is attached to what is not. (476e-477a)

(2) Opinion lies between knowledge and ignorance. (478c)

∴ (3) From (1) and (2), opinion depends on whatever lies between what is and what is not. (478d-e)

(4) The Form of $X$ is always $X$. (479a)

(5) Beautiful things are also ugly, just things also unjust, holy things also unholy, double things also half, big things also little. (479a-b)

∴ (6) From (5), a particular $X$ thing is both $X$ and non-$X$. (479c)

∴ (7) From (4) and (6), a particular thing both is and is not, whereas the Form of $X$ is. (479c)

∴ (8) From (1), (3), and (7), the Form of $X$ is the object of knowledge, whereas particular $X$ things are objects of opinion. (479d-e)

A subsidiary part of this argument aims at showing the failings of the world of ordinary experience: the concise and crucial argument *against knowledge of particulars* (hereafter AKP):

(1) Knowledge of an $X$ thing is possible only if that thing is unqualifiedly $X$ (or 'always' $X$, 479a).

> (2) Individual $X$ things (for at least some properties $X$) are both $X$ and non-$X$.
>
> $\therefore$ (3) There can be no knowledge of individual $X$ things.

Glaucon accepts (1) without a murmur, when he agrees that knowledge must be knowledge of what is (476e). Along with (1) he accepts a broader unstated assumption:

⑫ Every level of understanding requires a corresponding level of reality in the object of understanding.

In this instance, it is knowledge that they want, and knowledge of an $X$ thing calls for that thing to hold its property $X$ unequivocally. (Later Plato's theory will draw out further implications of ⑫.)

Expressed abstractly, ⑫ might appear too vague to worry about. As soon as it is put in concrete terms it contradicts common sense. On a commonsense view of acquiring knowledge, you start out ignorant of a subject, then formulate opinions, and (if all goes well) come into the possession of knowledge – all concerning the same subject. You have no idea what sunrise is; then you think it is the sun coming up to orbit the earth; finally you know that the earth orbits the sun and spins to produce the effect of sunrise. You go from ignorance about the bloodstream, to a confused idea about blood sloshing back and forth in veins, to knowledge about the circulatory system of arteries, capillaries, and veins. Common sense ancient and modern sees the object of inquiry remaining fixed while the inquirer's cognitive state improves. What you don't know (sun's orbit, circulation) is just as real as what you have beliefs about and what you know for certain, just as it is the same person coming toward you who is first too far away to recognize, then might seem to be your friend, and finally gets close enough to identify beyond all doubt.

Plato seems to follow common sense when he describes the slow process of coming to know the Forms (516a–b, 521c, 533c–d). The Forms remain what they are as the philosopher's understanding of them improves. And here in AKP Socrates says the lovers of fair or beautiful particulars do not see 'the fair itself' (479e) – i.e. they are either ignorant of that Form or merely possess opinions about it. So one can be in a state other than knowledge even for what the *Republic* identifies as an object of knowledge.

Applying ⑫ literally to cases of studying a given object is evidently the wrong way to interpret it. But other examples elicit the philosophical intuition that drives this premise. Consider predicting

   (i)   the behavior of a Pisces;
   (ii)  the behavior of someone whose name begins with 'R';
   (iii) the week's weather;
   (iv)  the week's stock market;
   (v)   how many prime numbers will occur in the next 1,000 integers;
   (vi)  how the volume of a sphere will change when its radius doubles.

Regarding (i) and (ii) there is nothing to know. Fortunes and centuries have been wasted trying to learn something meaningful about people born in February and March. The letter 'R' at least really exists, but its appearance at the start of a name is a poor guide to what that name's owner will do next. So if you need to predict someone's behavior, but you only know an astrological sign or a first initial, you have no useful information.

In the next two cases, experts can predict (iii) or (iv) better than the layperson. But most investors and meteorologists admit that their knowledge is incomplete. A region's weather is described in a set of equations that cannot all be solved simultaneously. The stock market responds to some data on a consistent basis, but no experienced stock trader thinks a moneymaking prediction will be without risk. There is much worth knowing about seasonal changes and catastrophes in both cases, and never enough.

The differences between (v) and (vi) are subtle but important. The distribution of prime numbers follows a pattern, described in the prime number theorem, that estimates the likelihood that a randomly chosen number near a given large number is prime. Of course one can always go through all the integers near 1,000 or near 1,000,000 checking each one to discover how many are prime. The sphere in (vi) does not have to be approached so slowly: twice the radius means eight times the volume.

Different upper limits of understanding correspond to the different cases, thanks to the natures of these objects of understanding. No one knows what a Pisces will do or even has an informed opinion, because that grouping corresponds to no traits of its members. There are better and worse opinions about the weather, but nothing better than a good opinion, because local weather on any given day depends on an unstable cluster of forces and conditions. In the mathematical examples knowledge is possible thanks to the general predictability of prime numbers and the very concrete formula for a sphere's volume. Today one does not say that prime numbers have greater reality than tornadoes; but as long as you say there is something about them that makes the more-certain knowledge possible, you can agree with Plato that each type of thing admits of a different kind of understanding.

These six cases have avoided the scientific examples that would be classed as knowledge by modern scientists but that Plato calls opinion. Socrates warns that there is no truth to be found in astronomy, because the heavens are visible and changeable (530a–b). What is visible belongs in the middle category (see also *Phaedo* 96a–99c).

But the telling problem, on Plato's own terms, is that the higher-ranking objects only *permit*, do not *require*, higher-ranking understanding. No one can know what Raleigh and Roberta will do, but some people can be equally ignorant about the coming week's stock market and about the new sphere's volume. According to ⑫ it might seem that the distribution of prime numbers can only be a matter of knowledge, never of opinion. Obviously that is false.

For now, a weaker version of ⑫ can preserve what is true in it: each level of reality corresponds not to *exactly* one level of cognition, but to *at best* one level. AKP only needs to deny knowledge regarding particular objects, not also to deny opinion about the Forms. The weaker version of ⑫ will not fit every passage, but it is enough to make AKP work.

AKP also depends on its second premise, which charges individual X things with being both X and non-X. Here Plato has an argument, but one so compressed as to support various interpretations. Socrates says that each of the many beautiful things will also look ugly, each of the just things unjust (479a). The many doubles also appear as halves; so too, *mutatis mutandis*, for big and light things. It follows that every particular thing no more is what one calls it than it is the opposite (479b). Particular things lack genuine properties; they are only half real. Such things can't be known, if knowing them has anything to do with knowing their properties.

This argument inspires two questions. How does an $X$ thing fail to be $X$? And which properties both do and do not hold of a single object? To answer the first question is largely to answer the second, since the properties at stake will be those for which AKP's critique works. Given answers to these questions we can describe the Forms. They will be $X$ in a way that the many $X$ things are not, and there will be a Form of $X$ for every property $X$ to which the argument applies.

Socrates' argument is easier to understand if we set aside beauty, justice, and holiness, and look at the other properties he groups together with them. Things called double, big, or light are so called by comparison with other things. My arms may be *double* if I compare the pair of them to a single arm, also *half* if I compare them to the group of all my limbs. Doubleness is not a built-in property of my arms, but a property that depends on what I compare them to. The question 'Is this double?' needs to be given a context. Because any such context dependent or *relative* term never applies unequivocally, focusing on the individual things that have that property will not lead to knowledge of the property. I may study a big, thick, heavy mouse for as long as I like, but it will not reveal what bigness, thickness, or heaviness consists in. A Form, by comparison, is a pure exemplar of doubleness or heaviness, showing the nature of those properties without appeal to comparisons.

The simplicity of this argument, and its echo in Book 7 (523a–524a), has led some to conclude that things fail as exemplars of their properties when, *and only when*, those properties are relative terms, terms whose meaning depends on their contexts. Then we should go back and apply Socrates' critique of relative terms to the evaluative terms – beautiful, just, holy – in the preceding sentence. But the two sorts of properties are not similarly ambiguous. We do not praise a just law only by comparison with another one. In this sense of 'context,' evaluative terms are no more context dependent than color terms are. If they fail exactly as relative terms do, we must clarify the nature of their dependence on context.

The fault might lie not in the laws or people to which moral terms both do and do not apply, but in the bad generalizations that people make about those terms. When Cephalus defined justice as returning what was owed, and Socrates refuted him with the example of the madman's weapon, we may interpret Socrates as having shown that returning what is owed is just in one context and unjust in another. A single act both is and is not just.

Now justice looks more like doubleness. But while this interpretation is insightful, and sensitive to Plato's ethical project, it is also speculative. Plato never speaks of Forms in any passage that also condemns naive generalizations about moral terms.

In addition, the analogy remains imperfect. This account of evaluative terms extends the notion of 'context' from the clear sense of a basis for comparison to the more nebulous idea of a situation. We have lost the point that certain terms only mean something when one object is being compared to another.

Plato's *Symposium* says somewhat more, charging specific beautiful things with three kinds of shortcomings: their beauty exists in only parts of them; it waxes and wanes; it differs depending on who is looking at the thing (210e–211b). So alongside,

(1) An $X$ object is not $X$ *in every context*, but $X$ compared to one thing and non-$X$ compared to another,

we may name three more criticisms of particulars:

(2) An $X$ object is not $X$ *in every part*, but contains non-$X$ parts.
(3) An $X$ object is not $X$ *at every time*, but increases and decreases in $X$-ness.
(4) An $X$ object is not $X$ *to every observer*, but seems $X$ to one and non-$X$ to another.

Here are four grounds for calling $X$ things incomplete bearers of their properties.

Of the four, (2) accomplishes the least. It may even beg the question, for it asserts the imperfection of the world's contents, which this argument was supposed to prove.

(4) works especially well for ethical terms. Nor could anything be more widely observed than disagreement about justice. The Sophists had already argued that such disagreement demonstrated the emptiness of morality. If an action looks brave to one observer and cowardly to another, it cannot have any intrinsic property, whether courage or cowardice. Plato half agrees; only he does not take the disagreement to show that *nothing* is really brave or cowardly, but rather to show that no *act* will be either one or the other. This in turn only exposes the inadequacy of the world of opinion by comparison with that of the Forms, about which two informed people would never disagree.

This interpretation has a disadvantage opposite to that in the argument using (1). Whereas the argument about context applies neatly to relative terms and only metaphorically or obscurely to moral terms, (4) works well for moral terms but scarcely applies to others. People do not enter into disputes over whether a thing is light or heavy, is or is not a dog. Only issues of value produce intractable disagreement. So (4) alone will not account for the entirety of Plato's criticisms of the world.

(3), the most powerful criticism, condemns the physical world to imperfection for its changeability. Because the growth and decay of things prohibits them from holding any properties forever – animals grow from small to large, beautiful temples crumble into eyesores – no $X$ thing in the world of ordinary beliefs will exemplify $X$. It will be non-$X$ before you know it. Perhaps changeability explains why Socrates uses the future tense when he apostrophizes to the lover of sights: 'Now, of these many fair things ... is there any that won't also look ugly?' (479a). It may be why he says the Forms are *always* what they are (479a, 484b, 485b, 585c). Certainly the changeability of the physical world is at stake when Socrates describes that world as a place of generation and destruction (508d, 527b) or decay (485b). Since no one could deny the ubiquity of change, since Plato seems concerned to deny change in the Forms, and since the change of the world indicts every object in it, this argument may work as an elucidation of Socrates' brief comments.

It is also relevant to this reading of AKP that philosophers before Plato made the world's changeability central to their cosmology. Plato's *Theaetetus* (152d–e) calls this the dominant tradition in Greek philosophy, stretching back to Homer; but even if that statement goes too far, there is no doubting the presence and importance of Heraclitus. And the philosophy of Heraclitus contains two claims reminiscent of AKP:

(1) The flux: Objects possessing a given property will come to possess the contrary property. What is hot becomes cold.
(2) The unity of opposites (apparently presented by Heraclitus as a consequence of the flux): Every object that has some property also in some respect has the contrary property. What is hot is in some way cold.

*Because* of the flux, as well as for other reasons, objects may be said to hold contrary properties.

What matters here is not just that people before Plato spoke of the world's changes, and also spoke of the ambiguity of the world's contents, but that before him the changeability of the world had already been thought to demonstrate the incomplete predication that characterizes the world. For if Heraclitus made this argument against the stability of natural phenomena, Plato may be making it too.

Despite its pedigree, this broad critique of the physical world also runs into trouble as a reading of AKP. In the first place, the argument in Book 5 restricts itself to evaluative and relative terms. If Plato had an argument in mind that worked against everything on earth, it's curious that he did not name other examples. AKP would equally well imply a Form of Tree and a Form of Air. In the second place, the corruptibility of the sensible world does not apply clearly to morality. A courageous act does not decay into a cowardly one, and just laws do not fade into injustice.

AKP seems to turn on a spectrum of arguments, each one of which shows in a different way, and with respect to different kinds of properties, that an X thing is also non-X. The criticisms have different implications for what kinds of Forms there will be: if (2) or (3) is Plato's core argument, every observable property will have its Form. The changeability of the world implies that even the property of being a dog will hold only partially of any individual thing, since that thing is bound to die and cease being a dog. If Plato instead means to rely on such arguments as (1) and (4), there will only be Forms of relative and evaluative terms. (See Chapter 11 for more about this issue.)

Whichever argument is at work, a Form of $X$ stands apart from particular objects by dint of being $X$ under all conditions, to all observers, at all times. AKP has not proved that such entities exist as objects of knowledge, but that only they and nothing else *can* be objects of knowledge, *if* they exist. Nothing but Forms will serve as objects of knowledge, as individual things lack the necessary relationship to their properties.

One last word about Forms. They threaten to be such perfect objects that human beings cannot possibly know them. But the argument of Book 5 is more sanguine than that about our ordinary state. While opinion lacks philosophical insight, it also avoids the total absence of knowledge that characterizes ignorance. If opinion rather than ignorance is most people's state of mind, the transition to knowledge becomes significantly more plausible. For if the unschooled lack all awareness, their acquisition of knowledge must be a spontaneous and unmotivated leap into another state. But if the common human condition is some jumble of ignorance and knowledge, education has a place to begin. Rather than transform the unphilosophical into new beings, one need only prune away their ignorance.

## THE FORM OF THE GOOD (503E–518B)

In the last third of Book 6, Socrates returns to the young philosophers' education. Young guardians must be tested to see if they are worthy of learning about the Form of the Good (505a). The Form of the Good, again, is intended to unite the pursuits of philosophers, which all too often drift away from human concerns, with the ethical knowledge that makes life worth living (505a–b), and by virtue of which philosophers are qualified to rule in the ideal city.

Everyone wants what is good. In this respect the good differs from justice, since no one needs to be persuaded to seek it (505d–e). Like the English 'good,' the Greek *agathos* can serve as both a moral concept and a much broader term of approbation. Even wicked people want good food; we listen to good music without growing saintly. As Socrates says, every soul makes what is good the goal of its every action, but though people glimpse this 'good' they notoriously can't say what it is (505d–e). Given this universal inarticulate yearning for what is good, perhaps the ultimate strategy for defending ethics would involve unpacking the meaning of goodness to find a fundamental value on which everyone agrees.

The right word here is 'perhaps,' because the *Republic* does not go so far toward analyzing the good. Socrates contents himself with a sketch of its function as the supreme principle of metaphysics, and even that remains a sketch. Solid arguments barely enter into this image-laden section of the dialogue; the reader should bear in mind that Plato is trafficking in broad proposals, of which we should not ask more specific questions than they can answer.

The *Republic* provides several examples of Plato's figurative explanations. The noble lie of Book 3 casts the class structure of the city in terms of metals in the soul. The ship of state in Book 6 explains allegorically the hostility that politicians feel toward philosophers. The myth of Er that closes the *Republic* restates its defense of justice in a story about the afterlife. As familiar to Plato's readers as Jesus' parables are to readers of the Gospels, the myths, images, and allegories of the dialogues also resemble those parables in having three distinct purposes. Some *persuade* their audience to do what it already knows it should; others *teach* in concrete language what an unsophisticated audience would otherwise have trouble following; still others *speculate* about matters that no human beings have understood. The noble lie and the myth of Er illustrate the propagandistic function of Plato's images, while the ship of state and the tale of Gyges' ring illustrate their pedagogical function. The coming images show Plato speculating about the Form of the Good.

## THE IMAGE OF THE SUN (507C–509B)

Socrates once more assumes the existence of Forms (507b). Here he opposes them to the objects of human sight (507b–c), and this opposition between visible and intelligible suggests an analogy between the sun and some corresponding entity in the realm of the intellect:

| | |
|---|---|
| Form of the Good | sun |
| intelligence | eye |
| knowledge | sight |
| Forms | visible objects |

Just as the eye sees objects only thanks to the sun's supply of light, human reason knows the Forms only thanks to the intercession of the Form of the Good (508b–e). And as the sun, the source of all energy, also makes possible the existence of every living thing, the Form of the Good also causes the Forms to be in the first place (509a–b).

Socrates calls the sun a god (508a: incidentally this is not Apollo, who would not be identified with the sun until later in antiquity). If the sun represents the Good, shouldn't that Form also be a deity? The neo-Platonic movement that dominated philosophy later, during the Roman Empire, certainly found theology in the *Republic*'s Form of the Good, and their ancient and modern Christian readers drew inspiration from that theological interpretation. To a degree the interpretation is right. Plato's works make plentiful use of religious imagery and vocabulary, more than modern scholars acknowledge.

But while godliness is an important property of the Form of the Good, it is not the only feature of that Form, and the religious reading of this passage should not overshadow other questions about it – for example the question what kind of Form the Form of the Good is.

In some ways the Form of the Good resembles a Form of Form-ness, and if the *Republic* offered more details here it might be possible to spell out such a reading. For the uniqueness, self-predication, and nonidentity that characterize Forms are features of the Good itself. It is certainly unique; good, hence self-predicating; and Socrates says it is 'beyond being' (509b). The Forms belong in the domain of being if anything does, so the Form of the Good is not identical to any other Forms.

An account of Form-ness begins with the self-predication of Forms. The Form of X captures what it is to be X, in other words to be a *real* X; this is also what it is to be a *good* X. 'Now that is a real movie' one says after seeing a good movie. The Form of X, X itself, is the best X there is.

The Form of X cannot be all there is to being good, though, because other properties exist besides X. Even if 'justice itself' is the best that justice can be, it is not the exemplar of the even numbers. Nor is it piety or perfect largeness. When X and Y are unrelated properties, the Form of X will be the good X but not necessarily the good Y. This makes the Form of X both good and not good, not everything it is to be good. By comparison the Form of the Good is good regardless of context, observer, or time. It embodies, unequivocally, that property of being best that all other Forms possess. It is the Form of Forms, or Form itself.

Along these lines the Good might perform the function of a supreme principle of metaphysics, accounting for the many other Forms' existence. As the property of being best it could also make knowledge of those Forms possible. Looking for any best case, whether the Form of courage or of curvature, presupposes some orientation toward ideality as such, the best in general. The Form of the Good corresponds to the sun, which both causes visible things to be and makes our vision of them possible.

Against this interpretation of the Good comes, first, the trenchant observation that it is speculative. The *Republic* makes clear that the entity in question is a Form of some kind, playing these two roles in the realm of Forms. The rest goes beyond anything Plato wrote.

A second problem: What does this have to do with ethics? The city's philosophers study the Good in order to rule wisely. How can the supreme principle of metaphysics and epistemology also justify and explain the human pursuit of value? This arch-Form might complete the structure of the intelligible world, but it does not seem to be ready for service as the goal of life.

This second problem is likely to hamper any reconstruction of the Good. Socrates himself stops referring to any role it plays in human ethics after having introduced it with that purpose in mind. It will be hard enough to find a clear theory of reality and knowledge in these pages about the Good; the connection to ethics all but disappears.

A third problem with seeing the Good as a Form of Forms follows from a technical feature of the theory. Almost without exception, Platonic Forms cause the existence of particular objects' properties by virtue of perfectly instantiating those properties. The Form of piety makes every pious act pious, to the extent that the act is pious, because the Form is perfectly pious to begin with. Causation by Forms is a causation of resemblance. For this reason Plato's dialogues often illustrate the relation between Form and particular with the metaphors they do. Things 'share' in Forms, i.e. they are a little *like* the Forms that cause their properties. Forms 'participate' in things, which is to say they are partly or briefly present in those things. Aristotle will object that such words are metaphorical and obscure (*Metaphysics* I.9, 991a19–32); still the motive behind them is clear, that what is already $X$ (and nothing else) can make another thing $X$.

This principle of metaphysical causation then suddenly fails when Socrates says, in one of the *Republic*'s grandest pronouncements, that despite its own status 'beyond being' the Good causes being in other objects, presumably the Forms (509b). Being (which almost translates to existence or reality) is the supreme characteristic of Plato's intelligible objects. And yet it is absent from the cause of those objects. Causation by resemblance ought to work here, at the top of the system, if it works anywhere; but right here is where it fails, and with it (probably) any attempt to reconstruct a metaphysical architectonic accounting for all beings. The Form of the Good will have to function more as a guarantor of knowledge than as a ground of being.

## THE DIVIDED LINE (509D–511E)

### The argument from analogy

In the remainder of Book 6 Socrates returns to his distinction between objects of opinion and objects of knowledge, complicates that distinction, and arranges the entire structure into a path toward the Form of the Good. He describes an unequally divided line, with each part redivided into the same unequal proportions. The two segments resulting from the first cut correspond to the objects of knowledge and opinion. The objects of opinion, or

visible things, are then separated into ordinary physical objects
and their shadows and reflections (509d–510a). The higher class
of objects is divided too (510b), into Forms and mathematical
objects ('the odd and the even, the figures, three forms of angles,'
510c). Assuming that greater length corresponds to greater
intelligibility or clarity, the Divided Line looks like Figure 2.

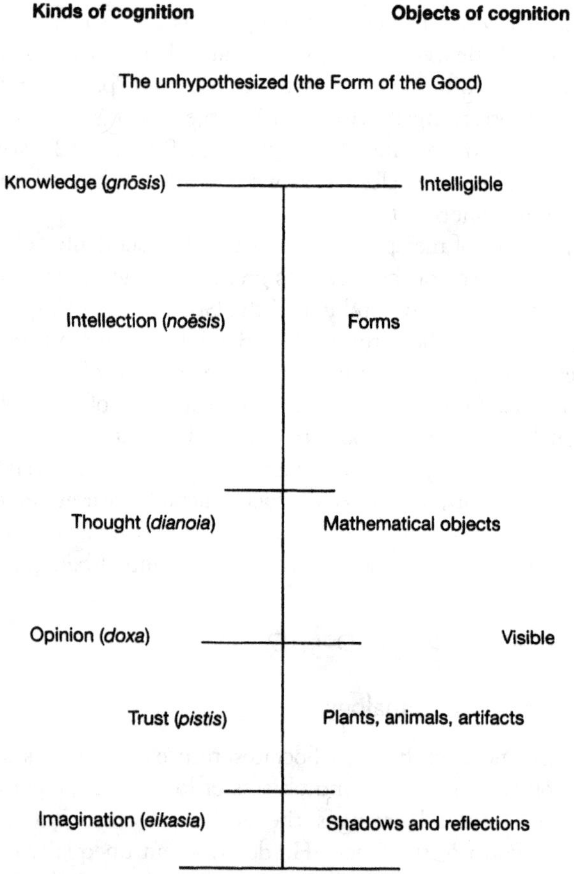

**Kinds of cognition**     **Objects of cognition**

The unhypothesized (the Form of the Good)

Knowledge (*gnōsis*) ———————— Intelligible

Intellection (*noēsis*)          Forms

Thought (*dianoia*)          Mathematical objects

Opinion (*doxa*) ———————— Visible

Trust (*pistis*)          Plants, animals, artifacts

Imagination (*eikasia*)          Shadows and reflections

*Figure 2*

(The question whether to organize the Line vertically or horizontally, and whether to make its longer segments or shorter ones correspond to greater intelligibility, goes back at least as far as the ancient authors Plutarch and Proclus.)

What began as a simple comparison between the sun and the Good has become a bewilderment of analogies. This complexity results from Plato's desire to use the Divided Line to make two points at once. First, it explains to an unphilosophical audience how the objects of opinion are related to objects of knowledge, by inviting that audience to see the visible world as a mirror-image of another, truer place. The reflection relationship uses an ordinary conception of greater and lesser reality, a conception we appeal to every day, to gesture beyond ordinary experience toward a greatest kind of reality.

At the same time, the Line lets Plato find a special place for mathematics, which he has set above all other skills as a preliminary to philosophy. This double function of the Divided Line gives rise to architectonic rococo, but it finally issues in a unified account of all objects and our grasp on them.

On this last point – regarding the relationship between objects of cognition and kinds of cognition – the Divided Line passage is sometimes elusive. But it closes with an emphatic assertion of ⑫:

> As the segments [of the line] to which [the affections of the soul] correspond participate in truth, so they participate in clarity.
>
> (511e)

The question will be whether Plato can make the Divided Line work in all these ways.

## Kinds of cognition and their kinds of objects

Plato wants to retain some bridge connecting objects of opinion with objects of knowledge. He also insists on the difference between the two, so that philosophical knowledge may remain superior to what ordinarily passes for knowledge. The very idea of a Divided Line reflects this tension: as a *line* it emphasizes the continuity between higher and lower realms; as something *divided* it sets them apart. To have it both ways, Plato will need to explain the relationship between sections of the line in terms that express both kinship and difference.

Hence Plato's appeal to the relationship between an original and its *eikôn*, 'likeness, image.' In Platonic terms, the things in the physical world possess a more substantial reality or being than their reflections do. My reflection depends on me for its existence, but not vice versa. I make a more reliable object of knowledge than my reflection. Mirrors may distort my appearance. Yet there is no denying the similarity between us. No house would have mirrors in it if reflections did not bear their special relationship to the thing reflected. The metaphor of likeness and original tells non-philosophers what they are missing when they wallow in the world of the senses, and also hints at how they might come to attain it.

Mathematics belongs to the realm of knowledge because the truths it discovers do not concern objects of sensory experience. To know that adding seven chairs to five makes a new group of twelve chairs is to know something not about chairs, but about the properties of numbers, which are 'intellected but not seen' (507b). Children who add by counting on their fingers have grasped this Platonic insight. Anything you count is as good as anything else. Thus numbers and geometrical shapes belong with the Forms.

Mathematics remains beneath metaphysics because (1) mathematicians treat their objects as known, when in fact the elements of mathematics call for further investigation (510c); and (2) mathematicians rely on diagrams in their work (510d). This use of visual aids does not condemn mathematical practice to the lower segments of the Divided Line, for mathematicians use those diagrams 'as images' (510b, e, 511a), only as guides to the real entities at stake, just as I use a mirror to shave my flesh-and-blood face, not the reflected one.

Plato evaluated mathematics on the basis of mathematicians' methods. In Book 5 the X things of this world were themselves at fault; here the fault lies not with triangles, but with the complacency with which mathematicians think about them. Likewise, those visible things that had seemed to consign anyone who looked at them to the level of mere opinion, apparently do not have that effect on mathematicians, because mathematicians use those objects as images. Mathematical practice is elevated on the one hand, downgraded on the other, on the grounds of the cognitive relationship between mathematicians and the objects they talk about.

But now what happens to ⑫? Do objects determine the levels of cognition about them or not? Plato cannot say they do, because then everyone would be stuck at the level of opinion. Everyone begins life perceiving only visible objects of experience. There would be no hope for philosophy; mathematics could not exist. So Plato grants that there are different ways of treating one and the same object, therefore that a single object can lead to different states of the soul in different observers. But in that case, why speak of different classes of things, instead of different views of a single class? Plato does not want that either, because philosophy should concern itself with something more real than the objects of unphilosophical scrutiny. Packing mathematics into the Divided Line, and trying to make each division the image of the one above it, creates puzzles that call for much more complex solutions.

## Destroying hypotheses

The most debated issue concerning the Divided Line has to do with the faults of mathematics. What distinguishes the Line's third stage of understanding from the fourth? Dialectic, by contrast with mathematics, neither rests content with hypotheses nor uses sensory images (510b, 511b–d), but investigates its own basic principles until it has arrived at an unhypothetical starting point (510b, 511b). Later Socrates calls this investigation the work of 'destroying hypotheses' (533c). Once in possession of that first principle, philosophical argument 'goes back down again to an end' (511b).

What are these hypotheses, and what do they have to do with visual images? Socrates ties the hypothesis-mongering of mathematicians to their unwillingness to give accounts of mathematical objects, 'as though they were clear to all' (510c–d). Numbers, figures, and other mathematical objects need to be given more complete accounts. This is still vague, because the further account can be either a *proof* of basic postulates about those objects, or a *definition* of the objects themselves.

The geometry of Plato's day could have been accused of lacking both proofs and definitions. Even Euclid's *Elements*, written after the death of Plato, treated certain statements and terms as given. The best-known example is the Parallel Postulate, the claim that through a point not on a line exactly one line passes that is parallel to the line. The Parallel Postulate is a complex assertion about geometry, but it goes unproved in the system that spells out demonstrations for every statement about lines and figures. If we draw lines and points on flat surfaces, we might never notice that the Postulate even needs proving. Only with the flowering of non-Euclidean geometry in the last 100 years did mathematicians appreciate its arbitrariness. It needs a better account, though geometers' reliance on visual images blinded them to this need. So unproved assertions about mathematical entities might be what Plato means by hypotheses.

But Euclidean geometry also contains undefined or inadequately defined terms. Euclid gives no good account of what a point is, but anyone engaged in reasoning about points and lines would consider their meanings to be clear enough. Again, non-Euclidean geometry put the lie to such confidence when it showed that points, lines, and planes admit of radically divergent interpretations. We may interpret a plane as the surface of a sphere, instead of the flat surface we are used to. This openness of the terms of geometry to rival interpretations means that no sound definitions have yet been provided. If 'line' had a precise definition, it could not have been interpreted in a new way. Therefore, undefined terms exist in geometry, and produce an obscurity in the discipline that Plato may have had in mind when he complained about mathematicians' hypotheses.

Once we know which complaint Plato means to make, we can say what he expects from the highest philosophy and the Form of the Good. If the problem with hypotheses is the absence of proofs for fundamental assertions, then Plato is calling for dialectic to discover a philosophical foundation for mathematics. Ascending from the hypotheses amounts to finding more fundamental principles from which they can be derived. The unhypothetical beginning will be a super-axiom requiring no proof, from which every truth about the Forms and about mathematics can be derived. Philosophers find increasingly powerful principles until they reach this axiom, then 'go back down again' to prove the truth of those lower principles that mathematicians had accepted as postulates. More broadly, they will return to ordinary discourse and test what their dialectical inquiry showed them, maybe the way Socrates comes back to moral discourse with his new definition of justice.

This picture of the ascent up the Divided Line, the axiomatization theory, has captured many imaginations, especially given the quest for logical axiom systems in the late nineteenth and early twentieth centuries. Just as Frege and Russell searched for axioms from which they could prove the elementary truths of arithmetic, Plato wants to find a foundation for all mathematics, and somehow for metaphysics at the same time. One must not press this historical analogy too far, but we may ascribe to Plato a desire for unwavering truth, what we now call logical certainty (477e).

The greatest problem for this interpretation arrives when we try to describe the unhypothetical beginning, which seems to be the Form of the Good. Nothing in any of Socrates' remarks, here or elsewhere, about the Form of the Good or about Forms in general, lets us think of the highest entity of metaphysics as a super-axiom. Still less does it seem capable of generating the basic truths of mathematics.

A competing picture, which begins by seeing hypotheses as undefined terms, takes the ascent up the Divided Line to be a quest for definitional *clarity* rather than for axiomatic *certainty*. Socrates has said the segments of the Line depict the different *saphêneia* 'clarity' of the objects in them – but as often happens in philosophy, 'clear' is a more metaphorical term than it first appears to be, and the great challenge is to say what makes one object clearer than another. If mathematical objects lack further accounts in the sense of remaining undefined, then dialectic will define each one on the basis of simpler, broader, more abstract terms. Plato's *Phaedrus*, *Statesman*, and *Philebus* all describe dialectic as a method of reaching definitions, and though the process of finding definitions at work in the *Republic* might differ from the one those dialogues lay out, it would probably be, as they are, a search for ever more general terms, under which we subsume more and more specific terms until everything is defined on the basis of one unhypothetical concept.

This reading possesses a pair of advantages over the axiomatization reading. First, it comes closer to many depictions of Socrates at work. When he elicits definitions from his interlocutors in some dialogues, he often criticizes them for defining a virtue too narrowly. He seeks to elucidate moral terms in the broadest language (*Meno* 72a–c, *Euthyphro* 6d–e, *Laches* 191c–d). At one point he even suggests that all specific definitions must be guided by knowledge of the good (*Charmides* 174b; compare Socrates' comments about 'the good' at *Laches* 199d–e). Although this 'good' cannot be exactly the same as the *Republic*'s Form of the Good, the similarity of terms might mean that Plato saw affinities between the *Republic*'s systematic enterprise and the piecemeal approach pursued in the shorter dialogues.

The second advantage of this reading is that it is a more natural interpretation of the Form of the Good. Hopeless as an axiom from which to derive the truths of mathematics, the Form of the Good has a chance of working as the broadest concept in the realm of knowledge. If mathematical objects bear any resemblance to the Forms, it is their quality of being ideal. A triangle understood in strict geometrical terms is something superior to any drawing of a triangle. The proof that every triangle's internal angles add up to 180 degrees will apply only roughly to drawings, but to the triangle as strictly defined the proof applies perfectly. Again, a line, as defined, has no width; but the nature of physical marks guarantees that any line I draw will have some width. Hence the triangle and line conceived as abstract entities are better than the ones drawn on paper, precisely as the Form of Justice describes a better justice than that found in any person or institution. If the Form of the Good captures the ideality of Forms, then it will also capture the ideality that characterizes mathematical entities. The Form of the Good will therefore play an indispensable role in every definition of objects of knowledge; we may call it the ultimate term in all theoretical definitions.

Destroying hypotheses means destroying the 'everyone knows what it is' attitude that mathematicians hold about the primitive terms of their enterprise. To a modern audience this interpretation may seem too modest, if dialectic leaves mathematical postulates clarified but not proved true. And we need to exercise caution about insisting on any reading of this passage. Nevertheless we have a clearer sense than before of what Plato expected from philosophy, and how he thought it might grow into a unified discipline on which all his philosophers could work together.

## THE ALLEGORY OF THE CAVE (514A–517C)

The Allegory of the Cave brings real relief after these puzzles about geometry. Here again is the *Republic*'s rhythm of an abstract point for specialists succeeded by a popularization. The Allegory of the Cave translates the Line's distinctions among kinds of knowledge back into the imagery of sun and light that first illustrated the Form of the Good. The four stages of things that the liberated prisoners see – the shadows (cast by firelight) of the statues of things; the statues themselves; shadows (cast by sunlight) of those things of which the statues are images; then the things themselves – correspond to the four stages of objects of cognition in the Divided Line.

For a better understanding of how the Allegory works we need to press two questions:

(1) Is the Allegory an image of all human life, or only of life outside the good city?
(2) How well does it match the Divided Line?

The Allegory of the Cave returns the conversation to political questions by illustrating the political consequences of the hierarchy of knowledge. Since the Allegory depicts a prisoner being led out of the cave and returning to help the other prisoners, it may be said to translate the static imagery of the Divided Line into images of education and governance. So it sounds like an image of life in the ideal city. Socrates' language at 519b–520d and 540a–c shows that he imagines the cave's escapees as the guardians of his city. But we can hardly square this interpretation with the bitterness of 516e–517a, which pictures the enlightened thinker stumbling back into the cave, forced to compete with his unfreed companions, and ridiculed by them for his ineptitude at worldly affairs. If these remarks allude to Socrates, then the cave's perpetual prisoners must represent Athenians, not citizens of the unfounded city. (Hence Socrates' discouraging words at 515a, 'They're like us.') Perhaps Plato means the Cave as an image of all human life, whether ideal or actual.

But if the cave represents life in all cities, the great majority of human beings will always find itself bound to the lowest sort of experience. According to the Divided Line, that lowest level is 'imagination' or 'image-thinking' (*eikasia*), restricted to the sight of reflections and shadows and presumably the sound of echoes, which even the poor standards of this world of opinion judge as only virtual reality. Surely Plato has erred in claiming that most human beings remain beneath even empirical knowledge. Has he overstated his case so egregiously in a furious wish to insult ordinary experience? Or has he imagined an image to the Divided Line that works only in its broadest outlines, and fails when we try to work out the details?

Either guess may be right. But we may also read *eikasia* metaphorically, and accuse the general run of humanity not of gazing at reflections, but of occupying itself in some other way with the images of visible things. When Socrates is not speaking technically, he uses *eikôn* 'image' in the *Republic* to refer to his own metaphors and stories (375d, 487e–488a, 489a, 514a, 531b, 588b–d). The word seems capable of describing any nonliteral use of language, often with no pejorative connotation. But 'image' also covers nonliteral language that *is* inferior. In Book 3 Socrates calls the imitative poet's creations 'images' (401b, 402c), and though he will not use the word in Book 10's condemnation of poetry, that condemnation would let imitative poetry take its place alongside the images of Books 6–7.

Now, in the Allegory, Socrates equates the cave's shadows with issues disputed in court (517d–e). Since Athenian legal disputes were famous for their rhetoric (*Phaedrus* 272d–e), it is safe to identify figurative language as the imagery that most commonly captures the public's attention. All their lives people take in mere allegations about important issues, colorful poetry grounded in ignorance, and every artistic or political performance that, by drawing more attention to the flash of its form than to the solid matter of its content, leaves its audience more ignorant than ever. The prisoners who squint at and squabble over shadows represent all those citizens who believe what politicians and artists tell them.

If the Allegory describes the state of all human beings, inside the ideal city or out, it implies that even given the best political institution, most of a city's members will mill around poets and demagogues. The Platonic city will be as full of the ignorant rabble that Plato wants to escape as Athens ever was. Either the Platonic city remains far from utopian, kept by inevitable human weakness from becoming a perfect community, or else Plato has not worked through the implications of his analogy.

A greater problem with accommodating the Cave to the Line arises over the existence of mathematical objects. Socrates distinguished mathematics from dialectic on the basis of its practitioners' methods instead of its objects' reality. But the Allegory of the Cave identifies a specific kind of thing for every step on the Line. Geometry corresponds to the reflections (outside the cave) of the trees and animals that correspond to the Forms. But mathematicians had not been said to study objects with less being than the practitioners of dialectic did. Whereas the Line loosens the hierarchy of knowledge and being to permit emphasis on humans' approaches to what they know, the Cave adheres to the strict assumption (⑫) that for every kind of knowing there exists a separate thing that is known. The Allegory does not exactly match the Divided Line, but papers over its complications regarding the objects of cognition.

## AN EDUCATION IN METAPHYSICS (521C–539D)

Once Socrates shows his best guardians progressing toward dialectic, he will have completed his argument for the philosophical city, and he can come back to the species of injustice he had promised to catalogue. Amid the curricular proposals in these pages, a few arguments allude to the Divided Line.

## THE PROBLEM WITH PARTICULARS, AGAIN (523A–525C)

In search of studies that lead the soul to higher thinking, Socrates distinguishes between objects that 'summon the intellect to the activity of investigation' and those that do not (523b). The former involve relative terms. Here Socrates takes the inferiority of particular things to prove the merits of arithmetic:

(1) Because a finger does not also appear *not* to be a finger, sense perception suffices to form the true judgment, 'This is a finger' (523c–d).

(2) Because a large, thick, or soft finger also appears small, thin, or hard, sense perception cannot make clear judgments about those properties. (523e–524a)

∴ (3) In the case of the latter properties, the intellect needs to examine the properties apart from perceptions of them. (524c)

(4) Every number appears not to be true of a particular thing at the same time that it appears to be true of it. (525a)

∴ (5) Arithmetic, which is concerned with numbers, leads to the truth. (525a–b)

This argument is close enough to Book 5's argument about knowledge and opinion to be a further implication of that argument. As such, it supports the view that only relative terms will have Forms. Since the inferiority of individual things in Book 5 rested on the ambiguity of their properties, this passage would deny the existence of a Form of Finger.

Mathematics enters the argument because numbers are a special case of opposable properties. They appear in particular things in the same confusing way that other relative terms do. Premise (4) might mean that my hand is simultaneously one (hand) and five (fingers). But numbers belong to existing disciplines. Philosophers dream of an education that leads to the systematic study of justice and beauty, but they can take heart in the existence of some disciplines that have already studied confusing terms without reference to their empirical manifestations.

The tone of this passage, a dramatic change from the belittling language of Book 5, suggests inconsistency in Plato's view of the physical world. How can the bigness of a finger both condemn the student of the sensory world to a life of mere opinion (479d–e), and also be the stimulus that leads that student up to being (523a)? It depends on the observer's orientation toward that property. If I take the physical world to be the sum of existence, then the incomplete way in which certain predicates apply to that world will leave me possessed of mere opinion. But if I seek theoretical understanding of those predicates in a realm beyond the physical,

I stand a chance of reaching knowledge. Images have epistemic merits, as long as we value them not for their own sakes but for their capacity to point beyond themselves to greater knowledge. The world of the senses is like a marionette show that deceives only those who do not think to look for the puppeteers.

We are back at the problem of objects of cognition (⑫). The critique of particulars in Book 5 presupposed that attention to a kind of object commits a person to the corresponding kind of cognition. The present passage allows the knowledge available from an object to vary with the investigator's method of studying it. The same finger can leave me swamped in my confusion or guide me out of it. But if this last claim is true and my level of awareness determines which thing I am thinking about – Form of Thickness or one thick finger – then ⑫ cannot be true in any form that permits the argument of Book 5 to work. This concession to the investigator's frame of mind means, as the discussion of mathematical objects in the Divided Line also did, that Plato's distinction among kinds of objects muddies the waters more than it clarifies them.

## DIALECTIC AGAIN (531D–537D)

Plato returns to dialectic, the final phase of a philosopher's education. We see, first, that although Socrates' praise of mathematics had seemed to forget the earlier criticism of mathematical method (529c–e, 530e–531c), he takes it up again when speaking of dialectic. Given their adherence to unexamined hypotheses, mathematicians only dream about reality (533b–c). Dialecticians destroy those hypotheses in order to lead the soul to superior knowledge (533c–e). So including mathematics in the curriculum does not imply a change of heart about its truth.

Secondly, the Form of the Good is named as the goal of dialectic (534b–c; cf. 532a). The unhypothetical beginning at the top of the Divided Line is, as we had thought, the Form of the Good. And here Socrates links dialectic to the ability to form an 'overview' of every other subject (537c). Since an overview, or a most general possible statement of the nature of each thing, is closer to a broadest term of definition than to a first axiom from which all others follow, this passage favors the definitional interpretation of ascent up the Divided Line.

## REVIEW OF BOOKS 5–7

Plato's motion back and forth between political and metaphysical discussions leaves these books of the *Republic* resistant to summary. As Aristotle complained (*Politics* 1264b39), much in Books 5–7 lies outside the main argument of the *Republic*. To some extent these books even threaten the rest of the dialogue, for they demote justice to secondary status in theoretical philosophy (504b–505a, 506a). If Plato really believes this, he must consider the *Republic*'s main argument a philosophical primer, suitable for those who cannot understand the Form of the Good, but a crude approximation for those who can.

Still, much in these three books is essential to the political and ethical arguments of the dialogue. As a document of political philosophy, the *Republic* needs to lay out the plan for a good state, in order to specify which features of existing states engender the injustices in which human beings find themselves. Without the details of Books 5–7, the *Republic*'s good city would be too vague to work as a model for political change. The equality of women and the abolition of property and family for the city's rulers clarify the degree to which a city must subordinate other interests to the pursuit of justice. Even if these changes seem repellent, they make the point that tinkering with details will never produce a just society. In this sense all revolutionary political thinkers owe a debt to Plato, for imagining radical change instead of reform.

Plato's boldest proposal, that philosophers rule the city, becomes indispensable as soon as he considers the practicability of his political dream. The city will not work without philosophers at its helm. But to say that is to grant the importance of the Form of the Good to the *Republic*, for in the Form of the Good Plato is able, however schematically, to unify the theoretical pursuits of philosophers with the moral expertise required of rulers. The Form of the Good promises to deny the distinction between the insight we find in morally wise individuals and the learning we attribute to scientists and scholars.

Thus the middle books give the *Republic* a good measure of its power as a political text. But the *Republic* is also an ethical text, an argument that the life lived according to moral principles is the life most worth choosing; and to this argument the digression is also essential. Reason acquires content in these books. In Book 5 it is the passion of philosophers, with its own motivational force (⑪). In Books 6 and 7 we learn what work reason accomplishes, drawing the soul away from the seductions of the physical world and toward an abstract principle of goodness. Book 9's closing argument for the pleasantness of a just life will turn out to depend on the conception of reason that these books make possible. So we return from the digression to the main argument with a better understanding of its elementary terms.

Where does the theory of Forms belong in this story? What is it a theory about? What work is it supposed to do: explain? predict? This is not just the complaint that we never see Forms. Every scientific theory contains entities, be they atoms or black holes, that do not turn up in ordinary experience, and have been hypothesized on the basis of observations. But in science we know what the theoretical entity might do: unite disparate phenomena under general principles; explain the properties of plant cells; predict where Mars will appear in the evening sky. We accept atoms and black holes because those things form part of a broad and instructive account of the world.

In one respect the Forms violate the most fundamental requirement of scientific theories, to explain or account for the world as it is. The theory of Forms describes theoretical entities that stand *apart from* the world of ordinary experience and judge its shortcomings. The Forms bear their properties in a manner that individual things cannot: the Form of $X$ is unequivocally and completely $X$, whereas $X$ things are only partly $X$. The Forms enjoy an eternal existence that no individual thing can match. It can seem as if the theory of Forms works only as a condemnation of the ordinary world, and hence accomplishes no more in the way of explanation than a geography of heaven would accomplish for earthly mapmakers.

But this is not all there is to Forms; for if it is true that an individual $X$ thing is not entirely $X$, it is just as true that the thing is not *non-X* either. The particular falls short of perfectly exemplifying what it is, but to some degree it does exemplify the property in question. So while the Form makes clear what the *X* thing is not, it also shows what that thing can be.

In this sense, the Forms are vital to more than the *Republic*. In Plato's conception of philosophy, every inquiry into abstract terms, which ultimately is to inform our vision of the nonabstract world, needs some object to study. The Forms offer something lucid and real to look at when the physical world, because of its ambiguity, incompleteness, or corruptibility, seems incapable of being studied. Understanding the justice of laws in our world, or the beauty of people, presupposes clear theoretical knowledge of justice and beauty 'in themselves.' The point is still to understand this world. But what *is* the justice of a law or a person? What do we study when studying a just law? Plato appeals to the Forms: the 'participation' of the Form of Justice in a person or law makes for whatever in that person or law is just. To put it another way, whatever is just in a person or law reflects the properties of the Form of Justice, much as the mass of a table, and the properties of that mass, are really the mass of its constituent atoms.

Then there is some similarity between the theory of Forms and a scientific theory. Our knowledge that fundamental physical entities exist assures us that all physical objects obey the same general laws. Tables and cows alike will be held to the earth's surface by gravity, and cast shadows. Plato's belief that Forms of disputable terms exist assures him that all examples of those terms will manifest similar properties, which is to say that there is a point to discussing the justice of laws or the beauty of colors, that such discussions amount to more than subjective taste (see *Parmenides* 135b–c).

## SUGGESTIONS FOR FURTHER READING

This is the chapter that the reader should respond to with the greatest caution, using it as a springboard toward deeper discussions. It is probably best to begin with one of the general treatments found in Annas, *An Introduction to Plato's Republic*, or Santas, *Understanding Plato's Republic*. Fronterotta, 'Plato's *Republic* in the recent debate,' offers superb summaries of the main debates over meta-physics that have lately occupied scholars. Two excellent and recent (but not introductory) discussions of the Forms in the *Republic* are Ferejohn, 'Knowledge, recollection, and the Forms in *Republic* VII,' and the relevant parts of Rickless, *Plato's Forms in Transition.*

For illumination of Plato's phrase that some things are and are not, see Kahn, 'The Greek verb "be" and the concept of being,' and Fine, 'Knowledge and belief in *Republic* V'; on Plato's epistemological concerns see Moravcsik, 'Understanding and knowledge in Plato's philosophy.' On the problem with particular things, the reader will profit from reading Allen, 'The argument from opposites in *Republic* V,' Brentlinger, 'Particulars in Plato's middle dialogues,' and Nehamas, 'Plato on the imperfection of the sensible world.'

On the Form of the Good and its ethical implications see especially Cooper, 'The psychology of justice in Plato'; also Santas, 'The Form of the Good in Plato's *Republic.*'

The Divided Line has inspired a quantity of interpretive effort; see Patterson, *Image and Reality in Plato's Metaphysics.* Numerous issues are treated in Morrison, 'Two unresolved difficulties in the Line and the Cave,' and Smith, 'Plato's Divided Line.' On the passage from third to fourth stage of the Line see Benson, 'Plato's philosophical method in the *Republic:* the Divided Line (510b–511d)'; Zhmud, 'Plato as "architect of science,"' contains historical background on the study of mathematics in the Academy.

The philosophers' education is much more important to these books than this chapter has represented. For an overview of the meanings that education acquires see Reeve, 'Blindness and reorientation: education and the acquisition of knowledge in the *Republic.*'

# 8

---

# INJUSTICE IN THE SOUL AND IN THE CITY (BOOKS 8–9)

Books 8 and 9 round out that overarching argument that began in Book 2 with the two goals of defining justice and showing its profitability. It might appear that by the end of Book 4, in which he described justice as a harmony akin to health (444d–e), Socrates had achieved both aims. But Glaucon wanted Socrates to demonstrate, not merely that justice in the soul is worth possessing – not merely that it is profitable – but that one would rather possess justice in the soul than any other psychological arrangement: that justice is the most profitable of all conditions, that the just soul is the happiest of all possible souls (⑧). So Book 8 begins with the announced aim of contrasting justice with every form of injustice, in order to show that each of these will generate less happiness than justice does, both in the person and in the city. Whether the *Republic* aims at showing that a just person will be happy no matter what the circumstances (as Plato's ancient readers believed), or (as today's readers mostly say) only argues that in any given circumstance the just are happier than the unjust: either way, justice must emerge victorious in the coming comparison.

Every part of a work as rich as the *Republic* suffers from being boiled down into a sequence of arguments. Books 8 and 9, which contain textured and perceptive accounts of both political history and psychology, suffer the most. They contain fewer arguments, and simpler ones, than the rest of the *Republic*, and this chapter's discussion of those arguments will leave out most of the anecdotes and examples that give these books such flavor. The theoretical structure returns in Book 9, when Plato finishes his catalogue of bad cities and people and looks only at the most just and most unjust individuals; at that point he introduces lines of argument conceptually unrelated to the preceding parade of vices, lines of argument which moreover take his conclusions in a direction we could not have foreseen at the end of Book 4.

## DEGENERATE FORMS OF THE CITY AND THE SOUL (544A–576A)

### THE FIRST DEGENERATION (546A–547A)

From the point of view of the *Republic*'s plans for an actually existing city, the first decline into imperfect political forms has special significance. Plato introduced the guardian class, and then made the ruler-guardians philosophers, in order to produce a social system that the natural system would tolerate: a human world not easily ruined by nature. He knows that these institutions, presented to ensure the city's possibility, themselves threaten to be impossible. He emphasizes the point. The hardest part of any political plan is the strategy for putting it into practice. The city's founders therefore confront near-contradictions to make their city happen, first keeping the army both gentle and ferocious, then making its rulers both politicians and philosophers.

Breeding plays the predominant role in resolving those contradictions. Plato's frequent analogies to dogs reveal what an extensive project of eugenics he has in mind. Generations of selection have brought the natures of dogs into agreement with their masters' culture. By breeding for socially desired traits, domestication overcomes exactly the difference between nature and culture that antimoral arguments like Thrasymachus' depend on.

The breeding of humans calls for despotic intrusions into their private lives. Plato can tolerate that. What troubles him is that even so, the domestication may not work. Sooner or later the rulers will miscalculate the mating times for guardian couples, and the next generation will yield a lesser crop of rulers (546a–547a).

The gratuitously obscure language of this passage, that business of squares of numbers and dates of birth, makes the point sound complicated. In fact Plato finds it depressingly simple. The good city will only exist given human interventions into the natural order to breed natures attuned to society's needs. Because those interventions ultimately fail, some gap will always remain between the natural order (how people behave) and the moral order (how they ought to).

## THE FOUR KINDS OF INJUSTICE

Socrates identifies the four main species of injustice (see 445c) with already existing forms of government: timocracy, oligarchy, democracy, tyranny. A psychological constitution corresponds to each form, so that we may speak of the oligarchic soul as naturally as of the oligarchic city (544a, d–e). After its disappearance in Book 5, the analogy between city and soul returns in full force.

It is not evident why Plato should have settled on *five* kinds of constitution, especially when he has Socrates admit that more variations could be described (445c). Plato probably bases his classification on an empirical observation of existing governments, as well he should. But we can guess that the five types of government will fit uneasily into his prior political analysis that all citizens fall into one of *three* classes. Five human characters should prove just as hard to describe theoretically, assuming only three parts of the soul. Many of the complications in the coming argument grow out of this awkward fit between the theories.

The account of timocracy works best, for cities and for souls. Both regimes arise when the rational part loses its hegemony over the whole (547b, 550a–b). The productive class in the city, and the appetites in the soul, insist on their claims to satisfaction. In a compromise between lowest and highest, the spirited part between them comes to rule. As he often does, Plato shows his respect for

Sparta, the second-best type of government (544c). We might think of Napoleonic France or the early Roman Empire, and Napoleon and Caesar come to mind as timocratic people, as Glaucon comes to mind for Adeimantus (548d). Although this form of life enjoys considerable stability, the fact that the spirited part comes to power in the midst of conflict shows that the timocracy will possess less unity than we found in the best soul and city.

With the transition to oligarchy, the third class or part of the soul takes the place of the second. Once the productive class takes charge, money becomes the dominant force in a society; thus it will be not all members of the producing class who rule, only the richest (551b). In the soul the desire for money takes charge, for out of all the bodily desires it is the one that most resembles an organizational force. Unlike lust and hunger, greed knows the value of discipline (however anxious: 554d) and long-term planning (however ignobly aimed: 554e–555a).

From these cases of degeneration we can generalize to three characteristics of vice. First, Plato fits his account of social decay into his claim that justice requires the performance of natural functions (⑥). Trouble begins when the wrong children enter the ruling class (546b–547a). Species of political vice are identified by the class that inappropriately rules the city. The worst social pathology – people who live off liquidated assets (552a, 564b) – is the one that most flamboyantly breaks the rule of distributed labor.

Secondly, bad constitutions possess only spurious signs of unity. The oligarchic soul controls itself as if virtuous, but it lacks the harmony that characterizes true virtue. A single appetite *dominates* the oligarchic soul, but that appetite can't *unify* it. Unlike reason, which inspects every motivation, then chooses which ones to permit, avarice rules by insisting on its own goals. Avarice knows no way of reining itself in: not having been born to rule, it lacks the capacity for self-examination. Plato would cite billionaires who crave money beyond anything they could spend, as proof of the unfitness of greed to rule the soul.

Finally, any value other than justice, once permitted to dominate, will bring the soul and city into worse injustice through an inner logic of the degenerative process. Every ideal pursued by these lesser constitutions – whether honor or money, pleasure in general or sexual pleasure in particular – poses as a goal to coordinate the city's actions. In this sense all unjust cities recall the just one. However corruptly, they acknowledge that a society must bring union to a scattering of persons. For this reason all cities but the very worst have been said to possess 'shadow virtues,' imperfect and provisional arrangements that substitute for genuine governance. But only the just city pursues an ideal that produces and enhances coordination. Every ideal other than justice engenders instability in the city that honors that ideal. This instability then resolves itself in a worse constitution.

For instance, the competitive spirit of the timocracy's citizens prompts them to accumulate private wealth (550e) and turns them into oligarchs (551a). When the oligarchy carries its avaricious ideal too far, it impoverishes its solid citizens (555d–e) and so encourages the licentiousness that characterizes democracy (555c, 556c–e). But if every configuration of the city aside from the best one grants pride of place to the very value that will degrade the city further, there is something inherently wrong with those configurations.

Democracy carries disunity to its logical extreme. Democracy presupposes disagreement, not as a temporary evil to be overcome in future unanimity, but as an inherent condition of society. No value predominates in the democratic city, unless it is the open, empty value of toleration (557b, 558a). Because the citizens can agree only to disagree, they appeal to no common value and encourage no public virtue. Their pact of mutual toleration is like a code they all adhere to, and playing by the rules is the closest thing to moral principle they know. But the very idea of harmony, or of a ruler superior to the citizens, has become repugnant to them.

Equally egalitarian, the individual democratic soul prefers not to choose among its desires – certainly not to condemn any objects of desire (561b) – but indulges each one as it arises. Desires may be necessary or unnecessary (558d–559c); and whereas the oligarchic soul also denied itself higher impulses in the service of desire, at least that desire originated in need. Having lost the power to tell necessary from unnecessary desires, the democratic soul has no principle to guide its steps, not even the crass and unlovely rule of greed.

There is still worse ahead, for Socrates has tyranny to speak of. The greatest dictatorship in the city arises out of the greatest anarchy (564a). In the soul, the democratic person's refusal to judge among desires brings one of those desires, lust (*erôs*), to outgrow all the rest (572e–573a). (Here Socrates seems to despise *erôs*. Elsewhere he recognizes its importance: 458d, 474d–475b. In the *Symposium* and *Phaedrus* Plato finds metaphysical significance in sexual love; the *Timaeus* lists the bad effects of celibacy at 91b–c; cf. *Laws* 930c.)

In one sense this development returns us to the oligarchic soul, for like it the tyrannic soul follows the command of a single desire. We see Plato working to make his psychological theory account for the phenomena: he draws yet another distinction among desires, this time separating unnecessary ones into the law-abiding and the lawless (571b). The worst of the lawless desires is lust, especially monstrous lust for forbidden persons, foods, and deeds (574e–575a). Unlike the oligarch's greed, this transgressive lewdness has nothing to do with self-control. It rules the soul wildly – indeed, it emerges as the dominant commitment of the tyrannical soul not by virtue of any deliberation on the person's part but *faute de mieux*, because it has out-shouted every other desire. It comes to dominate by being the most uncontrollable desire and not because it is suited to controlling; thus its rule is of all states the least recognizable as rule.

Of all the psychological portraits, this one (reminiscent of the elderly Baron de Charlus in Proust) sounds the most modern. Unfortunately, the portrait of a depraved soul, for all its realism, strains Plato's psychological theory. He needs to claim that someone compelled by one desire nevertheless experiences less unity than the person whose soul follows the promptings of many desires. Both the structure of the soul, and its disunity when unjust, have become confused by Plato's efforts to make every soul fit his theory. In reality, the political and psychological transitions from democracy to tyranny are not obviously symptoms of growing chaos. If anything, they show that chaos engenders a new order. In the case of the soul, Socrates' repeated distinctions among the various desires brings to mind a question that came up regarding Book 4, whether this category of 'desire' had any informative function, or merely gathered under a single meaninglessly broad heading motivations that had nothing to do with each other. If rule by the appetites can equally produce oligarchy, democracy, or tyranny in the soul, the appetites must have even less to do with one another than we thought.

## LIMITATIONS OF THE COMPARATIVE METHOD

Book 8 and its conclusion in Book 9 stand out for their psychological insight and their applicability to states and people beyond any that Plato knew. By the time the tyrannical soul has been described (576c) there seems to be little left for the reader to do but agree that Plato has laid out these cities and souls in order from best to worst, and that the good city surpasses its political competitors; the corresponding soul, all its psychological competitors.

But what has depicting this string of injustices accomplished? Grant that each city and soul is more prone than its predecessor to engage in unjust acts. We knew that before looking at the cases, since *ex hypothesi* each one was to be more unjust, or worse, than its predecessor. If Plato is to answer Thrasymachus, he also needs to show that what makes a soul worse makes it unhappier. In timocracy and oligarchy the power passed ever further from the rational part or class, which is most equipped to rule, to the appetitive, whose selfishness assures that its rule will never bring about the voluntary cooperation of the parts being ruled (552e). If every step into greater injustice could likewise be shown to follow from a further loss of unity, we might have the basis for an argument: harmony in the soul being pleasant, and inner conflict a source of unhappiness, the arrangement that produces good works will simultaneously lead to happiness (⑧).

But this growing disintegration ends with the tyrant. The parts of the soul then cease to illuminate, since Plato complicates the desiring part beyond recognition. And although we know what Socrates means when he finds 'anarchy and lawlessness' in the tyrannical soul (575a), he has not shown that this lawlessness follows from the disunity that Book 4 warned against. Since Socrates' explicit comparisons of justice with injustice (576b–588a) use tyranny to represent all injustice, this deviation from the theme of unity is no small matter: unity of a sort we recognize disappears exactly when we are about to put the picture of disunity to work.

Other details also cause trouble. Each city is shown to follow by inevitable historical laws into the next, and each soul is put into a man whose son degenerates into the worse type. To what extent does Plato believe himself to be telling a causal story? The tale of generational decline is too simplistic; since Plato gives no hint of how upward progress might work, we have to assume this devolution to be terminable and irreversible, so that within five generations every human community would consist only of sex-crazed burglars. As a factual claim this is false, besides sounding like the oldest complaint ever made about younger generations.

Concerning the city, Plato knew that the transitions he speaks of are not the only ones possible. During his own adulthood Athens recovered from the Thirty Tyrants and returned to democracy. And he was even sixteen, old enough to notice, when the city went briefly from democracy to oligarchy in 411. So governments can grow out of worse forms into better. Moreover, if every city declines from a better one, then the best city, which would improve on every other, can never be born in this world whose history always travels from bad to worse.

Plato's 'history' makes better sense as a lively vehicle for presenting a hierarchically ordered series of governments. The fiction that each type slides down further from its predecessor permits Plato to look for the single characteristic that sets democracy apart from oligarchy, and oligarchy from timocracy. His argument would work just as well if cities changed haphazardly; to prove that justice benefits a city Plato needs only to show that each type *is better than* the one below, even if it does not *transform itself into* that worse type.

Unfortunately, translating the narrative of cultural decline into a taxonomy of governments turns a strong but false claim about politics into a truer but much blander one. We lose any sense that Plato locates the characteristics of various cities in specific material conditions. If this is not really history, we can ignore its accounts of political change.

One question about this aspect of the argument is whether Plato is registering any genuine interest in history. There is evidence that he read the two great Greek historians Herodotus and Thucydides, but Plato's interpreters today tend not to ask how he might have responded to their works. Is the primordial Athens imagined in the *Timaeus* and *Critias* an attempt at a Herodotean dramatization of the *Republic?* Then maybe Plato thinks some actual full-scale history can be told according to the *Republic*'s principles of constitutional change.

Even more relevant is the historical narrative that dominates Plato's *Menexenus*. Socrates summarizes a century's worth of Athenian wars and alliances, and three forces shape his story: Athens the truly Greek state, honorable and wise; the other Greek cities, which Socrates calls 'half-Greek,' whom Athens sometimes educates in courage; and the grasping tyrannical barbarians. This history runs from best to worst, as the *Republic*'s history of a city does. The three forces correspond to three parts of the soul along lines suggested in the *Republic* (435e–436a), and in many instances the transition from one international configuration to a worse one follows the same dynamic as the constitutional changes within the city. If the *Menexenus*' speech is not the joke that many scholars suppose it to be, these parallels between its international history and the decline of the city in the *Republic* show Plato seeking a method for philosophical history. He would have seen the intellectual value of both Herodotus and Thucydides, but neither one had organized history's events with the system that a philosopher could bring to the subject. It would be worth studying Platonic history more closely to see whether it does approach sound philosophy – whether Plato has in fact united the disciplines.

As for the analogy between the city and the soul, that originally promises to play an important role in Plato's argument. Glaucon's introduction expects bad regimes to shed light on bad kinds of people (544a–b). Socrates adds that each regime will be populated primarily by the people whose souls correspond to the form of government (544d–e; see 435a–c). If this is true, the timocratic soul will both share its general structure with the timocratic city, *and* turn up more frequently than any other personality type in the citizens of that city. Then individual psychology explains a great deal about politics, for a city will reflect the character of its citizens. Such a tight relationship between the city and the private person would retrospectively justify the *Republic*'s argumentative strategy, by unifying its treatments of souls and cities.

But the analogy breaks down. When Socrates imagines the development of timocratic and oligarchic men, he sets them in cities unlike either their own souls or their fathers'. The timocrat's father, the best sort of man, lives in a city that is not well run (549c), therefore not the best city that would correspond to his soul. The young oligarch grows up in a city swarming with informers and lawsuits (553b), which is to say in a city more like democracy than oligarchy. The tyrant offers the clearest disanalogy, for exactly by drawing attention to the special misery of a tyrannical person who gains a tyrant's power, Socrates is suggesting that this conjunction of pathology and power will be the exception rather than the rule (576b–c). So psychological tyranny does not have to have anything to do with dictatorship. Socrates expects tyrannical men to band together in a city (575a–c); but if they form a small group in *any* given city, they cannot be that city's representative types.

Furthermore, using the citizens' characters to explain the regimes they belong to makes a confusion of the changes that the two entities undergo. Family psychodynamics turn one character type into the worse type, while the city's degradation is caused by political and economic processes. It would take a strange coincidence to make personal histories all across a city transform the son of an oligarchic soul into a democratic type, right when the oligarchy's changing economy and property holdings bring about democratic institutions. Plato must be saying something more modest, that certain sorts of people resemble certain constitutions. There is something metaphorically democratic about a democratic person's soul and metaphorically oligarchic about the oligarchic soul. In practice this connection has only one definite consequence: 'With respect to virtue and happiness ... the relation between man and man [will] be that between city and city' (576d). The oligarchically souled will be more self-controlled people than those with democratic souls, as oligarchies in cities are more self-controlled, hence more virtuous, than democracies. We rank souls as we rank cities. This helps, but Plato could have shown one kind of soul to be worse than another much more directly than by constructing such a complex analogy. The analogy between city and soul, like the account of each city's degradation, fails as a literal statement, and as a metaphorical version of the truth it turns out to be less significant than it had first appeared. The general effect of this discussion is one of vast machinery being assembled and then sitting idle.

## THREE COMPARISONS BETWEEN JUST AND UNJUST LIVES (576B–587B)

This complexity of comparing souls and cities is especially striking when we bear in mind that Socrates narrowed down his immediate goal: not to show that each form of unjust soul is worse and unhappier than the just soul, but to contrast the soul of the most just person with that of the most unjust (545a). The narrower agenda reflects Glaucon's original comparison between the perfectly just and the perfectly unjust (360e–362c). So now Socrates drops the intermediate types and compares the lives lived at the two extremes, deploying three arguments to establish the superiority of the just life.

### THE PSYCHOLOGICAL PROFILE (576B–580C)

Look at the tyrannical soul, Socrates says. For all its delusions of wielding power, it represents the most enslaved human condition (577d). Like a city in a despot's hands, this soul lives in confusion, regret, and fear (577e–578b). A man with a tyrannical soul who has the bad luck to rule an actual city comes off worst of all (578b–580a).

This is more a recap of the catalogue of injustices than a fresh argument, emphasizing the disunity and instability in unjust souls. Thanks to guarding its possessor from the anxieties and obsessive desires that injustice brings to the soul, justice also surpasses injustice in its consequences as well as in itself.

As in Book 4, justice is conceived as a harmonious relationship among the soul's parts, on the basis of which the soul escapes inner conflict. By ruling the other parts, reason brings happiness to the person. The explicit argument in this passage comes at 577d–e:

If, then ... a man is like his city, isn't it also necessary that the same arrangement be in him and that his soul be filled with much slavery and illiberality, and that, further, those parts of it that are most decent be slaves while a small part, the most depraved and maddest, be master? ... Therefore, the soul that is under a tyranny will least do what it wants – speaking of the soul as a whole.

Justice is pragmatically desirable because just souls more often achieve what they want, as healthy bodies likewise pursue their goals more effectively. The task of reason in this passage, as it has been implicitly since the beginning of Book 8, is the supervision of the whole soul that we saw at work in Book 4. But now Socrates is about to complicate this conception of reasoning.

## THE PHILOSOPHER AS BEST JUDGE OF PLEASURE (580C–583A)

Here is another proof of the just life's superiority, says Socrates (580c). Each part of the soul has its own desires, and the pleasures that derive from their fulfillment. The appetitive part loves gain, the spirited part honor, and the rational part wisdom and learning (581a–c). Everyone ruled by one part of the soul will find the fulfillment of that part's desires the most pleasant experience (581c–d). This last claim follows from the *Republic*'s psychological theory: to be ruled by a part of the soul is to take the values of that part as the values of the whole person, hence to find the objects of its desires the most pleasant objects.

How to choose among rival pleasures and therefore among lives dominated by different parts of the soul? Such disputes need judges. But the best judge on any subject is the one with the widest experience; and since the *philosophos* 'lover of wisdom' knows the pleasures of bodily appetite and honor as well as those of learning, that will be the best judge of pleasure (582a–d). Because judgments rely on arguments, and philosophers use arguments better than anyone else does, they emerge again as the best judges (582d–583a). Having accepted philosophers' judgment as best, we must say that their own life, the life of the just, defeats the life of the unjust a second time (583b).

Socrates has turned his attention from the best life to the most pleasant. The pleasure in question should be understood broadly – not necessarily as a sensation common to all three lives and certainly not a physical sensation. Bodily pleasures tend to be universally acknowledged, but the very possibility of a dispute among pleasures implies that the philosopher's favorite objects will not attract people with tyrannical souls. The philosopher can enjoy the tangy flavor of pomegranate, but the gourmand might not even realize that a geometrical proof contains enjoyable elements.

At the same time 'pleasure' should not be read so broadly that it becomes vacuous, with anything one chooses to do considered (by definition) pleasant for that person. On that view, philosophers would find ruling the city pleasant simply by virtue of having agreed to rule. Pleasure has to be something more concrete for this argument, which is depicting the just life as something the just enjoy living. It is true that Glaucon's challenge in Book 2 did not specify that Socrates compare the pleasures available to the just and the unjust; but he did ask Socrates to show the better natural effects of a just life. If Socrates identifies pleasure as one effect, he has not strayed from his mandate.

The really bold step in this argument is not the appeal to pleasure, but the assignment of a characteristic *epithumia* 'desire' to each part of the soul. When Socrates first named the parts of the soul, he assigned all desires, properly speaking, to the third and irrational part (437d, 439d): the function of that part had been to yearn for and pursue objects, while the other two parts found their expression in behavior *not* aimed at objects. Now Socrates makes official his implicit premise of Book 6, that the rational part has desires of its own (⑪). This change significantly modifies the *Republic*'s psychological theory, by adding a second feature to reason that is much different from its original characteristic of serving as an overseer to the whole soul. Now that reason rules in the philosopher, and to all appearances in no one else, its desire for learning becomes specifically love for philosophy. We have shifted from just and unjust men to a contest between the philosopher and the tyrant; from moderate souls contrasted with souls lacking discipline, to the contemplative against the oversexed. Philosophical justice, in which reason not only presides over a harmonious soul but also pursues abstract learning, is the new form of good life being endorsed. (See Chapter 10 for more remarks about the *Republic*'s two conceptions of reason.)

## REAL AND UNREAL PLEASURES (583B–587B)

This last and most difficult argument continues to conceive the just life as the intellectual life, and tries to prove that the pleasures available to a philosopher exceed everyone else's pleasures in both truth and purity (583b).

First (583c–585a) Socrates distinguishes among the three states of pain, pleasure, and the intermediate repose that contains neither (583c). This middle state sometimes feels like pleasure and sometimes like pain, depending on what precedes it. Then the argument moves in two different directions, so tersely as to resist clear summary. Plato continues a point from the previous argument, that a philosopher makes a better judge of pleasures than anyone else. The middle state, because we experience it sometimes as pleasure and sometimes as pain, can't really be either one (584a); therefore, those pleasures brought about by relief from pain only *seem* pleasant. But if pleasures can be false – which is to say 'pleasant' only from an unenlightened perspective – we must acknowledge the possibility of expertise with respect to pleasure (584e–585a). That expertise will tell the true from the spurious, a task that reminds us of Book 5's portrait of the philosopher.

Plato wants to remove the subjectivity from discussions of pleasure. We may think that a pleasure is exactly as good as it feels, but the condition that now brings pleasure may bring pain on another occasion, or nothing at all. Even when ranking brute sensations, we have to defer to the expert; we will not accept the word of the unjust that their lives are more enjoyable than those of the just.

Next Socrates draws out what he calls an illumination of this point (585a–587b), although in fact it moves in a fresh direction. Most pleasures of the body and soul relieve a person not simply of pain, but specifically of the pain of emptiness (585a–b). If pleasure equals fullness, the pleasure will be a greater fullness if that which replenishes the person possesses greater reality. Because the objects that the philosopher studies are more real than those that a hungry person eats, the pleasures of the philosophical soul surpass those of the less philosophical body (585b–e). Pursuing intellectual pleasures offers permanent relief from the doomed cycle of desire and fulfillment. Thanks to their greater reality, the objects of philosophical knowledge will not evanesce as food does in the stomach, but keep the philosopher at a steady state of fullness.

This is ⑫ at work again. Kinds of understanding correspond to different levels of reality in their objects. Despite the trouble that ⑫ causes for an account of knowledge, it is essential to this defense of the philosophical life. The higher the cognitive state of the learner, the more substantial the objects acquired through learning, and therefore the greater the pleasure.

The two parts of this argument sit together uncomfortably. The first part calls for an expertise that judges among *all* the pleasures available to a person. Such expertise fits our image of reason as a coordinator of the demands that come from the rest of the soul, demands that all have some claim on the person. But the second half of the argument identifies true pleasures with the joys of the intellect, as if the appetitive part of the soul should *never* have its way. Now the intellect pursues its own special pleasures; and reason is performing its two distinct roles in the course of a single argument.

There is a more profound contradiction. For whereas the first half of the argument resisted praising any pleasure that follows from the relief of pain, the second half endorses the relief from ignorance as though it could lift a person up higher than the middle state of calm (586a). Nothing in the argument prepares for this claim, which feels like a gratuitous insistence on the pleasures of philosophy. It seems as if Plato wants so badly to demonstrate the superiority of the contemplative life that he will even downplay an essential characteristic of P-justice, namely that it gives each part of the soul its fair share of satisfaction.

## CONCLUSION (587C–592B)

Plato closes with familiar rhetorical gestures. Playing with mathematics, he has Socrates calculate the exact proportion between the lives of the just and of the unjust (587e). Always inclined to give his theory an image, he pictures the soul as the biological union of a human being, a lion, and a many-headed mythological beast (588b–589a). The fate of reason, represented as the only human part of our souls, is to find itself trapped with a dangerous if educable creature, and another, far more lethal and loathsome, which the little human can master only with the help of the intermediate beast.

Finally, most familiar of all, comes the disclaimer that although the good city might never exist, it is still valuable as a pattern that private citizens can use as guides for life (592a–b).

This closing passage reiterates the *Republic*'s general attention to the soul, to the person's cultivation of virtue, and to the happiness that human beings can win for themselves by caring for their souls. But although the last pages of Book 9 make a stirring conclusion about soul and virtue, it is also an unstable one, drawn both toward the divine and the quotidian human.

The *Republic*'s acknowledgment of the human is visible when Socrates proposes friendship among the soul's parts (589a, b). The *Republic*'s ethics sometimes sound puritanical, but this dialogue does not envision justice as a state of constant repression. Natural desires can find reasonable expression in the good soul. In the same spirit, Socrates calls the actions commonly thought of as just important to maintaining justice in the soul (589c–d, 590a–c). He claimed as much in Book 4 (444d–e), in the course of arguing for ⑦: the precepts of conventional morality, although they need justifications that only philosophers can provide, produce the justice that a philosopher praises. In the present section Socrates takes his respect for legal justice further. Not only do the rules of ordinary justice *happen* to conduce to Platonic justice, they were *made* to do so. Plato returns at the end of his praise for philosophical virtue to recognize the worth of virtue at its most unphilosophical.

But along with this heartwarming turn to the morality of ordinary life comes something very much like the opposite. The final confrontation between best and worst souls rewards just people with a pleasure that belongs to the soul as opposed to the body (585d; cf. 591b–c); and Socrates has begun associating the soul with incorporeality and immortality (585b–c). Does the just person's pleasure belong to the just insofar as they are not regular persons at all? It is hard to escape that suspicion when Socrates concludes by separating the soul into what is animalistic and what might be, as he says, *theion* 'divine' (589c–d). Even his word 'perhaps' soon disappears, and Socrates is speaking of the reason as divine (twice at 590d).

Book 9 concludes with language that might not absolutely have to be taken as religious, but has been read that way more often than not. Glaucon says the city they have been discussing exists in words, in principle, probably not anywhere on earth. Socrates suggests that the model city might exist in heaven, inspiring those who want to live according to wise principles (592a–b). Now the just soul seems otherworldly in the extreme, refusing to declare citizenship in any society known on earth, or to express loyalty to any such society. In these moments the just soul sounds like a religious mystic, improved by philosophical morality to the point of becoming divine.

## SUGGESTIONS FOR FURTHER READING

On the types of government and types of souls, see Guthrie, *A History of Greek Philosophy*, volume IV, for exegesis of the faults Plato finds in each stage. For a reading of the degenerate regimes possessed of shadow virtues see Hitz, 'Degenerate regimes in Plato's *Republic.*' Frede, 'Plato, Popper, and Historicism,' attacks the very idea that Plato could be treating these political forms historically.

On the comparison between best and worst souls see first the overview in Brown, 'Plato's ethics and politics in the *Republic.*' Russell, *Plato on Pleasure and the Good Life*, offers a powerful presentation of pleasure in the Platonic corpus that differs from the one presented here; relevant sections discuss the choice between just and unjust lives. On the tension between two conceptions of justice in Book 9, see Nussbaum, 'The *Republic*: true value and the standpoint of perfection.'

# 9

## ART AND IMMORTALITY
## (BOOK 10)

On a first reading of the *Republic*, going from Book 9 to Book 10 resembles turning off a highway to wind along twisted back roads. After a two-book-long strategy for comparing justice to injustice, which ties up the elaborate argument spanning the dialogue as a whole, comes a bag of arguments about the arts, apparently unconnected with one another or with Books 1–9.

Even more suddenly a discussion of tragedy lurches into an argument for the immortality of the soul; after this argument comes a myth, warning of the otherworldly penalty for leading an unjust life, that apparently takes back the *Republic*'s long and patient defense of justice in the terms of this world. Then the dialogue ends. It is almost as if someone had tacked on marginally relevant arguments to the preceding sections of the *Republic*, in the belief that more deep thoughts may as well go there as elsewhere.

But to complain seriously that Book 10 has in any sense been tacked on is to misrepresent the *Republic*, whose central ordering principle admits of ample asides. Moreover, Book 10 amplifies a dominant theme of the dialogue, that a good life requires the rule of reason. Socrates opens his critique of poetry, for instance, with the comment that the earlier censorship (398a–b) has found further justification 'now that the soul's forms have each been separated out' (595b), and this turns out to mean that poetry must be banned in order for reason to govern the person. Indeed, every issue in Book 10 reflects back on the *Republic*'s psychological theory (Book 4), and on the vindication of a life in which reason rules (Books 8–9). Given that Socrates has just finished defending the life of reason, it becomes less strange than it first appeared to see Book 10 going on about the nature of that life.

## THE ARGUMENT AGAINST ALL POETRY (595A–608B)

However difficult the details of the first half of Book 10, the general argument is clear enough:

    (1)  ⑬ Poetry imitates appearance. (595b–602c)
∴ (2)  ⑭ Poetry appeals to the worst parts of the soul. (602c–606d)
∴ (3)  Poetry should be banned from the good city. (606e–608b)

Despite his conclusion, Plato's interest lies not in censorship but in his new discoveries about poetic imitation. He gives no argument for the step from ⑭ to (3), considering it obvious that if he can show poetry to yield deleterious effects, he will have made the case for its abolition. (Free speech for views known to be harmful has no value for Plato – if anything, it reminds him of the licentiousness of democracy.) The work consists in showing where those effects come from. So he will first argue that poetry is a phantom (⑬), then use ⑬ to expose its psychological effects (⑭).

## IMITATION (595A–602C)

Book 3 already said that poetry presents its characters by means of *mimêsis*, imitation or representation (392d). Book 10 will enlarge upon this claim to say that artistic imitation is an imitation of appearance. The things imitated, and the bad species of imitation, remain the same in both discussions: poetry as it now exists imitates human beings (393b, c; 395c–396d; 605a, c), but in the ideal city it will imitate only the best of them (396c–397b; 604e; 607a). If Plato has changed his view about poetry from the earlier discussion to this one, the change concerns the nature of imitation. In Book 3 the process was left unexplained, but since that point Plato has introduced a theory of knowledge and reality that lets him analyze it more closely.

## PAINTING (596A–598D)

Socrates begins with an analogy between poetry and painting, both of which 'imitate' their subjects. This comparison suggests that looking at painting may clarify an elusive characteristic of poetry.

In the description of painting, the Forms arrive unexpectedly (596a–b) – not the Forms of Book 5, which corresponded to a few kinds of predicates, but Forms of everything. Whenever many objects share a name, a Form of them exists (596a). Such Forms are models for manufacture: the carpenter who builds a couch or table does so by 'looking to' the Forms of couch and table (596b). The painter of a couch or a table, by comparison, looks only at the individual things and copies their appearance (597e–598b).

Why bring in an unfamiliar version of the Forms just to show that imitation is inferior to other skills or professions? The *Republic* argues (598b) that painters are ignorant of the nature of the things they depict. Is that not enough?

But the Forms differentiate between two superficially similar activities. A painter and a carpenter might both be described as copying a particular table, the painter when making a picture of a table and the carpenter when making a table. But to the carpenter this table represents something more substantial, as the drawing of a triangle does for a mathematician (510d–e). Carpenters examine the construction of each joint, the cut of the table's legs: they 'look to' the Forms even by looking at a table. A table bears some relation to the Form of the table as $X$ things generally participate in the Form of $X$ (476d). So imitating a table as carpenters do still permits them to escape the table's idiosyncrasies; imitating as painters do, in ignorance of the Form, leads to an imitation of appearance alone, only a part of the imitated object (598b).

It might also matter that Plato refers to a god who makes Forms (597b), as a parallel to the carpenter who makes tables and painters making table pictures. People think of imitative artists as something divine, as if they made whole worlds (596c–d). This triad god/carpenter/painter puts the imitations at the furthest distance away from the divine status they claim for themselves. You can think of it as a religious argument – accompanying the metaphysical contrast between the objects these different creators make – to underscore how much is at stake in supervising a society's arts.

## POETRY (598D–601A)

Assuming the similarity between painting and poetry, we have arrived at

⑬ Poetry imitates appearance.

The problem with moving so fast is the vagueness of *mimêsis*. How can artistic imitation be the same in both art forms? This question leads to live issues in aesthetic theory: Can music also be representational? What is the difference between the representation of a person in drama and the 'same' representation in fiction?

But Book 10 can be understood without explaining imitation as such, for its emphasis falls on the *object* of imitation, namely the appearance of a thing as opposed to the thing's true nature. Even if the imitative relationships in the different arts have nothing to do with one another, this claim about appearance can still hold true. So all we need to say about poetry, to preserve the analogy, is that poets are as ignorant as painters about the truth concerning their subjects. They are focused on mere appearances as opposed to reality and truth.

That is the point Socrates turns to in his exposure of Homer's ignorance (599c–601a). Homer's ignorance betrays the merely apparent nature of a poet's understanding of human beings: Homer's skill lay in his ability to create convincing portraits of heroes in action, not in any comprehension of morality. Poets are therefore ignorant in the same way that painters are; hence they too imitate appearance alone.

The champions of art sometimes respond that ignorance is irrelevant, that one may be ignorant and still a splendid poet. Plato acknowledges that point; it is his own point. From Plato's perspective the problem is precisely that whether the poet is knowledgeable or ignorant makes no difference to the merit of the poetry. One cannot be ignorant of medicine and still be a splendid doctor; but Homer's ignorance shows that one can be a poet without being knowledgeable, therefore that it is not part of poets' imitative job to learn the facts about the things they write about. Since poetic imitation can be accomplished without appeal to the fact of the matter, it cannot be an imitation of the thing's true nature.

## USER, MAKER, IMITATOR (601C–602A)

Socrates now ranks the levels of understanding available to the user of a bridle or flute, to its maker, and to its imitator. The first possesses knowledge (601e) and the second one 'right trust [*pistis*]' or 'right opinion [*doxa*]' (601e, 602a), while the imitator, lacking both knowledge and justified belief, remains ignorant (602a).

This argument feels tacked on to what came before. Some readers even suspect that a later editor inserted the passage. But one thing is clear, that the new tripartition user/maker/imitator means to illustrate the epistemological differences in people paralleling the metaphysical differences among Form, table, and picture. So this passage shows how to tie the discussion of art to the Divided Line: the words for 'trust' and 'opinion' here are the same words Socrates used there to name perceptions of physical objects (511e; cf. 534a). Because the imitator possesses something worse than this trust, imitations must belong in the lowest part of the Divided Line, together with shadows, reflections, and all other 'images' (509e–510a). Works of art are objects of 'imagination' or image perception (*eikasia*), the cognitive awareness furthest from knowledge.

This passage also begins the move from artistic imitations *simpliciter* to their effects on their spectators. In what follows, Plato will argue that distinct states of the soul mark the audience of art, and that these states corrupt the soul. The excoriation of poetry's *epistemic* status is a preliminary to that *psychological* criticism.

Because the two triads in this part of Book 10 both put the professional maker in the second rank and the imitator third, it is tempting to try to reconcile them. But what became of the god at the top of the first ranking? A good answer to that question might draw the two passages together. As a first step toward an answer, consider the objects that Socrates uses in this argument. Flutes and bridles are two items whose origins are told in Greek myths: Athena made both and was the first to use each. (See Pindar's *Twelfth Pythian Ode* about the *aulos* 'flute' and his *Thirteenth Olympian Ode* on the *chalinos* 'bridle, bit.') Choosing these two examples might be an allusion to Athena as the ideal top-ranked personage in this second triad. Then the imitator winds up opposed to a god for a second time, and the poetry that Book 10 ultimately permits – hymns to gods, praise for good people (607a) – belongs in a larger religious conception of poetry's place in well-run and worshipful societies.

## THE AROUSAL OF UNREASON (602C–607A)

### Painting and the irrational (602c–603b)

Socrates asks what imitation works its effects on in people (602c). He contrasts the sense of sight, easily duped by artistic shams, with the calculating faculty that replies to illusion with measurement (602d–e). Since sight and reason disagree about whether a stick in water is bent, and since a single part of the soul cannot disagree with itself (602e), the part of the soul taken in by visual images must be distinct from the calculating part (603a).

This argument duplicates the passage in Book 4 that originally separated the parts of the soul, also on the basis of internal disagreement (436b). If the present separation of parts matches up with the earlier one, artistic imitation may be said to appeal to the lower impulses. Socrates has outlined a succinct argument for the depravity of imitation:

(1) ⑬ Art imitates appearance and not reality.
(2) Reality is the object of knowledge, perceived by the rational part of the soul.

∴ (3) From (2), appearance *without* reality appeals to a nonrational part of the soul.

∴ (4) From (1) and (3), art appeals to the irrational in human beings.

⑭ is only (4) specified to poetry; so if the argument applies to poetry, ⑭ is true.

As the argument stands, however, it plays off an ambiguity that threatens to keep its focus too narrow. In the case of painting, the 'nonrational' means the bodily organs that are susceptible to making mistakes about experience. This is a neutral sense of nonrationality, far from what we mean when we speak of irrational anger or fear. It is like saying that your stomach churns food without rationality. But the argument against poetry requires the irrationality encouraged by art to include all the passions that a person falls prey to. The problem is that while Book 4 separated the part of the soul that exercises self-control from the angry part and the lustful, thirsty part, the present argument addresses itself to the part taken in by optical illusions and the soberer part that remains unfooled. One's sense of sight may be fallible or even inclined to error, but not because it is inherently manipulated by desire. Plato needs to equate the propensity to error with the propensity to passion.

## Poetry and the irrational (603c–607a)

So Socrates abandons his analogy and turns directly to poetry (603b–c), to show how its imitative practice allies it with the soul's lower parts. (In these critiques of poetry Plato concentrates on drama, treating Homer as a grandfather tragedian: 595b, 598d.) Because Homer and the playwrights occupied pride of place among all poets, Plato has to attack them to show how far-reaching he means his criticism to be. The argument makes two distinct points: first, that poets tend to imitate the soul's worse impulses instead of its better ones (603c–605c), and secondly, that poetry leads its audience to foster and obey those parts of the soul that ought to be kept subservient (605c–607a).

The first argument sets the soul's deliberative faculty against its other impulses. In every crisis that leaves people torn between the desire to react passionately and the effort to forbid themselves the passions and control their reactions, the latter effort – which Book 4 called the work of reason (439c–d) – is the impulse to decide what really happened. Suppose a man's son dies. His reason will be the part of him that asks what human life amounts to (604b–c), while his grief flows from the part that 'believes the same things are at one time big and at another little' (605c), presumably the part that finds a death monumental when the young man is a son, incidental when he is a stranger.

The *Republic*'s two conceptions of reason are both at work. The soul's calculating faculty instinctively aims at controlling the other impulses, but also philosophizes. Philosophical inquiry is the source of self-control. The desires lack awareness of their own importance or insignificance; therefore, the impulses that do not come from reason will always make mistakes. So the expression of any passionate or desiring impulse rests on an error about the importance of that impulse's objects. Perhaps it is more accurate to say that the expression of any such impulse *amounts to* an error about the objects' importance. So now the soul's irrational parts resemble the sense of sight after all, because in the domain of human action they are the source of all misjudgment.

Reason takes on the appearance of an inner command that denies the importance of personal ties and desires to a healthy human life. Deliberating about his son's death requires a man to deny the very unabstract relationship between himself and his son, to treat himself impersonally as one more human among many.

Whether or not Plato wants us to become *that* detached from our desires, he certainly expects us to subject the desires to scrutiny, weighing each nonrational motivation against a philosophical evaluation of its worth. This picture of behavior illustrates ⑪, which first arose in Book 5 and then grew in significance in Book 9. The rational part of the soul has its own desires, not only governing the other impulses but also aiming at philosophical insight. Because the ruling part of the soul is also the part that looks philosophically at every issue, a well-run soul must force its irrational impulses to meet philosophical standards of appropriateness.

Plato supports his position by arguing, independently of the painting analogy, that poetic imitation appeals to and encourages the irrational impulses in the soul. He finds dramatic poets choosing to depict passions instead of the sober calculating agency that reins those passions in (604e–605a).

Plato's description of drama is true, regardless of his agenda. Playwrights and actors alike do shy away from perfect characters. To play an idealization is to leave out the bumbling and the vice, all the flaws with which actors show their skill. Plato knows how much the dramatic arts thrive on portrayals of imperfection; given that imperfection belongs in the domain of the irrational, he can hardly help seeing the dramatist's fondness for deviance as an unseemly preference for error over truth. He also recognizes that a good dramatist loves the virtuous and the vicious characters alike and writes each part trying to respect that character's motives and goals – sheer madness, Plato would say. (Considering Plato's antipathy toward the theater, we understand better why Socrates should have become such a stiff, saintly figure in Plato's own works of this period: Socrates' is the good and intellectual soul that no actor would want to portray.)

In his final argument, Socrates convicts the audience of poetry of the same perverse preference (605c–607a). For whatever reason, we let ourselves enjoy actions, passions, jokes, and drives in a dramatic or fictional work that we would never tolerate in our private lives. Such enjoyment privileges nonreason over reason, because every appeal to the emotions is a seduction away from the use of reason. Emotions by themselves are not bad. But preferring an emotional response to a rational one is like asking the army what its leaders ought to order it to do. And just as too many calls for votes in an army would weaken its officers' power, so too every indulgence of an irrational impulse leaves it stronger (606b–d; cf. 444c, 589c–d). The enjoyment of poetry leads to injustice in the soul.

## APPEARANCE VS. THE IMITATION OF APPEARANCE

The problem cannot be simply that the imitative arts produce objects possessing a low metaphysical status. Book 10 ranks poems with reflections, but surely mirrors and shadows should not be expelled from the city. Plato finds poetry dangerous, but his analysis of artistic imitation puts it on a par with the most insignificant objects imaginable. Why get exercised over trivial entities? How can artworks affect the soul when they are no more than shadows?

Plato must believe that imitations possess some additional quality that gives them a power unmatched by other images. Consider the painting of a table, in which the front legs are made longer than the rear. In one sense this misstatement about the world resembles a stick that looks bent in water. But while I might pull out the stick and hold it against a straight edge, it never occurs to me to measure the legs of the painted table. To enjoy a painting is to give up such pedestrian considerations as the actual proportions of the depiction. In this way the painting seduces me away from using my powers of calculation, as an apparently bent stick does not. Something about the artistic image holds my attention and keeps me from asking rational questions about it.

That 'something' is the added element that inspires Plato's mistrust of the artistic image. On his account, the special character of poetry includes the sweetness (607a) and beauty (598e, 602b) of representations, and the audience's pleasure (605d, 607d), but it goes beyond these. Poetry exercises what Socrates calls *kêlêsis* 'charm' (601b, 607c), an appeal tantamount to a magician's enchantment. The word evokes other references to sorcery and spells in the *Republic*, which condemn malevolent influences on the citizens (e.g. 412e–413b). A pleasant and naturally occurring image, such as the sharp shadow cast by a leafless tree, does not arouse the condemnation that Socrates directs at imitations, because no such image would seduce its spectator in the fascinating way that an artistic image has.

The reference to charm suggests a better argument. The products of artistic imitation lure the spectator into preferring those images over objects that might lead to knowledge. Their charm is the origin of their seductiveness. Plato seems to have acknowledged this charm earlier in the *Republic*, when he shows the guardians developing aesthetic reactions to good and bad deeds, with the help of moral lessons dressed in the attractive speech of poems (401b–d). There, poetic charm seemed a force capable of good; but this difference between the two passages only underscores the general difference between Books 3 and 10, namely the difference between Plato's earlier attempt to find some poetry that is good and his later suspicion that no such thing exists (see Chapter 12).

Assuming some explanation of charm, the argument might work. Socrates attributes the charm of poetry to its rhythm, meter, and harmony (601a), but that explanation begs the question of where those poetic devices get their appeal. And here the *Republic* is silent. In the *Ion* and the *Phaedrus* Plato tries to say more, accounting for the power of poetry with a divine madness, like what we call inspiration, that possesses the poet and gives every good poem its inexplicable attractiveness to its audience (*Ion* 533d–534e; *Phaedrus* 245a). Plato says nothing about divine madness in the *Republic*, probably because it would elevate poetry to a more exalted level than the *Republic*'s criticism permits. Instead the argument ridiculed the seeming divinity in artistic imitation and marked off a great distance between god and artist. But without some explanation of their charm that does invoke divinity, the danger inherent in works of art must also go unexplained. Either Plato must explain the bewitchment of art in terms that do not praise it, or he must concede that such error-riddled productions could never corrupt the soul.

## MORE CONSEQUENCES OF JUSTICE AND INJUSTICE (608C–621D)

The second half of Book 10 completes Socrates' discussion with Glaucon and Adeimantus with references back to the issues they had raised in Book 2. When they developed their original challenge, Glaucon and Adeimantus had made secondary points – Glaucon about the unfair wages that accrue to the just and the unjust, Adeimantus about the disrespect for virtue evident even in his culture's praise of it – that Socrates now addresses.

The *Republic* has defended justice on the grounds (1) that the just enjoy greater psychological peace than the unjust, and (2) that the intellectual pursuits to which the just find themselves drawn yield pleasures unknown to anyone else. Whatever the merits of these claims, we must recognize that to one kind of listener they will ring hollow. Someone whose life is concerned with fame and physical joy will easily shrug off the promise of psychic harmony, to say nothing of intellectual pleasures. Plato knows he cannot win over a reader who has not already begun to think philosophically: Book 5's lover of opinion cannot simply be told about the Forms, but first has to stop focusing on the things in the visible world. Through the *Republic* we have seen Plato respond to this gulf between his philosophical and unphilosophical audiences by offering two different arguments for a single point. The dozen remaining pages serve the same purpose: after arguing for the deep benefits of justice, Socrates says a few words about its superficial benefits, to satisfy the reader on whom those better arguments were wasted.

## IMMORTALITY (608D–612A)

First Socrates argues that the soul is immortal. Especially during the period of the *Republic*, Plato kept returning to this subject. The *Phaedo* devotes itself to seeking a proof of immortality; other dialogues include arguments in passing (*Meno* 81b–86d, *Phaedrus* 245c–d); still others assert immortality without argument (*Laws* 959b, 967d, *Timaeus* 41c–42e). The argument in the *Republic* follows a strategy not found in the other passages:

    (1) The evil connected with every thing is that which can
        destroy it. (608d–609a)
    (2) Injustice, licentiousness, cowardice, and ignorance make a
        soul bad. (609b)
∴  (3) Vice is the specific evil of the soul.
    (4) The presence of vice never results in death. (609c–d)
∴  (5) The soul is immortal. (610e–611a)

The motivating idea behind this argument appears in (4). A knife when it is blunt enough becomes no knife at all, but a soul gone bad continues living. Though moral badness means being *bad at* fulfilling the soul's task, and that task is living, nevertheless the unjust soul continues to exist. It lives despite not living up to its duties; but if badness can't kill the soul, nothing else can either.

An obvious objection: immortality might not be the only explanation of (4). Indeed you might want to use (4) to deny (3). Because vice does not destroy the soul it must not be the soul's specific evil. What are these claims about the soul's task and its defining badness doing in this argument?

These claims have appeared before, in the final argument Socrates deployed against Thrasymachus (352d–354c). The thing's specific evil in (1) can be seen as that which counteracts the *ergon* 'work' characteristic of that thing (⑬); and when Glaucon agrees to call moral vice the evil of the soul (3) he is asserting the inverse of something Thrasymachus assents to, that justice is the virtue of the soul (④). These two assumptions have traveled a long way through the *Republic*, justifying (respectively) the city's division of labor and the quest for happiness in the harmonious operation of the soul. Here they reverse, or almost reverse, the argument against Thrasymachus that justice means living well and living well equals happiness. Here injustice means living badly but living badly does not equal death.

Perhaps what keeps both arguments from convincing us is the vagueness of 'living well' and 'living badly.' The argument in Book 1 rushed to make justice the good working of the soul, and Book 10's argument simply helps itself to the same moralizing psychology. As closing arguments, both express deeper and more powerful intuitions about the soul than they can stop to examine.

## THE MYTH OF ER (614B–621D)

Having argued for immortality, Socrates fleshes out his argument with detail about the events to come after death. This too is a version of something found in other dialogues. Both the *Phaedo* and the *Gorgias* conclude with myths of otherworldly judgment, while the *Phaedrus* (246b–256e) depicts the starting point of the reincarnational cycle.

The *Republic* begins with Er, who died in battle. Rather than stay dead, he roused himself on his own funeral pyre and told of the afterlife. According to Er's story, all freshly dead souls travel to an unearthly junction, where they are judged and sent either up to the heavens for a thousand years or down into the earth for at least as long, depending on how incorrigible they are (614c–d). Meanwhile, other souls return from their millennial stays in the earth and heaven and tell of the rewards and punishments they received (614d–616a). These souls travel to a second place, located so that they can see the stars and planets from a point outside the visible universe (616b–617b). Here they cast lots and choose which human or animal life they want for their next trip into existence (617d–618b). Some choose well and others badly, but they all must live with their choices (619b–620d). Socrates enjoins Glaucon to heed the moral of this story, that a person ought to practice justice informed by practical wisdom (621c).

The myth of Er offers a supernatural incentive for justice, and also explains people's present situations in life. As an incentive, the myth satisfies both brothers' complaints from Book 2. Glaucon gets his reassurance that besides being its own reward, justice will generate further rewards for the just. All the deeds of our lives are rewarded and punished (615b–c), which means that even unreflectively decent people can enjoy a fair return on the moral effort they expended while alive.

Then the myth moves to a different point, because ordinary justice is not its only aim. One character (some read him as resembling Cephalus) chooses the worst life possible. His previous earthly existence of habitual virtue, followed by a thousand years' reward for those good deeds, lulled him into complacency about virtue and the soul (619b–d). His old goodness helped to bring about his next life's badness. Indeed, most souls acquire no lasting instruction from their successive incarnations, but swing from justice to injustice and back again. Only philosophical justice, which alone leads to a wise choice of future lives, offers permanent relief from his karmic pendulum. As conceived in Book 9, philosophical justice reflects not merely harmony among the soul's three parts, but a positive attachment, by the calculating agency, to philosophy. Only the just behavior that also entails theoretical understanding of justice will make one a good judge of lives (618b–e).

Socrates' warning about the complacency of those who are mindlessly just answers the complaint of Adeimantus, that traditional myths of reward and punishment insult what they pretend to praise, by describing disembodied lives in which none of the virtuous ever practice virtue (363a–e). Socrates has told a new kind of myth in which the greatest virtue needs constant exercise, as much in the next life as in this one.

Some readers feel betrayed that so much patient argumentation throughout the *Republic* has yielded to pious storytelling. To others the myth of Er is attractive but unfortunately unbelievable. They could all agree that the myth would promote virtue and philosophical reflectiveness among those who did believe it. Still this is only one of the myth's two purposes, for it also seeks to account for people's present station in life. To reward and punish behavior, an eternal afterlife suffices. Reincarnation brings the focus back if not to this *life*, then at least to lives in this *world.*

As cosmic explanation the myth is less successful even assuming it is true. For in the first place it does not quite convince its reader that human beings bear complete responsibility for the lives they choose. Too many factors in the selection process lie outside human control, from the order in which souls get to choose to the arrangement of new lives on the ground, for everyone to have an equal opportunity in the next life. Then there is the nature of the otherworldly reward, whose millennium of joy lulls those who had once been just into rushing toward injustice.

Indeed, if those who win long rewards grow lazy and return as villains, while former villains (having been chastened for just as long) come back to life as good people, the myth of Er seems to promise endless cycling back and forth, for which the souls deserve only partial credit or blame. Philosophers might emerge from eons of reward still ready to choose another life of virtue – a life that then lets them become philosophical again, and so on for eternity – but no one else can have the same good hopes for the next life. Freedom regarding life-choices fully exists only for philosophers.

And now things get a little worse. If those who had been habitually just choose injustice, and those who'd been unjust steer toward a well-ordered and unreflective life, the life of philosophy will only be chosen by – philosophers! Philosophers are those who have always been philosophers. So to this degree at least the myth of Er works like a noble lie for everybody in every city, making philosophers a permanent class of souls in the world. Among other things this means that the good city's philosophers do not owe any debt to that city that should make them willing to rule. They would have come back as philosophers under any regime. And for most of the world's souls it implies a hopelessness beyond the power of human choice to repair. The myth makes every circumstance of life the work of the gods, hence inescapable, but at the same time it pins the responsibility for those circumstances on the person living through them, so that one may not even resent the inescapable. This is one of the most conservative touches in Plato's work. It hints that even founding the good city would be wrong, inasmuch as that act would divorce a huge number of people from the circumstances of their lives.

Finally, the myth of Er is another Aristophanic moment in the *Republic*. Aristophanes' *Frogs* likewise ends with a return from the underworld; in the *Frogs* that return is prefaced by a debate between two rival tragic playwrights, Aeschylus and Euripides, whereas in the *Republic* it follows a debate between the tribe of poets taken together and the voice of philosophy that will supplant all of them. If Plato's first readers did think of Aristophanes here, the reference would have advised them what the otherworldly contest should really result in, and who deserves to be its victor.

## SUGGESTIONS FOR FURTHER READING

Readers curious about Plato's conception of imitation are advised to begin with Nehamas, 'Plato on imitation and poetry in *Republic* 10'; then they should read Halliwell, *The Aesthetics of Mimesis: Ancient Texts and Modern Problems*, which delves into the details of Book 10's argument as well as coordinating that argument with larger discussions of imitation in and after Plato. For an unorthodox treatment of Book 10, see Deleuze, 'Plato and the simulacrum.'

On other issues in Plato's critique of the arts, see Murray, 'Poetic inspiration in early Greece,' and Woodruff, 'What could go wrong with inspiration?' The interpretation spelled out in this chapter can be found discussed at greater length in Pappas, 'Plato's aesthetics.' Burnyeat, 'Culture and society in Plato's *Republic*,' shows how deeply the *Republic* integrates its arguments about art into its larger vision of human culture, both actual and ideal.

Plato's myths have inspired a range of interpretations. Partenie (ed.) *Plato's Myths* is an excellent and very recent anthology; on the myth of Er in particular it contains Ferrari, 'Glaucon's reward, philosophy's debt: the myth of Er.' Annas, 'Plato's myths of judgment,' reads the myth of Er against the backdrop of the similar myths in Plato's *Gorgias* and *Phaedo*; McPherran 'Virtue, luck, and choice at the end of the *Republic*,' presses the myth on the difficulties it creates for decisions of personal responsibility, very much the same difficulties gone over in the last part of this chapter.

# Part III

---

## GENERAL ISSUES

# 10

## PLATO'S ETHICS AND POLITICS

### WHAT IS THE CALCULATING PART OF THE SOUL (REASON)?

In Plato's *Phaedrus*, whose psychological theory resembles the *Republic*'s, Socrates depicts the soul as a charioteer steering two horses. One horse is gentle and heeds its driver; the other one, a crazed animal, tries to drag the entire team wherever it wants to go (246a–b, 253c–254e).

The image captures several features of psychological experience, but maybe most dramatically the sense people can have that reason by itself is powerless. Without the horses the charioteer would stand in a stalled chariot. Without some desires that begin outside the calculating part of the soul, reason might imagine what the person should do, but would not get beyond imagining. Reason can weigh one desire against the welfare of the whole soul; counsel against some irrational impulses; encourage those that conduce to the soul's overall health. But in itself it contains no source of movement.

On this view of the soul, reason is a second-order agency, only having something to do once the person experiences some other motive. I crave a fistful of bacon but I tell myself I'm better off without it, or else I lay the strips of bacon in a pan to cook them: either way my reason reacts to my hunger.

In the Platonically just soul, as Book 4 describes it, the spirit and the desires accept reason as their overlord. When the calculating part of a just soul tries to curb the person's anger or to counter any other temptation, the person listens. But on what basis does reason decide what to say? Here the charioteer may be a misleading image, because charioteers do not steer for the good of their horses. The *Republic*'s analogy between city and soul, while it still envisions reason in a second-order capacity, describes a more specific function for the tribunal of reason. The governing classes come into existence to serve the needs of the productive class, whether they work for this class in obvious ways – when the army protects the city – or in a way that only the rulers appreciate, as when they deprive all citizens of the delights of drama in order to keep the army both fierce enough to protect the city and gentle enough not to overrun it. It does not matter that the craftspeople never initiate public policy; not even that they may not grasp the reasons behind a policy. Their continued activity is the goal at which all policy aims.

To the extent that the good city reflects the good soul, its organization implies that within the soul, reason pursues the long-range satisfaction of the desires. The world is such that most desires have to go unsatisfied, and the ones that do get satisfied bring unwanted effects. The greatest satisfaction of the desires therefore demands that they be controlled. But desires express themselves unconditionally, lacking the ability to impose conditions on themselves. So reason acts on behalf of the whole person, but the person (we are told to this point) is moved by a cluster of appetitive desires; and it is these that reason serves.

We saw that when Socrates defined justice in Book 4 as a psychological state, he had to address the charge of irrelevance. For the *Republic*'s argument to work against the challenge that Thrasymachus posed, the P-just person must be the one who acts O-justly. Though Plato's response to this challenge is oblique and incomplete, it stands a chance of working as long as reason is a second-order critic of other motivations and supplies no motive force of its own. For then the essence of P-justice is thoughtful self-control. In that case it makes sense to see the P-just person as O-just, because self-controlled people can adapt to any rules; also to see the O-just person as P-just in turn, if that simply means that obedience to any sane moral system inculcates the restraint that lets reason's voice be heard. (Socrates seems to have this etiology of the ordinary virtues in mind when he says that they are 'produced by habits and exercises'; 518d–e.)

But the calculating agency does not remain at the level of practical wisdom. Socrates implies in Book 6, then asserts directly in Book 9, that the calculating part of the soul has its own desires, just as the appetitive and the spirited parts do, except that where they love gain and honor, respectively, it loves learning and philosophy (581a–c). The wisdom that resides in the calculating part of the soul (441e) now amounts to theoretical wisdom.

Why should Plato change his conception of reason halfway through the *Republic*? For one thing, the argument in Book 6 (485d) needs this premise for the purpose of demonstrating the philosopher's virtue. Being so passionate about wisdom, philosophers have less energy left for the attachments that lead other people into vice. But the possibility of rule by philosophers owes more to the expanded conception of reason than this argument alone would indicate. If reason had no desires of its own, the calculating faculty that directed traffic among the parts of the soul would possess only practical wisdom; it would be the rational agency of the sane person and the sound ruler, but the sound ruler would not have to be a philosopher too. Once reason has some purpose of its own to pursue – which turns out to be philosophy – then the same part of the well-integrated soul that manages its own efforts (and the city's, if it is the ruler's soul) will be the faculty that grasps abstract truths. The highest knowledge and the sanest personality go together. The philosopher rules.

The argument profits in a second way too. When reason can achieve its own satisfaction, it is easier to demonstrate the rewards of reasonableness. By Book 9, Socrates hardly distinguishes justice from philosophy. The comparisons between just and unjust lives (576b–587b) allegedly return to the challenge that Glaucon and Adeimantus had set Socrates in Book 2; yet the victorious (because

more pleasurable) life repeatedly turns out to belong to the philosopher in particular. (See 582e, which speaks of the 'lover of wisdom'
or philosopher as the best judge of pleasures; at 583b that argument
proclaims 'the just man' the winner, as if the two were the same.) If
the harmonious or P-just soul is also the one that hungers after
philosophy – call that the Φ-just soul – then all the delights of
intellectual activity automatically accrue to the P-just soul and
help to show that justice is profitable.

Now Plato faces a fresh charge of irrelevance. In Book 4 he could
be accused of changing the subject from O-justice to P-justice,
demonstrating merely that a certain state of character is worth
possessing, not that recognizably virtuous behavior is worth
doing. Φ-justice poses a similar problem, for the skeptic may
wonder whether the philosopher's soul will be the same as the
just person's soul. If it is, justice has been vindicated; if not, we
possess only an advertisement for philosophy.

To overcome this new threat of irrelevance, Plato needs to show that

(1)  the Φ-just soul = the soul of one who is more likely than
anyone else to perform O-just deeds.

The *Republic* has overtly recognized and asserted one component
of (1), namely the claim that

(2)  Φ-justice in the soul brings about regular O-just actions.

Testimonies to the philosopher's virtue recur through the second
half of the *Republic*, most obviously at 485a–487a. Philosophers
are moderate (485e), brave (486b), and in every other respect
(487a) the right sorts of people. But these claims only do half the
work. For the pleasures of contemplation redound to the credit of
all just people only if all just people have philosophical souls – only
if, that is,

(3)  the regular practice of O-just actions implies a Φ-just soul.

Because he needs (3), or something as close as possible to it, Plato
makes a bold claim on behalf of ordinary morality:

> [The] laws have made the distinction between noble and base things on
> such grounds as these: the noble things cause the bestial part of our
> nature to be subjected to the human part – or, perhaps, rather to the
> divine part – while the base things enslave the tame to the savage.
>
> (589c–d)

The laws in question are not only such perfect laws as the good
city's rulers will establish, but all those decent precepts that everyone knows, condemning lies and thievery and the offenses of every
day. One who follows those laws comes to be ruled as the *Republic*'s
finest city is ruled: 'all the soul follows the philosophic' (586e).

The extravagance of the claim is hinted at in the words 'divine
part' (already commented on at the end of Chapter 8). Reasonable
governance might even foster what is godly in human beings,
turning obedient citizens into new divinities.

Plato knows that his argument needs some version of (3) if
Book 9's praise of philosophic pleasures is to promote the just
life. So he makes the claim (589) and seems to think he can
defend it. We would need to see the empirical support before
believing him, but at least the *Republic* does not fall unwitting
into the fallacy of irrelevance.

It goes without saying that (3) is extremely hard even for
Plato's sympathizers to accept. Does plodding adherence to law
and custom really make a soul philosophical? Then it's surprising
there are not more philosophers in the world, as even Plato grants
that many people lead upright lives, however blindly they may do
so. If (3) is true there is no virtue without philosophy.

Indeed, (3) claims more than Plato himself often says. It contradicts, to name only one example, a significant passage in the myth of
Er. When one sorry soul inadvertently chooses the life of a tyrant,
Socrates remarks that he had lived 'in an orderly regime in his
former life, participating in virtue by habit, without philosophy'
(619c–d). The warning to the complacent Cephalus in all of us is
that only philosophical enlightenment can give virtue the foundation
it needs. But if we need to heed that warning, we must be able to
achieve virtue without philosophizing – which makes (3) false.

But again, if (3) is false then $\Phi$-justice is not O-justice, and
then Book 9's advocacy of higher pleasures brings no comfort in

the face of the threat of immoralism. If (3) is false then Plato must give up on the greater hope of redefining justice as philosophy, and specifically give up this hope by denying reason its own desires. And then there can be no philosopher-rulers.

Premise (3)'s promise that all those who live lawfully become philosophical makes other problems as well. In Book 7 Socrates says that philosophers who come into existence in ordinary cities

> grow up spontaneously against the will of the regime in each; and a nature that grows by itself and doesn't owe its rearing to anyone has justice on its side when it is not eager to pay off the price of rearing to anyone.
>
> (520b)

This loophole seems concocted to excuse Socrates. Can it work? If any legal system can bring its citizens into a just psychological state in which their calculating agencies predominate, and therefore into a state of studying philosophy, then all philosophers owe their enlightenment to the regime they were born into. Philosophers like Socrates are as indebted to the states they grew up in as the ruling philosophers are to the *Republic*'s philosophocracy.

Note the fatality of this last problem to the *Republic*'s grandest proposal. To justify rule by philosophers, Plato expands his conception of reason. His expanded conception of reason makes justice in the soul something further removed from just behavior than it had been, and thereby commits him to the claim that the practice of ordinary justice makes one a philosopher. But then we lose the striking contrast between how philosophers come to be in the ideal city and how they have come to be in actual cities; and when that contrast is lost, so is the argument compelling the good city's philosophers to govern. The claim that comes in to show why philosophers *ought* to rule undermines the argument that should *persuade* them to.

## POSTSCRIPT ON TWO PHILOSOPHERS

The cheap and easy accusation says: Plato the philosopher over-values philosophers. All the trouble with the *Republic*'s politics begins with that massive collective self-regard that philosophers are prone to. Such accusations are unfair and personalize serious questions. But there is even more wrong with them than that. They accept 'the philosopher' as a unitary concept in Plato when in fact many of his works, including the *Republic*, are divided between two different ideas of what philosophizing is and what people philosophize.

Sometimes the philosopher's activity is the quintessential human activity. If other people do not think about virtue and the integrity of their words, they should. Or they think this way for a while, talking to Socrates, and forget to keep doing so after Socrates walks away. Such philosophizing amounts to moral integrity, and the philosopher resembles the sage, the good person, or the hero: a purified version of what everyone can be and a model for everyone to follow.

As the great human possibility, philosophy gains importance; but also loses the claim to expertise. Philosophical theorists or experts ought not to exist if philosophy comprises what everyone ought to know. But the *Republic* clearly envisions some knowledge as the object of specialized lifelong study. The experts who pursue that knowledge separate themselves from nonphilosophers (503b–d). Their inquiry is something distinct from the pursuit of justice, even from the study of justice (504b–505b). When the good city's philosophers die they receive memorials suitable to minor deities (540b–d) in recognition of their difference from the ordinary human standard.

Philosophy in the first sense, the essentially human capacity, employs the deliberative sort of reason as defined in Book 4. Philosophy as superhuman expertise employs reason in the contemplative sense. In part the *Republic*'s two conceptions of reason run together because the figure who masters each one is such a compelling vision of the philosopher.

## IS THE *REPUBLIC*'S POLITICAL PHILOSOPHY PATERNALISTIC?

In legal theory, a law is said to have a paternalistic justification if the law exists for the good of the person whose behavior it regulates.

Motorcyclists have to wear helmets on the grounds that the benefits of helmets are too great to be canceled by the rider's desire (judged an unimportant desire) to ride a motorcycle without one.

The political structure spelled out in the *Republic* is unquestionably autocratic; but not every autocratic state is paternalistic. (See the next section on the tyrannical paternalism called totalitarian.) And Plato does acknowledge the importance of citizens' moral decision-making, when he insists on a state that governs without the threat of force (548b, 552e). The productive class should freely consent to being ruled by the guardians – the city's moderation requires their consent (432a) – so the city's goodness may be said to rest on an acquiescence in being governed. If the city's goodness requires such consent, its citizens must possess a substantive power of consenting.

But this rock-bottom act of consent, however significant it is, does not gainsay the paternalism that pervades the Platonic state. The city of the *Republic* goes beyond strict centralized governance into paternalism when it refuses to recognize citizens' capacity for moral authority over their own lives. And in fact it refuses to recognize that capacity at every turn.

It is for paternalistic reasons that Plato bans mimetic poetry, for example, and proposes arranged marriages among guardians. The latter is an especially paternalistic move, in that it gives one group authority not trusted to another. Sex is necessary as drama is not, so the rulers can cast comedy and tragedy out of the city altogether, forbidding it to themselves as well as to the other citizens. Artistic imitation is a pollution of the intellect to which the rulers consider themselves as susceptible as anyone else. It is not unduly paternalistic to deny everyone access to a toxin.

The breeding laws, on the other hand, divide the guardian population into those whose marriages are secretly arranged and those who do the arranging. What the former must never find out about their marriages the latter must always bear in mind: this absolute divide (a divide, remember, not between the city's guardians and those less-able craftspeople, but among the elite) assumes an absolute difference in moral reliability between those entrusted with the secret and the rest.

Plato does not include the city's huge productive class in the guardians' communism or breeding rituals. That class only feels the effects of censorship accidentally, in the sense that poetry must be denied to the whole city in order that it not corrupt the guardians. Indeed, aside from general restrictions on how much money laborers and artisans may accumulate (421d–422a), or what they can do with their property (552a), they will live as people always have, owning goods and belonging to families. Many of them will appreciate having professionals in town to take over the tedium of governance and the perils of warfare – so cheaply too – while the productive class busies itself making private fortunes.

But while the superior life that the city makes possible will keep the productive class freely loyal, another kind of paternalism comes into play for them. Life in this class will never feel like autonomous life, for its members will not participate in the city's governance. The price they pay for privacy is a loss of autonomy.

## THE ROOTS OF PLATONIC PATERNALISM

Paternalism turns up frequently in the dialogues' political arguments. In the *Crito*, Socrates describes a hypothetical expert who would function in the moral domain as a doctor does with bodies – an expert who must be obeyed regardless of the nonexpert's opinion (48a). Socrates' claim that we should only listen to 'the one who knows' (47a–48b) means that individual moral deliberation is at best a necessary evil for circumstances in which we have not identified the expert.

As if talk of a moral expert did not announce Socrates' paternalism clearly enough, he closes the *Crito* with an analogy between the state and a parent. The laws of Athens provide for marriage, the nurturance of babies, and education; so the city performs the childbearing and child-rearing functions of the parent, which makes it a super-father (50d–51b). The *Crito*'s argument for citizens' obligation to the state therefore begins with the assumption of a sharp divide between the citizens' moral authority and the state's.

The *Crito* is much shorter and simpler than the *Republic* and dated earlier; the *Statesman* is assigned to a later period. Socrates is not its main speaker, and the *Statesman* sets stricter limits on how much is possible in human politics. Still paternalism is at work.

Plato compares rulers to doctors again, now emphasizing that the right commands are good for people even imposed by force (293b). The dialogue's leader, the Eleatic Stranger, calls statesmanship an art of herd-tending (261d–e). He depicts rule by consent of the governed as a nightmare of incompetence (298a–300b). Above all, the ideal of rule by the perfectly knowledgeable statesman (see 293d–e, 301c–d) makes it clear that the Eleatic Stranger dreams of a city in which moral deliberation by the citizens has withered away.

There is a larger issue that is relevant here but with no space to do it justice: the state's moral education of its citizens. Plato's dialogues speak to this subject even in nonpolitical contexts. Athenian democracy as presented (for instance) in the Funeral Oration of Pericles saw its own virtues arising spontaneously; moral education implied the laborious training that Spartans subjected themselves to. The dialogues' numerous attacks on Pericles fault him for just this democratic reluctance to educate. For Plato education means moral education first and foremost, in which the teachers claim authority, evidently on the grounds of their superior virtue and their superior understanding of what virtue is.

Almost everyone agrees on the existence and value of moral education when the teachers are parents. Plato's vision of the state as the great educator, obvious in the *Republic* and *Laws* but present in many other dialogues too, turns that unobjectionable process into a strong and controversial kind of paternalism.

## RULE BY PHILOSOPHERS

Expertise always grounds Plato's paternalism. That expertise takes its most dramatic form in the *Republic*, whose philosopher-kings derive their legitimacy from having studied the Form of the Good. A full examination of paternalism in the *Republic* – to avoid loose generalizations about Plato's writings – would lead into how the theory of Forms proposes to make governance a mathematical science. But the guiding impulse behind rule by philosophers, behind Plato's call for not only justice in the good city but also the knowledge of justice, may be something simpler than the developed theory of Forms.

When Socrates has described the first city, in Book 2, that Glaucon will call a city of pigs, he asks Adeimantus where that city's justice and injustice would be. 'I can't think, Socrates,' Adeimantus answers, 'unless it's somewhere in some need these men have of one another' (372a). And although the more plausible reading of this answer is that the village only fails as a display case for justice – that it is perfectly good in itself as a human community, bad merely as a philosopher's illustration of justice – Plato might be suggesting that the first city contains neither justice nor injustice; that such a simplified society has no room for either one. In any case it is surely true that this first city cannot know that it is just even if it should happen to be. Only a philosopher can know whether or not a city is just, and what Socrates calls the true city will have no philosophers in it.

Why should it matter that the city know its own justice? Because merely habitual justice – justice without such knowledge – is the kind of virtue we see in Cephalus, and hear warnings about in the myth of Er (619c–d). For the city as for the individual human, politics means not only practicing justice but also understanding it, because without an understanding to moor that practice it will not last.

Socrates makes the point about cities early in his defense of rule by philosophers:

> Those who look as if they're capable of guarding the laws and practices of cities should be established as guardians ... Does there seem to be any difference, then, between blind men and those men who are really deprived of the knowledge of what each thing is; those who have no clear pattern in the soul, and are hence unable ... to give laws about what is fine, just, and good, if any need to be given, and as guardians to preserve those that are already established?
>
> (484b–d)

Because justice without understanding falls so far short, Socrates speaks of the irreplaceability of philosophical governance: 'There should be no other leaders of cities than these [philosophers]' (485a). But if that first city had leaders they would not be philosophers.

Here begins the road that ends in philosophy. The best city will have philosophers in it, because it is the philosopher's task to understand justice. But a just city with philosophers in it will be a city in which they rule – and we set foot on the slippery slope to paternalism.

## AUTONOMY

Suppose we grant Plato that moral expertise exists in the form he envisions and therefore that it is conceivable to have rulers whose decisions about our private lives would be superior to our own. We might still protest that the process of making and obeying our own principles is essential to the human moral function. Paternalism keeps us from being full human beings.

The *Republic* too considers the capacity for moral deliberation essential to humans. Reason governs in the just soul exactly because it is the person's deliberative faculty. But we acquire the power to reason by first obeying the commands of moral superiors; those who can't make themselves better should keep obeying (590d). This desirable condition of being able to think for oneself may be attained, might even be *best* attained, through paternalism.

Autonomy through deference sounds like a contradiction. Maybe it is. But realize that Plato would find the modern democratic position contradictory. If mature moral deliberation is so important, then why not subject citizens to the guidance that makes such deliberation possible? The antipaternalist has good answers available to Plato's challenge, but they are not trivially easy.

## IS PLATO A THEORIST OF TOTALITARIAN GOVERNMENT?

### EVIDENT AFFINITIES

Since the rise of modern totalitarianism, its enemies have pointed out its resemblance to the Platonic state. Their argument has only been made more persuasive by Nazi and Stalinist books that claim Plato for a predecessor. Between the big family of the city and the powers available to its rulers, we feel ourselves on creepily familiar ground.

The popular image of communism comes to mind when Socrates depicts the guardians' lives together, property-less in dormitories. Other specifics of the city will recall the fascist fetishism of unity. Under fascism, the state has an identity above and beyond the collection of individuals constituting it. In many instances the state gives itself over to military organization. When not at war or planning for war, the state expresses its militaristic nature in the rigid hierarchy of civil society.

Much of this sounds like the alleged good city in the *Republic*. Most worrisome is the *Republic*'s organic conception of the state, the sense that for Plato the state counts as an individual. The very possibility of an analogy between person and city presupposes a reality to the city's existence that will not let it remain merely a set of human beings. Add Plato's dream of eradicating the family, so that the emotional attachments once pulling people toward private goals now conduce to social oneness, and every feature of the worship of the state is in place.

The Platonic state also reproduces totalitarian regimes in the control it imposes on its citizens. Typically the desire for complete control has meant that totalitarianism (1) restricts speech, (2) denies its citizens participation in government, (3) subjects the young to an indoctrinating education, (4) selects a self-perpetuating ruling class or cadre, and (5) enforces its rule by punishing any citizens' acts of disobedience or subversion.

Many of the same features appear in the *Republic*'s city. The philosophers' knowledge of the Form of the Good licenses their complete domination over the other citizens' lives. Free constitutional debate makes no more sense to Plato than asking children to vote on the multiplication table. As every government does, the guardians will make laws about contracts, libel, and insult, will levy taxes and regulate trade (425c–d). But we also see them lying to the people about their births (414d–415a), and to the guardians about their breeding partners (460a); planning the reproduction of the guardians in accord with eugenic theories (459a–e); restricting the speech and poetry permitted in the city; indoctrinating young guardians. Of the five characteristics listed, these clearly account for (1)–(4).

An unsympathetic reader will immediately think of the possibilities for abuse and blunder, assuming rulers with either character flaws or imperfect knowledge. Here lies the puzzle; for Plato acknowledges both the potential for character flaw in his rulers, and the imperfection of their knowledge about guardian-breeding. Socrates describes batteries of tests to separate the upright guardians from their unworthy siblings (413d–414a, 535a, 537a), institutes penalties for those who have not learned their moral lessons (468a–469b), and warns of the young candidates' corruption if they learn dialectic too early (537c–539d). As for error, the excellent city begins its decline because of these rulers' mistakes about breeding (546a–547a). To grant them the power they have on the grounds of either their goodness or their intelligence betrays a willingness on Plato's part to invest rulers with power even when they go wrong. This willingness appears to tend toward veneration of the state.

## DISSIMILARITIES

Not all apparent resemblances mean what they first seem to. Especially because some labels ('fascist,' 'communist') are heavily charged, a comparison between Plato's city and modern totalitarian states should look closely at the differences between them too. The organic unity of the state; the emphasis on citizens' loyalty; the completeness of state power: from a distance these features appear alike whether in ancient or modern manifestations. But from a distance a planet looks like a star.

And first there is a general accusation that needs to be gotten out of the way. Plato believed that moral propositions can be known as surely as mathematical ones; therefore he thinks like a totalitarian. But if this much can make Plato totalitarian, it also condemns most religious believers (and secular moral theories as well). Plato's confidence in moral truth might be false and might even be dangerous. To call it totalitarian is itself dangerous – disregarding important moral distinctions – and is false to all those who have believed in objective moral values without once falling into totalitarian practices.

### State unity

The *Republic* does portray its city as an extended family, but this is a commonplace in classical Greece, not some new fantasy of

Plato's making. Most Greek cities saw themselves as descended from a single lineage. Plato has accepted the platitudes of his own time, which feel more natural to a small city than they do in large modern countries.

Plato seems to have breathed in Athenian nationalistic prejudices too: belief in the superiority of Athenians over other Greeks and of Greeks collectively over the foreigners spoken of as 'barbarians.' Acquiescing in this prejudice is culpable in a way that wanting to picture your city as one large family is not, and the *Republic*'s simplistic ethnic distinction in Book 5 (469b–471b) comes as a disappointment after its independent-mindedness on other topics. The *Menexenus* funeral speech elaborates on the Greek–barbarian difference, though Plato also deserves credit for dissolving that distinction in the *Statesman*.

## Loyalty to the state

The *Republic* insists that the city think as one, even inscribing this insistence in one of its two foundational principles for all human society (⑤). Is this the blind loyalty that fascist governments call for? Plato presents the singleness of mind as no more than a necessary condition for human society, but we have seen how far the argument develops unanimity beyond that first friendly cooperativeness.

Of course the citizens of democracies often call for unanimity too, especially during a crisis. Democratic agreement is free, not coerced – but then Plato takes pains to prevent the city's army from terrorizing its populace. This brings us to (5), that very important feature of totalitarian states. They use considerable force to maintain their rule. But Plato says that a good state bases its legitimacy on persuasion, not force (548b, 552e). Even the loyalty that the good city expects is not supposed to be blind loyalty. If the philosophers living under existing regimes do not owe their cities public service (520b), political obligation must be something earned by the city. Indeed Socrates says one owes loyalty only to the well-run city, or to the model of it in one's soul (591d–e). Sensible people won't pay attention to political affairs in cities as they are (592a–b). A theory that calls for civic sentiment only in the best of all states is not a theory demanding irrational obedience.

Here it is important to remember that the Platonic city distinguishes itself from both Athens and Sparta. Both cities contained destabilizing tendencies toward civil unrest, and in Plato's time both had known violent civil war. Most of the *Republic*'s readers today live in some version of an Athenian constitution, divided between democratic and oligarchic powers; so we notice how Plato seeks to transcend both sides of the political opposition in a new harmony to which 'politics as usual' becomes irrelevant. This principled distaste for political opposition does anticipate modern experiments – totalitarian experiments – for bringing politics to an end.

Sparta's civil wars, however, pitted a small class of warriors against the Helots, the Spartan slaves. Plato wants to avoid that internal violence too. The Helots spent their lives in productive farm labor or craftwork, lived in poverty, and hated their Spartan masters. The *Republic*'s city will contain a large class that does the Helots' work, but they will consent to be governed by the city's guardians – perhaps because of the opportunities they will have for getting rich in this city.

As an anti-Athens the *Republic* does bring tyrannical modern regimes to mind. But as an alternative to Sparta, whose revolts Plato equally wanted to avoid, the new city repudiates precisely the rule by force those modern regimes are known and loathed for.

## State power

On the subject of the city's strong centralized authority, it should also be borne in mind that its extreme powers mostly affect only its ruling class. Every totalitarian state has a ruling elite, but none yet has imposed intrusive laws only on that elite, letting most people live as they used to. Not one has divorced economic power from political power.

One final difference might be what matters most in practice. Totalitarianism could only exist in the modern age, because only this age gave it the tools it needed. Telephones, television, and guns let a state spy on its subjects, bombard them with misinformation, and kill large numbers of them at once when it has to. This is not to mention faster or fancier tools of the modern state. In the absence of such technology, even a centralized military state like Rome under Augustus tolerated a fair degree of free thinking, free communication, and free movement among its people.

If Plato had envisioned modern technologies he might have also envisioned them at work in his city. As it is, the absence of modern tools from his arsenal leads him to sketch a political entity that differs in kind, not merely in degree, from the worst modern states. In another world he may have proposed a more terrifying state apparatus. In the world he lived in he could no more describe a totalitarian state than he could write an English sonnet.

## A LINGERING WORRY ABOUT PLATONIC POLITICS

One last worry is worth raising about Plato's style of political thought. He belongs with political philosophers of the Enlightenment in believing that tradition does no useful work in thinking about politics.

When Socrates calls for everyone over ten to be expelled from a city, and philosophers to indoctrinate the remaining children (540e–541a), he removes all doubt as to the value of traditional culture in the Platonic state. (And we may assume that during this interim regime the rulers might need to use force to get all those adults out of the city.) Book 2's dismissal of poetry that contains false allegations about the gods has already made this attitude evident; or consider the language with which Socrates speaks of women guardians exercising, his unconcern that people will laugh (452a). The *Republic* retains a role for Delphi (427b–c, 461e, 540b), but otherwise it has no place for the traditions that Plato's contemporaries took pride in. Totalitarian government wants no brakes on its progress toward a new society. Tradition, whether for good effect or bad, has a retarding effect on social change. Plato ushered into political philosophy a disregard for the customary that it has never abandoned, and that shows itself today in those fruits of political philosophy we call totalitarian governments.

# 11

## PLATO'S METAPHYSICS AND EPISTEMOLOGY

### HOW DO THE *REPUBLIC*'S TREATMENTS OF FORMS COMPARE TO ONE ANOTHER?

The reader who wants to study Forms more closely should supplement the *Republic* with passages in the *Symposium* (210e–212a) and *Phaedo* (74a–75d, 100b–106e). Their more direct presentations help one return to the *Republic* with a better sense of what Plato is up to. After the *Republic* every reader ought to consult the first pages of the *Parmenides* (128e–135d), in which Plato criticizes his own theory. For in the process of criticizing the theory, the *Parmenides* (in that initial discussion) is often refreshingly direct about what Forms can and cannot mean.

But before traveling so far afield, we need to make the best sense we can of the *Republic*'s three arguments about the Forms (Books 5, 7, 10) and one additional mention of them (Book 6), all of which have some detail to add to the picture.

As Table 1 shows, certain clear similarities emerge, such as the Forms' uniqueness. We may surmise that Plato had made up his

*Table 1* Arguments for the Forms

| | Book 5 475e–480a | Book 6 507a–b | Book 7 523a–524d | Book 10 596a–597d |
|---|---|---|---|---|
| 1 Properties for which Forms exist | Fair, ugly, just, unjust, good, bad; also Double, half, large, small, light, heavy (476a, 479a–b). | Fair, good (507b). | Big, little, thick, thin, soft, hard (523e). | Couch, table (596b). |
| 2 Features of particular objects | (1) Many (476a); (2) Never X without also holding the contrary property non-X (479a–c); (3) Objects of opinion (479d); (4) Likenesses of the corresponding Form (476c). | (1) Many things that share a single name (507b); (2) Seen but not intellected (507b). | (1) [In the case of specific properties X,] both X and non-X (524a–c); (2) Visible and not intelligible (524c). | (1) Many things that share a single name (596a); (2) 'Like' the corresponding Form (597a). |
| 3 Features of Forms | (1) Unique (476a); (2) Really X for every property X (476b–d); (2a) Always the same in all respects (479a); (3) Things that 'are' (476e); (4) Objects of knowledge (476d). | (1) Unique (507b); (2) Intellected but not seen (507b). | Intelligible and not visible (524c). | (1) Unique (596b, 597c); (2) Made by a god (597b). |

mind there could only be one Form per relevant property (597c). Also note the symmetry that holds between Rows 2, 'Features of Particular Objects,' and 3, 'Features of Forms,' in every column: the characteristics of Forms named in a passage are antitheses to the characteristics of particular objects named in the same passage. Do the many things of experience hold their properties equivocally? Then the Forms will hold them unequivocally. Are particulars seen but not intellected? The Forms are intellected but not seen. *Plato defines his Forms in opposition to the things of this world.* This opposition always automatically implies the Forms' nonidentity with particulars, and usually also captures their self-predication, their characteristic of perfectly exemplifying their properties. So Table 1 bears out the observation that uniqueness, self-predication, and nonidentity constitute Plato's most general descriptions of Forms.

Some of the columns match one another better than others do. The mention of Forms in Book 6 is intended as a digest of the argument in Book 5, so it is no wonder that the characteristics of Forms and non-Forms outlined in Book 6 reiterate points from the earlier argument. As for the discussion in Book 7, it is not really about the Forms at all, but about a pedagogical value in the properties that can hold of individual things. What Book 7 has to say about particular objects is compatible with the argument in Book 5.

The misfit is Book 10, which in some ways repeats what the earlier passages say, in other ways violates their consensus. The things of experience are still called 'many,' as in Books 5 and 6; they are 'like' their corresponding Form, as Book 5 asserts. But in Book 10 Socrates says that the Forms are made by a god, the only such claim to be found in the dialogues: as a rule Plato says that gods find the Forms already existing and contemplate them.

Book 10 also says that there are Forms of Couch and Table, whereas other mentions of Forms in the *Republic* name only evaluative and relative terms. But set aside the question which types of properties correspond to Forms; consider the third difference between Book 10 and the other passages, namely the justification that Socrates offers for the existence of Forms. 'We are ... accustomed to set down some one particular form for each of the particular "manys" to which we apply the same name' (596a).

The idea behind this 'one-over-many' argument (hereafter OM) is simple. Consider any group of things – horses, just laws, large objects – called by a single name. The predicate applied to all the members of this group does not belong in the group: 'that which all horses have in common' is not another horse, but what you may call the essence of horses. As the set of properties common to horses, yet itself not a horse, this essence satisfies the three conditions of uniqueness, self-predication, and nonidentity. So it is a Form.

The OM is well ensconced in Plato's metaphysics as a way of generating Forms. Row 2 of Table 1 might suggest OM at work in Book 6, where Socrates says, 'there is a fair itself, a good itself, and so on for all the things that we then set down as many' (507b). This *need* not imply an instance of OM; 'the things that we then set down as many' might signify the X things of Book 5, in which case Socrates is saying that there is a Form for each set of many things *of a certain sort*, not that belonging to a set of commonly named things suffices to generate a Form. But the *Parmenides* (132a) also announces OM as an argument for Forms, and Aristotle's testimony confirms that Plato used that, along with other arguments, to generate Forms (*Metaphysics* 990b9–17, 1078b17–1079a4).

Plato therefore has more than one argument for the existence of Forms. Different ones turn up in different contexts. Book 5's AKP (argument against knowledge of particulars) (479a–e) produces a Form for every property that is borne by objects in a qualified or context-dependent way. Whatever the reason is that things fail to bear their properties – whether because they decay or because they rely on comparisons with other objects – AKP only establishes corresponding Forms for the properties that invite doubt or disputation. According to AKP, that is, it is only necessary to posit a Form when something has gone wrong with the ordinary predication of properties.

OM generates Forms much more permissively than AKP. As long as a property applies to many objects, there will be a Form of it. Thus OM yields a Form for every general predicate.

It would be strange to condemn a philosopher for having more than one argument for an important doctrine. We might want to see Plato as deploying his arguments for the Forms strategically. In

Book 5 he seeks to demonstrate the superior clarity of philosophical knowledge, so he appeals to the argument that makes the Forms unambiguous bearers of their properties in all contexts. In Book 10 he wants paradigms of knowledge against which to pose a wide range of artistic images, and uses the argument that generates the greatest range of Forms. There must be a Form, if possible, as the counterpart to each imitation. In both passages, the purpose of the theory is to find support for a disputable moral vocabulary, to find moral truths that will not vacillate as ordinary talk about good and bad does. If we know anything about the Forms, it is that Plato used them to continue Socrates' project of defining ethical terms, so that the general statements Socrates looked for about virtues might be true of some ideal objects (Aristotle, *Metaphysics* 987b1–14). As long as that remains his goal, he may use more than one argument to reach it.

But what if the arguments prove incompatible with one another? AKP works as an argument in favor of the Forms by criticizing the many $X$ things of this world. Just and large things cannot teach us unambiguously about justice or largeness. Either Forms exist, and are the things we know about when we understand those properties, or we have no knowledge about the most important matters. If this critique of $X$ things is right, it poses Forms as the only escape from a variety of skepticism. OM, despite producing a wealth of Forms, fails to make a similar case for them, because it develops no critique of non-Forms. Horses are not all called horses, because they fall short of being what they are. The contrary seems more likely, that they get the name of horse precisely by virtue of *being* horses. (Recall that the passage in Book 7 asserts the full standing of a finger – and, by implication, a horse – in its species.)

This difference in the efficacy of the two arguments points to the deeper discrepancy between them. While the Form of $X$ produced by OM does stand 'over' the many $X$ things by virtue of not being a particular object – it is their metaphysical better – it does not clearly hold the property of being $X$ in a superior way. On the contrary, OM is consistent with every particular $X$ thing's being perfectly $X$, since it yields a Form of $X$ as long as more than one thing is $X$. On this account Forms are *universal terms*, and not obviously the *exemplars* or *perfect versions* of properties.

Understanding the two arguments this way makes it baffling to imagine Plato's taking OM and AKP both to be arguments about the same entities. His attraction to OM makes sense, given its power in generating such quantities of Forms so rapidly; but the argument becomes much less attractive by lacking a critique of non-Forms that demonstrates the need for Forms. OM also opens the door to the 'Third Man Argument' (*Parmenides* 131e–132b), which reduces the theory to absurdity by generating an infinite number of Forms. And it commits us, as Aristotle argued, to Forms of negative properties. Because the predicate 'not human' applies to a number of things, there would have to be a Form of the Non-Human, a property so vague that it could hardly have an ideal version. We have seen how hard it can be to interpret AKP, and it is far from a complete justification of Forms, but at least it avoids these defects.

## WHAT SORTS OF PROPERTIES HAVE FORMS ASSOCIATED WITH THEM?

This issue needs to be treated carefully. The passages in the *Republic* and other dialogues that mention Forms tend to give different sorts of examples of the properties that have Forms associated with them. Although the examples are not arguments, and so do not *commit* Plato to different metaphysical theories, the range of examples does *suggest* that he did not hold to a single scope for his Forms.

The examples given are also relevant because within the confines of a specific passage Plato largely restricts his examples of Forms to those implied by the argument that that passage either sets forward or hints at. If the examples fit the argument, they can help us see which version of which argument Plato is attached to.

For example, the only Form named in the *Symposium* (211a–b) is beauty, not the largeness that pops up so frequently elsewhere (*Phaedo* 100e, *Republic* 479b, *Parmenides* 131c, perhaps *Statesman* 283d–e). In the *Symposium* Socrates claims that individual beautiful things fail, in part, because beholders disagree about whether the things are beautiful. The argument from relativity to observers really only works for evaluative terms; hence its appearance here, when the only Form named represents an evaluative term.

Table 1 shows that no two *Republic* passages name exactly the same properties to which Forms correspond. Book 10 stands out, its couch and table rather dingy specimens next to the abstract thinness or lightness of Book 7; Book 6 does not mention those concepts, but only evaluative terms. The evidence from other dialogues compounds this complexity. Some mention of the Forms, explicit or implicit, has been claimed for the *Cratylus*, *Euthydemus*, *Euthyphro*, *Hippias Major*, *Laws*, *Meno*, *Parmenides*, *Phaedo*, *Phaedrus*, *Philebus*, *Protagoras*, *Sophist*, *Statesman*, *Symposium*, *Theaetetus*, and *Timaeus*; and the examples listed in those dialogues cover a broad range of properties falling into four groups: (a) evaluative terms; (b) relative terms and more specifically mathematical ones; (c) naturally occurring things; and (d) human artifacts. (Aside from Book 10, artifacts only come up again at *Cratylus* 389b–d.)

Some of this divergence may be the result of offhand remarks, but not all of it. Indeed, the dialogues that examine the Forms in the greatest detail pull in opposite directions. The *Phaedo*, which apart from the *Republic* is the closest thing to a sustained defense of the Forms, counts only evaluative terms, and such very general relative concepts as equality and inequality, as terms to which Forms correspond (74a–b, 100b–e). The *Parmenides*, Plato's sustained *attack* on the Forms, expands the catalogue to include nearly everything: probably such terms as 'man,' 'fire,' and 'water' (130c), maybe even such ignoble ones as 'hair' and 'mud' and 'dirt' (130c–e). When two reliable sources yield such different answers to our question, we know that the problem does not lie with the *Republic* alone, nor only with Plato's penchant for informal and nontechnical language.

It is noteworthy that the four types of object for which Forms exist are not on a par with one another. Rather, each category presupposes the existence of Forms for the preceding category. That is, when Plato has Forms of plants and animals, he also has Forms of mathematical objects; when he names relative terms as Forms, the group also includes terms of praise or blame. So the question of what things have Forms is a question of more Forms or fewer; and every list contains Forms for ethical and aesthetic terms.

But here we need to exercise the greatest care regarding Plato's arguments. Given Book 10's use of OM, we may take an easy way out and associate that argument with the large set of Forms, and AKP with a much smaller set, perhaps restricted to evaluative and relative terms. This is too easy. Though the *Republic*'s two sets of examples roughly go together with the two different arguments Plato uses for generating Forms in that dialogue, the connection does not have to be as close as it first appears. In the first place, the range of lists of Forms we have just looked at cannot be reduced to Plato's choice of AKP and OM. The dialogues that contain widely divergent extensions for the theory of Forms do not all use different arguments for the Forms.

In the second place, AKP by itself can produce varying sets of Forms. Which Forms AKP produces is not determined by its accusation of particular things' ambiguity, but also depends on how Plato *interprets* that ambiguity. We have seen how hard it is to decide just how Plato takes the world to fail; so appealing to AKP does not settle the question of which Forms exist. If an $X$ thing fails at being $X$ by virtue of the decay that infects the whole physical world, AKP might support the existence of a Form of $X$ for every property $X$; in that case, AKP and OM yield the same list of Forms. If the $X$ thing fails at being $X$ because of disputes that people have over its $X$-ness, AKP only underwrites Forms of evaluative terms.

In short, even if we leave aside the more abstract complexity that results from Plato's use of more than one argument for Forms, we still have the concrete complexity before us concerning how he uses AKP. The scope of the Forms, as well as their intrinsic nature, depends on what Plato takes to be most decisively wrong with the world of appearances.

# 12

## PLATO'S ABUSES AND USES
## OF POETRY

### HOW DOES THE EARLY CENSORSHIP OF POETRY
### IN BOOKS 2 AND 3 COMPARE TO THE FINAL
### REJECTION OF ALL ARTISTIC IMITATION?

Table 2 covers most of the points at which we need to compare the *Republic*'s two discussions of poetry. It would be ridiculous to deny the differences between the two passages' argumentative strategies and assumptions; at the same time, the remarkable degree of agreement between the table's columns shows that the differences will work toward a single common purpose. Both these sections of the *Republic* reject the majority of Greek literature, both ban it from the good city, and both justify their censorship (at least in part) by spelling out that literature's effect on its audience. The differences between the two arguments may mean that certain poems will fail by the standards of one and not by the standards of the other. But such puzzle cases are inconsequential by comparison with the sameness of intent in both passages, namely to show that the great prize and pride of Athenian culture, far

*Table 2* Arguments against poetry

| | Books 2–3<br>377a–398b | Book 10<br>595a–608b |
|---|---|---|
| 1 Authors at fault | Homer (377d, 379d–e, 381d, 383a, 386c–387b, 388a–c, 389a, 390a–391b, 393a); Hesiod (377d,e); Pindar (381d, 408b); Aeschylus (380a, 383a); Sophocles (381d); tragedians as a group (394c–d, 408b). | Homer (595b, 598d, 599c–600e, 605c, 606e–607a); Hesiod (600d); tragedians as a group (595b, 598d, 605c). |
| 2 Audience susceptible to poetry | Children (377a–c), but also the adults of the city (378a, 380b–c, 383c, 386a, 391b). | Children too (598c), but mainly adults (604e, 605b), 'even the best of us' (605c). |
| 3 Problem with poetry | (1) Its falsehoods about the gods (377d–e, 379a); worse,<br>(2) Its bad effect on the guardians (378a, 386c, 387b–c, 388d, 391e). | (1) Poetic imitation is an inherently ignorant process (598c–601b, 602a–c); worse,<br>(2) It corrupts the soul (604d–606d). |
| 4 Bad effects of poetry | Disrespect for ancestors (378b, 386a); disunity among citizens (378c, 386a); laughter (388e); lamentation (387d–e, 388d); cowardice (381e, 386b, 387c); indulgence of appetites (389d–e). | Laughter (606c); lamentation (605c, 606a); indulgence of appetites (606d). |
| 5 Process of imitation | (1) The poet's impersonation of a character's way of speaking (393a–b, 395a);<br>(2) The actor's enactment of a character (396b). | (1) The painter's imitation of the appearance of an object (598b–c);<br>(2) The poet's impersonation of the appearance of a person's behavior (604d–e). |
| 6 Subjects of imitation | Human beings (392b, 393b–c, 395c–396d). | Human beings (604e, 605a–c). |
| 7 Bad effects of imitation in particular | Bad habit (395c–e). | Arousal of the low parts of the soul (605a, 606a–d). |
| 8 Permissible poetry | Imitations of the best men (396c–398b). | Hymns to the gods; imitation and celebration of the best men (604e, 607a). |

from conveying wisdom, delivered its teachings so confusingly as to accomplish more mischief and mystification than enlightenment.

Thus, two of the prima facie differences fail to translate into any practical inconsistency. Books 2–3 appear interested in excluding bits of specific poems, or at most certain genres, from the city, while Book 10 plunges into its argument without concern for such niceties; but in practice this difference will be negligible. Both passages censor nearly every line of Homer and nearly every word spoken on the stage. What does not offend Socrates in the earlier discussion with its dubious morality is banned for its imitative form. Aside from Book 10's concession to religious hymns, the two purges will leave the city with the same few scraps of poetry.

Truth and falsehood seem to matter more in Book 2, while Book 10 addresses the psychological effect of poetry. But as Socrates warms to his discussion of the young guardians' education in the earlier discussion, he makes clear that apparent untruth in a poet's tales of the gods and heroes only matters insofar as it corrupts the poem's hearers. Nor is the charge of untruth absent from Book 10, for the analogy between painting and poetry establishes the deep inevitability of poetic ignorance.

The two treatments do consider different audiences for poetry. Books 2–3 are meant to map out a new curriculum, so they dwell on how children hear poems. Even though the censorship that Socrates advocates for young guardians spreads to include all the city's residents, still one might accuse him of thinking of the adults *as* children, hence as incapable of grasping what poetry is doing to them.

But in Book 10 Socrates is wrestling with the more complex phenomenon of an educated, virtuous adult's response to sophisticated poetry. No simple warning about bad role models will do justice to that phenomenon, so Plato uses all the intellectual theories he has developed in the *Republic* to account for his harsh judgment of poetry.

This mention of the *Republic*'s technical theories leads to the lines of Table 2 describing imitation, the principal feature of poetry in both discussions. The two accounts belong to different worlds, and the predictions of the *effects* of imitation also differ. Whereas in one case imitation acts neutrally on its audience, in the other it is inherently inclined to produce bad effects. To put it another way, Books 2–3 identify a number of faults in existing poetry, but rather than blame poetry itself Socrates points the finger at the poets who have thus far written, the bad apples who spoil poetry for everyone else. Even imitation comes in for blame largely because it has thus far presented poor models to the young. Book 10 expects all imitation to go badly, as though by its nature it sought out those poor examples, as though imitation of good people were the oddity (see esp. 605a). Book 10 argues for two positions that Book 3 never thinks of suggesting:

(1) Imitation may be described not simply in terms of its literary form, but more deeply in terms of its epistemic status; it is the imitation of appearance.
(2) Imitation is naturally inclined to imitate bad people and appeal to bad parts of the soul; hence, poetry is not a neutral form that might hold any content, but tends to hold the worst sort.

These differences take us to the most difficult parts of Plato's aesthetics. For one thing, it is notoriously difficult to nail down what he means by *mimêsis*. 'Emulation,' which seems to have been its original primary sense, does not come close to covering the uses Plato puts the Greek word to. Nor does 'imitation,' nor does 'mimicry'; 'representation' is so vague that it translates the problem into English without settling it. In Book 3 alone, Plato stretches *mimêsis* to cover both a poet's creation of a believable character, and an actor's enactment of the character. In Book 10 the first imitator identified is the painter; when the subject changes to poetry, the imitator is no longer confined to drama. Plato's example becomes Homer, with the tragedians as his heirs.

In a broader sense, Book 10 refuses to approach imitation as Book 3 had; for while Book 3 is trying to define a term in order that the reader might recognize imitation, Book 10 assumes that the reader recognizes it, and sets out to explain what everyone has already seen.

The two developments in Book 10, the epistemological diagnosis of imitation and the claim of its inevitable depravity, depend on propositions about the Forms and the soul that Socrates argued for in the books between the two discussions. In Book 2 poets looked accidentally error prone when they talked about the gods; in Book 10 the error is built into their enterprise, thanks to what we have learned in the meantime about the physical world's susceptibility to equivocation. In Book 3, dramatic imitation threatened to mislead the young when it showed them inappropriate role models; in Book 10 we see the fascination with wicked characters as a natural aspect of poetic imitation, because Plato's psychological theory has prepared us to call any unphilosophical activity the work of a soul's nether regions.

Although Book 10 makes clear that Plato's warning about poetry requires his division of the soul into parts, that much psychological theory will not suffice. For in the course of his critique of art, Socrates assumes 'the calculating part in a soul' to do the work of weighing and measuring (602d–e). This assumption deviates from the original definition of reason, which had assigned to it only the work of calculating the relative worth of different desires (439c–d). Reason could take on the task of weighing and measuring only after it grew – implicitly in Book 5 and explicitly in 9 – from a simple overseer of the soul into a philosopher. The crucial premise ⑪, which granted reason its own desires, paved the way for the expanded conception of reason that Book 10 calls for.

But the changed face of reason does not settle questions about the psychology in Book 10. Unreason too is at work in this argument as it is not in earlier passages about the soul. On most traditional readings, Book 4 describes a three-part soul (although Chapter 5 considers rival interpretations of that section); some readers insist on a number much greater than three. Even deflationary interpretations question the real division of the soul in Book 4 but then concede that Books 8–9 see the soul as tripartite. And here, in the argument of Book 10, we find only two motivations relevant to poetry and imitation: reason, albeit in the expanded role it has had since Book 5; and something else, the other part, something lower in the soul.

To say that Book 10 draws on the psychological theory of Book 4, is therefore true as far as it goes, but only that far. Besides using the insight that the person is more than one, how does Book 10 use the *Republic*'s psychological theory to expand its argument about poetry?

Here is a proposal. When Book 10 looks back at preceding discussions of the soul, it might be looking not all the way back to the first appearance of psychology in the *Republic*, or to the revised depiction of reason a little after that, but only a few pages back to the comparison between best and worst lives, late in Book 9. The worst soul, the tyrannical type, is ruled by a single irrational principle, the extreme opposite to the philosophical soul in which reason reigns. The things the worst soul feeds on are illusory: Socrates calls them 'idols' and painted images (586b). The tyrant stands at a third remove from the oligarch, a soul that in turn stands third below the 'kingly man' (587c–d). Ten pages later Book 10 will rank the imitator third from the king and from the truth (597e, 602c). Book 9's concluding word against injustice in the soul combines the workings of a single low motivation with unreal appearances; since those are the telling features of the irrational soul in Book 10, it might prove profitable to ignore those separations between books and practice reading straight through from Plato's analysis of tyrannical souls (ruled by unreason, fed on illusion), to his appraisal of the poetic form that tyrants first established in Athens and that the *Republic* associates with tyranny (568a–d), the poetry that feeds illusions to its audience and fosters rule by illusion in their souls.

The errors inherent in imitation are also informed by the theory of knowledge that the *Republic* outlined between its two critiques. This is a matter of cognitive failings independent of the effect that imitation has on the soul. Whether we focus on the distinction between intelligible and visible objects (507b–c), or on the intellect's need to investigate further where the report of the senses proves self-contradictory (523a–524c), we find an opposition in place between better and worse understanding, with the former connected to the Forms and the latter to objects of unphilosophical experience. Any such opposition will license a condemnation of the arts, as long as Plato can claim that the fundamental artistic process always yields objects of the lower class. Here is where Book 10 relies on the picture of reality developed in the Divided Line (509d–511e). The Line ranks every object on the basis of whether it is an original or the image of an original. Copies of copies of Forms belong at the bottom of the Line. Because a host of similarities link the 'imitation' (*mimêsis*) of Book 10 to the 'image' (*eikôn*) of Book 7, the fate of art has been sealed as soon as Plato identifies imitation as its essential property. We might even say that by introducing the language of original and image into his explication of the Divided Line, Plato has left himself little work to do in Book 10: purposely produced copies could stand little chance in a system whose most opprobrious word is 'image.'

## HOW IS PLATO'S VIEW OF ART RELATED TO HIS VIEW OF BEAUTY?

One short dialogue, the *Hippias Major*, contains Plato's most sustained examination of beauty. Three features of the dialogue's argument capture the essence of all of Plato's discussions of the subject. (1) The beauty under investigation resembles the entities that Plato elsewhere calls Forms. Socrates asks Hippias about an abstract property that encapsulates the beauty seen in all beautiful things, and that makes those things beautiful (286d, 289d, 292c, 297b). (2) Beauty bears some relationship to the good, even though Socrates argues against equating the two (e.g., 296e ff., 303e ff.). (3) Both Socrates and Hippias cite artworks as examples of beautiful things, but never treat them as the central cases (290a–b, 297e–298a). The inquiry into beauty goes on at a distance from the inquiry into art.

### BEAUTY AND ART

The *Symposium* contains Plato's only other extended treatment of beauty, in the climax to Socrates' discourse on love. Diotima outlines the philosophical soul's erotic progression from one body to all bodies, then through all beautiful souls, laws, and kinds of knowledge, up to universal beauty (210a–211d). In all this talk of beauty, with its acknowledgment of beauty's varied manifestations, only two passing remarks suggest that artworks might be beautiful (209a, d).

Similarly, the *Philebus'* examples of pure sensual beauty explicitly exclude pictures, admitting only certain colors, simple shapes, and 'series of pure notes' (51b–d).

Meanwhile, when Plato speaks of the arts, he barely mentions beauty. The *Sophist* admits that some beauty exists in mimetic works, but only as a sign that those works are false representations, hence needing to be praised for reasons that have nothing to do with their truthfulness (235e–236a). More significantly, the *Republic*'s arguments against poetry contain several reminders that Plato does not want to associate it with beauty. The *Republic*'s first discussion of poetry censors poems that corrupt the young (377b–398b); yet soon we find Socrates insisting that young souls are trained by exposure to what is beautiful (401b–d; cf. 403c), as if they could not find beauty in poems. In Book 10 Socrates compares the sayings of poets to the attractive but not really beautiful faces of some young men when they lose the bloom of youth (601b). Poetry looks beautiful (602b) and exercises charm (601b), but without its language and rhythms it is plain. Beauty has attached itself accidentally to artworks.

What makes the divorce between art and beauty most frustrating is that at times it does not even seem to serve Plato's own purposes. The argument of Book 10 could have made productive use of some appeal to beauty. Plato wants to say not only that poetry is ignorant and misguided, but also that it seduces us into the same ignorance. He could have blamed the seductiveness of poetry on its beauty: so why is there no account of beauty in Book 10?

## THE FORM OF BEAUTY

Plato has no quarrel with beauty. The Form of beauty makes its greatest appearance in the *Symposium* (210d–212a), which does not even mention another Form. Philosophers meet this beauty in a mystical experience in which they both consummate their deepest love and attain the loftiest knowledge. Such elevation for beauty, however, prohibits it from sharing in art's shame.

Many passages in Plato claim that beauty has a Form (*Cratylus* 439c, *Euthydemus* 301a, *Laws* 655c, *Phaedo* 65d, 75d, 100b, *Phaedrus* 254b, *Parmenides* 130b, *Philebus* 15a, *Republic* 476b, 493e, 507b). Indeed Plato mentions beauty as often as any other intelligible property of things. He conceives of a beauty whose nature can be articulated without reference to the natures of beautiful particulars. Certain objects might be intrinsically beautiful (*Philebus* 51b), thanks to their proportion and unity (*Philebus* 64e,

66b, *Statesman* 284b, *Timaeus* 87c–d), but even these occurrences of beauty in the world of appearance do not gainsay that its grounds lie in the intelligible realm, where proportion and unity themselves get precise definitions.

Beauty is so often cited as the example of a Form because it fits perfectly into Plato's conception of Forms. In the first place, beauty is an evaluative term as much as justice and courage are, and it suffers as much as they do from disputes over its meaning. As the theory of Forms mainly exists to guarantee stable meanings for disputed evaluative terms, then if anything has a Form, beauty will.

Recall that a Form of $X$ differs from an individual $X$ thing in that $X$ may be predicated univocally of the former (the Form $X$ *is* $X$), only equivocally of the latter (the $X$ thing both is and is not $X$). One reason that beauty makes a perfect example of a property for which a Form exists is that Plato's explication of the ways that $X$ things are equivocally $X$ echo ordinary observations about beautiful objects. They fade. They require an unlovely detail, like a dissonant chord. People disagree about them. Objects lose their beauty outside their proper context (adult shoes on childish feet).

The ordinariness of these worries about beautiful things points to the second way in which beauty is a paradigm Form. Physical beauty inspires Platonic philosophizing more easily than other properties do. The *Republic* says that equivocally $F$ things bear signs of their own incompleteness, so that the inquisitive mind responds wanting to know more (523c–524b). But while large or unequal items, and drawings of triangles, might inspire minds that already have an abstract bent, beautiful things affect every soul. So do their inconstancy, complexity, and controversiality. Beautiful things attract our attention and remind us of their mystery as no other visible objects do, and in his optimistic moments Plato welcomes our attention to them.

Beauty's pedagogical effects make one reason for Plato's testimonies to its goodness and good consequences (*Laws* 841c, *Philebus* 66a–b, *Republic* 401c, *Symposium* 201c, 205e). They also explain the gulf between beauty and art. Beauty might lead its viewer into dialectics; art only misleads. No feature of the experience that artworks offer can serve as a bridge to philosophical knowledge. If the study of art were centrally about beauty, artworks would stand in Plato's system alongside just acts and wise laws: respectable in themselves, as far as ordinary people are concerned, and stimulations to higher knowledge. Since imitation inclines toward the quirky and grotesque (*Republic* 395d–396b, 605a), it lacks that defense.

## HOW CAN THE REJECTION OF POETRY BE SQUARED WITH PLATO'S OWN USE OF LITERARY DEVICES, MYTHS, AND IMAGES?

Some version of the question occurs to most readers of the *Republic*. Even as Plato banishes poetry, his plans for telling tales to the citizens find him smuggling poems back into town. Given the low place of images on the Divided Line, and given Book 10's hostility toward the arts, it ought to follow that the noble lie, the parable of the ship of state, the Allegory of the Cave, and the myth of Er remain excluded from philosophy. Plato's reliance on image, metaphor, and myth either dooms his philosophical enterprise, or demands an explanation why those tropes should not count as the kin of poetry.

Defending Plato requires finding a distinction between his literature and the poetry he is so eager to expel from his city. What stops the dialogues, or the myths and allegories in them, from being imitations of appearance? To say that Plato's imitations imitate reality rather than appearance is attractive but misguided. Book 10 argues that every artistic imitation, by its nature, imitates appearance alone. To say that a Platonic dialogue imitates only a good person (Socrates), with as little drama as possible, has some truth to it. But you don't have to look beyond the person of Thrasymachus to see that Plato can include hugely imperfect characters in his dialogues.

It may help to return to a question about Book 10: How do appearances differ from imitations of appearance? Poetry was said to possess 'charm' (601b, 607c). The *Republic* does not speak to where that charm came from, but its effect is clear enough: the defining characteristic of artistic imitations resides in their power to stop their audience from asking rational questions about them.

By comparison, images that are not works of art may or may not lead their viewers into inquiry. A mason or physicist will treat the triangular tile pattern on the floor as a visible and physical thing whose significant properties include mass, hardness, brittleness, and so on. A geometer will treat the same object as a visual aid for thinking about and demonstrating the properties of triangles. I may use my reflection in the mirror to see if my coat is on right (treating the reflection as a means to finding out about the thing reflected), or focus on the blemishes in the mirror's surface (in which case I ignore my coat). Mirrors and floor tiles do not determine a single response. Paintings and poetry do. Geometers who measured the dimensions of an object represented in a painting could be accused of misunderstanding the nature of painting, in a way that they could not be said to misunderstand floor tiles for treating them in the same way. Floor tiles, unlike artistic images, leave themselves receptive to rational inquiry. They allow themselves to be transcended, while artistic images make that transcendence impossible or unappealing.

For Platonic literature to stand apart from poetry, it has to leave itself receptive to inquiry. Plato tries to stop artistic imitation from working its effect, and thereby to reclaim control over the imitation. Artistic images produce a world of their own, an aesthetic domain in which the realities of life no longer hold, where only the internal principles of the painting, the melody, or the plot determine its details. Plato produces literary images that draw attention to their own inadequacy.

This can only be a hypothesis. I will content myself with pointing to two passages in the *Republic* designed to induce inquiry unseduced by the charms of imitation. As it happens, both passages are connected with astronomy – a nice coincidence, because the *Republic* understands astronomy as a study that can treat visible images either productively or unproductively, either as aids to solid geometry or enticements for the eyes (529d–e).

(1) In the myth of Er Socrates explains the structure of outer space (616b–617b). But rather than mention stars or planets, he describes eight concentric bowls mounted on a spindle; we understand these bowls to be the spheres in which first the stars, then the planets, then the sun and the moon all

revolve. To understand this description one must already know how to think about celestial bodies and their orbits in terms of their geometric properties. The more that my interest in the afterlife draws me into the myth, the more I am inspired to decipher this account of the heavens. My attraction to the myth and its images leads me to find the mathematical pattern behind it. So the myth of Er accomplishes what Socrates has said all studies of astronomy should. It describes the orbits of heavenly bodies in terms of solid geometry, rather than acknowledge their material natures. To dig into that myth is to improve one's powers of intellection.

(2) A passage from Book 7 serves a similar purpose. Glaucon praises astronomy for directing the soul 'upward' (529a), and Socrates rebukes him. Glaucon confused the upward drift of the soul in philosophical education with what is physically above (529a–c). Mindful of the misleading potential of metaphor, Socrates undercuts the image he has relied on, according to which greater abstraction corresponds to greater elevation. In reminding Glaucon that this is only a metaphor, Socrates thereby undercuts the Divided Line and Allegory of the Cave, both of which picture greater reality and clearer knowledge 'above' ordinary experience.

This exchange reminds the reader that metaphors are very well in their place, as shorthand for elaborate accounts or first descriptions of what a student will later grasp more fully. When they begin to deceive the student the images do more harm than good, and a teacher needs to discard them. The dialogues differ from poetry by reminding their audience that there is a higher tribunal than the literary imagination, that even the most vivid images need to yield to the progress of reason, that in the world Plato dreams of inhabiting every likeness of reality will meet the same fate, and human life will keep every other goal subservient to its achievement of the Good.

## ARISTOTLE ON PLATO AND POETRY

Certain points of emphasis in Plato's condemnation of poetry become clearer by contrast with Aristotle's equally sensitive and emphatic, and more powerful, *defense* of the poetic arts. Although Aristotle (uncharacteristically) hardly mentions his teacher's name in the *Poetics*, that work assembles a comprehensive answer to Plato's attacks; so that looking at the *Poetics* reveals what Aristotle thought the main points of those attacks were. And because Aristotle retains some of Plato's descriptions of poetry but rejects the antipoetic conclusions Plato drew from them, his argument shows the deepest legacy of Plato's aesthetic theory, namely the basic points about poetry that centuries' worth of critics agreed with, even if they rejected Plato's views.

## ARISTOTLE'S DEFINITION OF TRAGEDY

Early in the *Poetics* Aristotle defines tragedy, the genre that most occupies him, as

> the mimesis of a serious and complete action of some magnitude, in language that is embellished in various ways in its different parts, in dramatic form (not narrative), that achieves, by means of pity and fear, the catharsis of such passions.
>
> (*Poetics* 1449b24–28)

Some of these terms need to be explained before the definition makes complete sense. But it is not too early to say that three of the terms – catharsis, mimesis, action – join to produce the core argument of the *Poetics*. And all three bear on Aristotle's reply to Plato.

## CATHARSIS OF PITY AND FEAR

Aristotle's works say almost nothing about what catharsis is. The *Poetics* only offers the cryptic phrase in tragedy's definition, that tragedy aims at a catharsis of pity and fear. Aristotle's *Politics* says a bit more concerning catharsis and music, but how to apply that material to the *Poetics* and tragedy has proved controversial. What the definition of tragedy says about pity and fear reinforces Plato's vision of tragedy as an emotional tempest: the strategic presentation of characters and their adventures in tragedy will excite fear and pity to the highest pitch they can reach (1453a10). Heroes must be decent enough to earn a spectator's compassion, but not so fine that they don't deserve the misfortune that befalls them (1452b34–36), so that we may feel as much pity as possible.

Doesn't it feed the irrational part of the person, Plato asked, to get so stirred up about tragedy's heroes? Catharsis is Aristotle's answer. Whatever the process is, exactly, it incorporates the arousal of pity and fear that Plato spoke of into some beneficial ethical effect.

The Greek word *katharsis*, literally a 'cleaning,' lends itself to more than one natural interpretation, and traditionally Aristotle's modern readers took him to be describing what ancient Greek doctors called *katharsis*, which is a purgation (a laxative or enema). Tragedy flushes out unruly passions by letting them flow until one returns to a calmer, untroubled state.

This interpretation has generally been supplanted by a view of catharsis as clarification. On the dominant contemporary reading of Aristotle, the emotions that tragedy arouses are here to stay, not to be purged; they only need to be calibrated to fit the real-world situations that call them forth. One clarifies pity and fear by coming to see exactly what they feel like and what makes them appropriate. So catharsis is the understanding of pity and fear. When tragedy excites these passions by means of a simpler sequence of events than we find in real life, it teaches us about pity and fear. Plato is right to find strong emotions in tragedy. But where he concluded that those emotions overpower our ability to reason, Aristotle finds us reasoning about the emotions. Catharsis, understood as part of an adult's moral education, makes the difference between merely getting spectators worked up and setting them to work thinking about their emotional responses.

## MIMESIS

It is worth reiterating, because it gets forgotten, that Plato does not confine himself to condemning tragedy for its arousal of the passions. Several dialogues (*Apology, Ion, Protagoras*) accuse poetry of ignorance, falsehood, and fatal obscurity, without mentioning a single emotion. A thorough rebuttal of his aesthetics must likewise reach beyond matters of emotion, to the question of poetry's knowledge.

Aristotle's treatment of the knowledge in poetry begins with his un-Platonic account of imitation. Where Plato considered image-making an odd, even perverse activity, Aristotle calls it natural to human beings (1448b6), and moreover natural and pleasant because it is a way of learning (1448b13). He will not automatically condemn an image-maker for falsifying an object, since a falsely simplified image can help us learn about the original.

But Plato has no interest in any teaching that directs the human soul to scrutinize particular objects in the visible world. He may not deny that tragedy's audience undergoes some recognition; he only laments the particularity of the recognition. The painted bed of Book 10 (597d–598c) is as lowly an imitation as it is because the painter does not possess what the bed's user and maker both do (601c–602a), namely knowledge of beds in general. The look the painter's imitation has captured is the look of this one bed. But what is the good of bringing somebody to see what one bed looks like?

Because Aristotle's first remarks about mimesis speak vaguely of knowledge, without specifying whether it is knowledge of particulars or of universals, those comments only begin the task of rehabilitating mimesis. They do not yet constitute an answer to Plato's charge that poetry dwells among the idiosyncratic. Aristotle still needs to explain why what we recognize in a tragedy – at least in the best ones – enjoys the status of a general truth. So he adds, to his description of tragedy as mimetic, that it be the imitation *of an action* (1449b25, 36; 1450a15, b3).

## ACTION

Aristotle's exact claim is that tragedy represents events and not persons. Plot, not character, is the soul of tragedy. This claim turns out to mean that a good tragedy must contain a unified plot, a plot whose parts are properly connected to each other. Each incident must follow the one that preceded it, 'either necessarily or probably' (1451a13, 38; 1452a20). So a good plot rests on causal principles about human action (1455b1–3), and to grasp the sense of the plot – why the story turns out the way it does – is to recognize a general truth about how human beings behave. Poetry is therefore 'more philosophical than history' (1451b6).

Thus Aristotle's account of tragedy pivots on his claim that tragedy represents action. Plato took drama to represent persons (*Republic* 393b–c, 395c–d, 396c; 605a, c–d), an assumption that lent itself to his criticism of dramatic poetry as focused on particulars. Aristotle's insistence to the contrary, that tragedy is more a matter of plot than of character, therefore deprives Plato of a crucial anti-poetic premise, and paves the way for the claim that poetry has something to say and something to teach. Tragedy communicates knowledge that even philosophy must call legitimate.

# 13

## THE AFTERLIFE
## OF THE *REPUBLIC*

It would take a book or two to spell out the *Republic*'s place in the history of thought, and this chapter will not try to. But for the reader who wonders what happened next – who read the *Republic* and to what effect – this chapter can mark off the general territory, indicating where to look for more details.

Because the *Republic* was barely known in western Europe for almost a millennium, this chapter divides into an ancient story continuing down to 600 or 700 of our era, and a modern one that begins around 1484.

### PLATO IN LATER ANTIQUITY

What became of the *Republic* in the centuries after Plato's death is sometimes hard to say. The surviving evidence is spotty and sometimes contradictory. But scholars know a fair amount about Plato's general influence in antiquity: about the Academy and the different ways that institution represented his legacy; and about his indirect legacy through other schools, especially that of the

Stoics. Later, and mostly separate from Athenian schools of philosophy, come the philosophers now known as antiquity's Middle Platonists, and after them the neo-Platonists.

As the late ancient world became the early Christian world, Plato's influence had its most familiar effects. The theologians of early Christianity warmed to Plato more than they did to other Greek thinkers, and they adopted so many doctrines and arguments from his dialogues as to render Christianity itself the final ancient phase of Platonism. Nietzsche was sneering when he called Christianity 'Platonism for the people,' but not misrepresenting either the religion or the philosopher.

The story begins at home, which is to say Plato's home of Athens, in 347, when he is believed to have died at around the age of eighty. By then the Academy had been in existence for at least a few decades; his posthumous legacy began in that school, with Plato's friends and students.

The Academy may have been more a place for scholars to meet than a modern college with curriculum and designated lecturers. It is a sign of the paucity of our evidence that historians have to turn to Athenian comedy for clues about what the philosophers used to do. In one surviving fragment from the playwright Epicrates, Plato and his friends are debating the definition of a pumpkin. So perhaps (the reasoning goes), if this was the joke, then in real life the Academy was engaged in a project of defining plant and animal species.

The rest is still more obscure. Did the Academicians function as a religious group? That is debated. We know that a gymnasium had existed before Plato's time outside the city walls of Athens, named 'Academy' after a local hero. Plato bought land on the grounds of that gymnasium or very close to it and lived on that land, perhaps with colleagues. Scholars arrived to associate with Plato, and evidently young scholars came to learn from the senior figures – most famously Aristotle, a student of seventeen when he arrived around 367, and still in attendance (aged thirty-seven) at the time of Plato's death.

Besides the method of definition that comedy found it fun to parody, the doctrines that predominated in Plato's later years seem to have had less to do with the Forms known from the *Republic*, instead developing abstract principles of number. After Plato's death, number in general and specifically the Monad and Dyad (the One and Two, or the indefinite Two) must have figured large in Academic discussions. Aristotle's references to the Platonists in *Metaphysics* I.9 emphasize these principles out of proportion to the time that Plato's dialogues spend on them. Number might have been the ongoing research program that Plato's nephew Speusippus took over when he became the 'scholarch,' head of the school, after the death of his uncle. Then Xenocrates was head after him, and under Xenocrates the Academy began to systematize the tenets of Platonic philosophy.

Soon Platonism in Athens split into divergent legacies. Other schools were founded near the Academy, including the school of Aristotle's named after another gymnasium, the Lyceum; also the Stoa 'Porch' founded by Zeno, whose members would be known as Stoics; the school at the Cynosarges (yet another gymnasium) that produced the Cynics; and the Garden of Epicurus. Because Aristotle had studied at the Academy for decades, his school retained connections with Platonism, though the Lyceum rejected many Platonic doctrines, and it was Stoicism that most overlapped with the doctrines in Plato's dialogues. According to legend, the first Stoic, Zeno, had been inspired to begin his school when he read about Socrates. And for all its magnificent later developments in logic and epistemology, Stoicism always oriented itself around some principles of Socratic ethics: the pursuit of *eudaimonia* 'happiness,' control over the passions, and a clear distinction between soul and body. Because these features of Socratic ethics received their first explicit formulation in Plato's dialogues, it is not tendentious to call Plato the ancestor to Stoicism.

Socrates also inspired the Cynics, though in this case it seems to have been some mixture of Socrates as Plato portrays him and the Socrates his friends knew. The Cynics especially loved the unconventional and charismatic free spirit (though indeed most admirers of Socrates, including the Christians later, were drawn at least partly to his willingness to reject mores). Plato would have been acknowledging his ties to Cynicism, as well as distancing himself from that group, if he truly said the words that one ancient story attributes to him, that the most famous of the Cynics, Diogenes of Sinope, was 'a Socrates gone mad.'

With Stoicism appropriating the inspiring hero Socrates together with systematized ethical principles from the Platonic dialogues, it could become a rival to the Academy. Not coincidentally, as the prestige of Stoicism grew, the Academy (which was now being run by Arcesilaus and Carneades) went back to the dialogues for a fresh look and distinguished itself from Stoicism. This time the official Platonists found special inspiration in the example of Socrates the cross-examiner, the brilliant negative spirit who mocked intellectual pretensions as he shredded other people's beliefs. During this period the Academy (sometimes called the Skeptical Academy) developed no systematic theories of reality or virtue; rather they dissolved philosophical doctrines in the critical spirit that they understood as the true Socratism. Even as Stoicism constructed an epistemology containing claims of great certainty, the Academy undid comforting certainties in the name of permanent skepticism.

The period from the death of Alexander the Great until Rome conquered all Greek-speaking lands (and became an empire) is called the Hellenistic period. In this period, which lasted nearly 300 years, the Greek language became common in the eastern Mediterranean, and philosophy written in Greek grew into a powerful cultural force. Newer schools of thought eclipsed the traditions founded by Plato and Aristotle: Stoicism and Epicureanism of course, but also Skepticism of several varieties, and the anarchic Cynics. The original Academy apparently came to an end in the first century BC, although philosophical Platonists continued to study and teach in Athens even when there was no more Academy. During this same century the writings of Plato and Aristotle again grew popular. This period, from late Hellenistic times into the early centuries of the Roman Empire, is the time of the philosophers retrospectively referred to as the Middle Platonists. Needless to say they would never have called themselves such a thing; but they fit historically between the Platonism practiced in the Academy that Plato had founded and the very different doctrine that would develop later, a longer-lasting and more famous school of thought known as neo-Platonism.

Although the Middle Platonists did not band together or form a school, they shared a commitment to understanding Plato as a systematic philosopher with a set of positive doctrines. Plutarch is the best known of this group, which also includes Posidonius and Antiochus of Ascalon, significant because he would later be Cicero's teacher. Some authorities also include Philo of Alexandria, a prolific and original philosopher and one of the first Jews to be prominent in classical Greek-speaking philosophy: Philo's works sought to make Platonic philosophy compatible with the Biblical books of Moses. In general the Middle Platonists emphasize the ethical doctrines in Plato and play down political theory, as other ancient readers would do after them. And they emphasize one strand in Platonic ethics and psychology that the neo-Platonists and Christians will make much of, though it plays a negligible role in modern Platonic studies: the soul's divinity.

Neo-Platonism made its first prominent appearance in the third century AD. Compared to Middle Platonism it amounts to a new start at reading Plato, or as some say a bold new misreading of his dialogues. Neo-Platonism flourished in several regions of the Roman Empire, often stronger in different parts at different times. First and most notably it appeared in Rome, in the third century; then Syria in the century after that; in the fifth and sixth centuries, Athens and Alexandria. Plotinus in Rome was an early neo-Platonist and almost single-handedly defined the school, though by all accounts he did not invent it. Other major names include Porphyry the student of Plotinus; Iamblichus in Syria; and Proclus the last great voice of neo-Platonism, who taught in Athens at what seems to have been a new version of the Academy, founded shortly before his arrival in Athens in the 400s. The new Academy, a neo-Platonic institution, survived until the year 529, when the Byzantine emperor Justinian closed all non-Christian schools of philosophy in Athens.

(Rome had fallen in the preceding century, and politically speaking it was Rome's collapse that signified the end of antiquity. But Justinian is said to have brought antiquity to an intellectual end when he closed the schools of Athens.)

The historian of philosophy who studies neo-Platonism dwells on its complex effort to synthesize Platonic and Aristotelian philosophies. But to readers who come to these works with less expertise, neo-Platonism creates the impression of grand abstract principles related to one another through mysterious processes such as 'overflow' or emanation. The One emanates Mind, which then emanates Soul. Neo-Platonism develops the side of Plato expressed in the *Republic* by the comparison between the sun and the Good, and by the mapped-out Divided Line. To the modern reader this all sounds 'metaphysical' in the popular sense of that word: theological, mystical, and at the same time highly organized, concerned to identify the boundaries between all the spiritual beings and states of existence.

The cross-examinations of Socrates are a long distance away from neo-Platonism's concerns. These readers do not seem to have noticed the memorable characters populating the dialogues, or the details that locate Socratic conversations in real-life Athens. And as far as the *Republic* is concerned, political thought – at least at first glance – seems to have secondary importance to the neo-Platonists. They honor ethics, but theirs (like the ethics of many Middle Platonists) is a spiritualized code of life that orients the soul toward its disembodied existence and makes the soul a divinity. Plotinus called the contemplative soul's liberation from this world 'the flight of the alone to the Alone' (*Ennead* 6.9.11), which locates the soul's true home in another realm of being at the same time that it stresses the solitary preparations the soul must undertake while visiting in the world of matter and sensory experience.

Despite the hostility of many neo-Platonists toward the new religion that they saw growing up around them, in fact neo-Platonism was a philosophy that early Christianity learned from and put to productive use. By the time the Emperor Constantine made Christianity legal throughout the Empire in 313, the dominance that neo-Platonism had achieved over other philosophies, together with its suitability to Christianity, led to a fertile exchange between the two systems of thought – so the strongest and longest effect that Plato has had on the history of thought probably comes through Christianity.

The congeniality between Platonism and Christianity has to do with their common otherworldliness. Especially as read by the neo-Platonists, the dialogues express piety toward a moralizing religion, sometimes a disapproving regulation of sexuality, the promise of life after death. These beliefs appear in other religions and ethical systems too. But looking into the details of the similarities shows how specific the connection could be.

Consider the ineffability of the divine: Plato's dialogues contain passages, much amplified by the neo-Platonists, that impose limits on what human beings can know and say about God or gods. In the *Phaedrus* Socrates denies that any mortal can describe the area above heaven (247c); the *Republic*'s placing the Good 'beyond being' (509b) likewise suggests the *negative theology* that would become a powerful theme in Christianity as well as in Judaism and Islam. Because God's positive attributes exceed what human beings can comprehend, even respectful adjectives distort and falsify; better to say *'un*limited,' *'in*visible,' *'un*caused,' and so on. What these negative descriptions lose in specificity they gain in truth, and they will not distract the embodied soul, which always tries to visualize God's attributes with concepts drawn from sense experience.

Otherworldliness also meant division between the soul and the body. Here again the philosophers of antiquity emphasized a theme one can find in the *Republic* as well as other dialogues, that the soul not only differs from the body, not only exists apart from it, but is even divine. Recall the closing pages of Book 9, in which Socrates calls reason 'divine' (589c–d, 590d). In Book 10 Socrates promises that the gods will not neglect the person who tries to become like a god by behaving virtuously, to the extent that human beings can reach that goal (613a–b; see 383c, 500c–d, 501b–d). Other Platonic passages include *Theaetetus* 176a–b, which urges human beings to escape the world by becoming 'like a god.'

To atheists the divinization of human souls sounds like an extravagance of emptiness, attaching the nonexistent property of divinity to those nonexistent things called souls. Many adherents to monotheistic religions will say that such a claim is blasphemous. But the Middle Platonists and neo-Platonists certainly found the divinization of the soul in the dialogues and prized the doctrine, and early Christian theologians found something similar in Biblical claims about humans being 'gods' (John 10:38, quoting Psalm 82:6) or children of God (John 1:12, 1 John 3:2), and participating in the divine nature (1 Corinthians 15:53, 2 Peter 1:4).

Aristotle, by comparison, denied the soul's immortality and God's creation of the universe. His ethics mostly do not honor human attempts to become divine; more generally his ethics are not radical about social convention as the ethical theories are that are more directly influenced by Socrates. In different ways the Stoics and Cynics especially would demonstrate their unconcern for mere social convention. The newly legal Church still saw itself at odds with the ways of the Greek and Roman world, hence unconventional, and would have felt less at home with Aristotelian thought. Finally Aristotle's reputation for precise definitions, and as the first expositor of logic, probably earned him more suspicion than respect from the early Church, which faced repeated crises over heresies brought on (or so it must have seemed to the Christians) by excessive logic-chopping.

Platonism did change when it became Christian. It had already changed when neo-Platonism highlighted some themes in the dialogues and muted others; and again before that, when the Stoics made Socrates their founding hero seeking to duplicate his virtuous self-control. The details surrounding many of these transformations have disappeared. Looking back on the 900 years that passed between Plato's founding of his Academy and the day the last Athenian schools were closed, we can make out some moments clearly, most of the rest remaining a jumble. This inconsistency in our information is almost worse than not knowing anything, because it makes the works and philosophers that do survive appear more significant than they might have been in reality. But it is safe to say that the ancient world took three broad points, or areas of emphasis, from the Platonic dialogues:

(1)  A priority to evaluative issues within philosophy: individual morality, public justice, worldly and otherworldly beauty. Moral and political principles are fixed, not merely social or legal constructs, and one can hope to ground them in truths about the human soul.

(2)  A temptation toward ambitious metaphysical speculations: Form, number, ratio. One can hope to map out the domains of the unseen world, and often the logical theories

about these abstractions merge into mythological descriptions of other planes of being.

(3) A practice of logical question and answer: definition, refutation. One seeks rigorous explanations for the vague concepts so often talked about; sometimes hoping for newfound clarity in those concepts, sometimes to humble those who pretend to possess knowledge, sometimes to show that all human knowledge is impossible.

Of the three, (1) is always present to some degree, although some philosophers stressed the psychological foundation of ethics in the soul and others stressed moral practice. Ethics sometimes includes political philosophy, sometimes not (as the next section will discuss further). The other two features of Platonism work against one another, some philosophers inclining toward excess of metaphysical system and others toward universal negative arguments. Although it seems obvious to us today that some ancient readings come closer to what the dialogues really say than others do, none of the ancient versions of Platonism should be stigmatized as a perversion of Plato's thought, because all three features of Platonism find some justification in the dialogues.

This is not to say that 'you can make Platonism be whatever you want.' Some interpretations really do fit the dialogues more accurately than others. But the Platonic corpus stands out among philosophical bodies of work for containing a variety of topics, claims about those topics, and methodological approaches to philosophy at the same time that a recognizable philosophical voice runs through all the dialogues. A philosophy that was easier to pin down would probably not have remained so compelling for nine centuries and more of ancient thought.

And even though some inheritors of the Platonic legacy refused to agree that they shared a philosophical pedigree with certain others – picture a Platonic Skeptic rolling his eyes at some neo-Platonist's exuberant speculation – the fact is that a significant common core unites them all: Socratic independence of mind, Plato's optimism about the power of reason to guide a life, and throughout a dissatisfaction with things and thoughts as they are.

## THE *REPUBLIC* IN LATER ANTIQUITY

The *Republic* contains all three elements associated with Platonism. This is one reason that readers today give the dialogue the special place it has. Modern readers want to identify a single work as a given author's masterpiece, and a dominant modern conception of the masterpiece is the work that contains all of the author's signature characteristics. The *Republic* fits the bill for Plato better than any other dialogue.

In antiquity, many Platonists paid more attention to the *Timaeus*, because that is the dialogue that speaks of 'first things': how the universe came into existence, what the world's most basic particles are. Those readers would have valued the foundational work over the most characteristic one.

But again, if you do want a dialogue that represents Plato in the round, there is nothing like the *Republic*. Book 1 features Socrates the master of cross-examination who leaves no beliefs standing. Platonic speculation appears in the images of the Good in Book 6 and in Book 10's astronomical afterlife. And no other work of Plato's spells out the connection between the moral and the political as completely as the *Republic*, or the way that both the moral and political orders rest on psychological theory. The Stoics would have seized on the dialogue's individual-centered ethics and its promise of happiness regardless of external circumstances (Books 4, 9); but the *Republic* also specifies its political proposals (Books 5–7), as if human happiness called for the correct external circumstances.

The *Republic*'s compendious nature makes it even harder to trace its influence through antiquity. Some Platonisms only need to be stated to give away their debt to a distinctive dialogue like the *Philebus*, *Timaeus*, or *Symposium*; but if every type of Platonism can find a home in the *Republic*, the expression of one type rather than another does not prove that its author had read the *Republic*.

To add to the trouble, Plato's readers in antiquity and the early Middle Ages did not distinguish his dialogues from one another as modern scholars do. An ancient author might attribute a view to Plato that comes half from the *Euthyphro*, half from the *Meno*.

Some specific evidence does come down from the centuries after Plato – some of it already from the generation that succeeded him in the Academy. It is fairly clear that the Academics read the *Republic* despite emphasizing a metaphysical theory different from the one argued for in that dialogue, and despite identifying themselves more with the *Timaeus*. Crantor wrote the first known commentary on any Platonic dialogue, some fifty years after Plato's death, and it was about the *Timaeus*; on the other hand we know that Speusippus – the first scholarch after Plato – wrote dialogues of his own, one of them titled *Cephalus*. That name appears in other dialogues too, but its most obvious association is with the *Republic*.

At around the time of Speusippus, Philippus of Opus is said to have written the *Epinomis*, an appendix to Plato's *Laws*. The content of the *Epinomis* draws on the *Laws* but also on the *Republic*, thus attesting to Philippus' familiarity with both works. And the philosopher Heraclides of Pontus, who probably came to study at the Academy toward the end of Plato's life, wrote a dialogue *On the Woman Who Had Stopped Breathing*, whose title character comes back to life to report what she saw while wandering in the afterlife, much as Er does in the *Republic* after leaping up off his own funeral pyre.

Aristotle is a special case. Naturally he belongs in the first generation to succeed Plato. Volumes of his writings survive, and they show how closely Aristotle had studied his teacher's works. But the very size of his corpus creates interpretive difficulties that do not arise for brief statements of the form we have about other philosophers, e.g. 'This philosopher wrote two dialogues called the *Republic*.' Moreover, Aristotle tends to read all his predecessors with an eye to where their views led to his and in what way they failed to achieve the complete theory that he worked out. Aristotle read Plato, as he read everything, with his mind on his own philosophy.

Without doubt Aristotle did read the *Republic*. He devotes a section of his *Politics* (II.1–6) to the political reforms associated with Book 5. Some Platonic arguments for Forms, perhaps including arguments from the *Republic*, are touched on in Aristotle's barrage of counterarguments in *Metaphysics* I.9. More obliquely, Aristotle's theory of soul in *De Anima* rejects Platonic claims argued for in the *Republic* (and elsewhere), but also contains a new three-part classification of souls that broadly evokes the *Republic*'s tripartite psychology. And Aristotle's *Poetics*, while barely mentioning Plato, returns to tragedy and *mimêsis* – Platonic topics specially connected with the *Republic* – to develop a new and favorable treatment of poetry. In fact the *Poetics* reads as a response to the challenge Socrates poses in Book 10, when he invites the lovers of poetry to defend her with prose arguments (607d).

The *Nicomachean Ethics* alludes to the *Republic* at countless points. The argument from human function with which Socrates silences Thrasymachus in Book 1 of the *Republic* reappears in new form in *Nicomachean Ethics* I.7, though it is still designed to show that virtue is natural for human creatures. The *Nicomachean Ethics* defines the virtues, dwells on the special case of justice, considers what combination of ethical theory and good habit best engenders virtue, sometimes teeters between conceiving human reason as practical guide to action and envisioning its highest calling as philosophical contemplation. These are of course the *Republic*'s ethical concerns. And yet the answers and approaches could not be more different. The *Nicomachean Ethics* best illustrates what the other Aristotelian works just mentioned also show, that Aristotle knew the *Republic* intimately, and that it identified many topics he took up as philosophically significant, usually serving as the esteemed opponent against which he could define his own views.

Of all these points of contact between Aristotle and the *Republic*, his critique of its political proposals is the most specific, but it promises a later influence for the *Republic* and debate over its politics that scarcely took place. Modern readers, for whom the *Republic*'s political proposals are the most relevant to contemporary issues (thus the debate over whether Plato was a totalitarian), need to bear in mind that ancient readers would have had the contrary response, finding nothing *less* relevant in it than its politics. This is because the *Republic* assumes the unit of political organization to be the *polis*, the freestanding city that functioned as an independent state. In Plato's time Greece contained hundreds of such cities, and Aristotle in the subsequent generation argued that they ought to be seen as the goal of political development. But the autonomous Greek *polis* disappeared as a political possibility during Aristotle's lifetime, thanks to Philip II of Macedon who defeated the Greek cities at Chaeronea soon after Plato's death. By the time of Aristotle's own death his former student Alexander, Philip's son, had conquered vast areas to the east and south, unifying them into a new kingdom to which the *polis* ideal was irrelevant. The subsequent centuries, in which Athens and most other Greek cities belonged to the large Macedonian kingdom, and then again later when Rome had conquered that kingdom, were times of less enthusiasm for a theory of the finest stand-alone city. What could the fantasy of a *polis* matter to Hellenistic or Roman political realities?

At least on the standard story of late ancient thought, the disappearance of the political entity that Plato considered essential to political philosophy steered philosophers away from debates over forms of constitution, or the state's relationship to the family. Cities continued to exist, but their power and their range of activity could not compare to what they had been in the old days, when Athens sailed hundreds of ships over the Aegean, or Sparta negotiated its own treaties with the Persian Empire. So Plato's readers, and specifically the philosophers who studied the *Republic*, were less likely to respond to the dialogue as a whole, structured around its quest for a most excellent city. They might address the *Republic*'s account of the soul, its promises concerning virtuous life, or its metaphysics of the Good.

It helps the *Republic*, in this connection, that its contents permit an 'apolitical' reading that would be impossible for Plato's *Statesman* or *Laws*. As this book has emphasized, the *Republic* mainly holds to its double argument of soul and city. The extended analogy permits readers who are wary of the politics to translate the *Republic*'s conclusions into statements about the soul.

The Socratic legacy, which ancient philosophers continued to honor, would have reinforced the apolitical reading of the *Republic* that one finds among the Middle Platonists and some neo-Platonists. Socrates set the example of personal responsibility; virtue no matter what the laws said. Plato's ancient readers would have wanted to keep this Socratic ideal alive as they studied the longest dialogue in which Socrates speaks.

Finally the *Republic* can be read as endorsing two claims that undermine its political argument. (1) There is the premise, noted above (p. 270), of the wise person's becoming godlike. The human being who achieves this better-than-human condition will not profit from living in a good city; so political philosophy matters only to the lives of those lesser beings still a long way down from divinity. (2) Even if a human does not become divine, the *Republic* can be read as promising happiness to the virtuous *under all circumstances*. The Middle Platonists and many Stoics did read the argument this way, as promising *not* that virtuous people will be happier than vicious people when placed in the same circumstances, rather that *regardless of external conditions the just are happy*. The former reading, the *comparative* promise of happiness, is a plausible claim, but it could still leave people needing good cities to live in. If the *Republic* espouses an *absolute* promise of happiness, it denies the need to live under a just regime. If virtuous people can be happy in a tyranny, reformers have less reason to do away with tyranny. Bad people and those of middling morals might still prefer life in the best city, but those are not the groups that political thinkers most want to provide for. That first and most persistent element in Platonism, its concern for a steadfast moral order grounded in psychological nature, is represented in its narrower form as individual morality.

Zeno the founder of Stoicism continues our historical sequence after Aristotle, probably coming to Athens in the generation after Aristotle died. Zeno wrote a work of his own titled the *Republic*; it has not survived, but it seems to have been a response to Plato's dialogue. Certainly the longest existing passage from Zeno's *Republic* alludes to Plato a great deal. This passage seems to emphasize the acquisition of moral virtue, not the necessity of political institutions, as if Zeno had already begun – soon after the year 300 BC – turning the *Republic* into a text on individual morality.

Some controversy does surround such claims about Zeno. (Many claims are controversial regarding authors from this period whose works exist in such tatters.) In Zeno's case it is sometimes argued that his *Republic* advocates utopian politics but that the influential Stoic Chrysippus, one generation later, set Stoicism on the path it was to follow, focused on the personal virtue of individuals to the exclusion of politics. Either way, Stoicism did not pursue the politics in Plato's *Republic.* The astonishing thought is that the Stoics might have begun, as an institution, by silencing the politics in the *Republic*, even in the midst of a close engagement with it.

Roughly speaking, as Stoicism declined in importance during the third and fourth centuries of our era, neo-Platonism ascended. Being as it was the ancient school of thought most associated with asceticism and withdrawal from 'the world,' neo-Platonism might be expected to carry on the Stoic and Middle Platonist emphasis on the soul and individual morality to the exclusion of political thought. This has long been the standard view of neo-Platonism, though some scholars argue that it was a more capacious body of knowledge than the stereotype implies, that it was capable of honoring both the Platonic quest to improve the soul, even up to divine status, *and* the *Republic*'s proposals for improving the city. In that case there would be no bar to the neo-Platonists' reading the *Republic*, nor any special inclination on their part to read it with apolitical selectiveness.

The Roman neo-Platonists refer to the *Republic* the most often. Plotinus repeatedly quotes a phrase about 'habituation and practice' that appears in the *Republic* (518e), and the writings of his student Porphyry and the later Macrobius show them to be familiar with the dialogue too. Porphyry wrote a now lost commentary on the *Republic*; Macrobius wrote a commentary on Cicero's *Dream of Scipio* – a text that is itself based on the myth of Er – and his commentary frequently cites the *Republic* in explicating Cicero.

Those words that Plotinus chose to repeat are telling. He seems to be following the *Republic* in believing that the soul benefits when it acquires political virtues, which is to say the virtues expressed in society and instilled by good laws. A good city's laws can initiate the process of restraining desires; thus the laws foster self-control, bringing the soul further along toward virtue. This is politics for the sake of ethics, to be sure, with ethics understood as psychic harmony or balance. Plotinus continues to read the highest good as the attainment of divine contemplative virtue in the soul. Nevertheless his interest in laws points to the false dichotomy that is at work in simple oppositions between ethics and politics, for example in the belief that divine souls would have no need of well-run cities. For if you believe that a sound constitution can make citizens more virtuous, then even those best contemplative souls ascending to godliness will want to live in a good city. And for most people it is the good city that will launch them on the long journey that ends with the alone's flying to the Alone.

The Roman Emperor Gallienus was fond of Plotinus, and with his encouragement Plotinus tried to found a new city, Platono-polis, run according to Platonic principles (Porphyry, *On the Life of Plotinus* 12). He had to abandon the project, as Plato had abandoned practical politics before him, so we have no way of knowing whether the principles he sought to bring to life came from the *Republic* or the *Laws*. But the anecdote shows that Plotinus did not despise philosophizing about politics. And given that he knew the *Republic*, his willingness to engage with political questions meant he took the dialogue on as a whole: the religious mysticism in the story of Er, the super-metaphysics of the Good beyond being, but also the training of philosophers and soldiers who could run a happy commonwealth.

Away from Rome it is sometimes hard to say which neo-Platonists read the *Republic*, or how much they emphasized it among the dialogues – let alone what they made of it. A few odd facts stand out, for instance regarding the school of Iamblichus. This collection of Syrian neo-Platonists read Plato at length and assigned their students an exclusive diet of Platonic dialogues, organized by subject matter. But the *Republic* does not appear on the list. For their introduction to political philosophy the students read Plato's *Gorgias* instead.

And oddly, something similar is said to have happened in Athens in the following century; for the anonymous work *Prolegomena to Platonic Philosophy* says that Proclus removed the *Republic* from his curriculum because it was not written 'in dialogue' (26.6–7). And yet Proclus wrote a commentary on the *Republic*!

Surely this last fact is more relevant. Neo-Platonic commentaries should count for more than anecdotes from scattered countries. And here the evidence testifies to the *Republic*'s popularity. We know of some twenty commentaries that the neo-Platonists wrote on individual dialogues, although often only their titles have survived. Of those twenty a full five were on the *Republic*, including the commentaries by Porphyry and Proclus. The Platonists of late antiquity did not neglect this work.

A final example comes from the later neo-Platonism that had become Christian. A shadowy figure, pseudo-Dionysius the Areopagite, writing around the year 700, spelled out the hierarchy for an idealized Christian church. His ecclesiastical structure seems to have taken the *Republic*'s good city and translated it into Christian clerical terms, so that the Church is now the city brought to earth. Pseudo-Dionysius is a completely unknown figure, and it is impossible to say whether he read the *Republic* or only other authors' synopses of it. But either way, some philosophers after the fall of Rome, and after the end of the Athenian schools, were still reading the *Republic* as a plan for a political order.

Outside the official schools of thought, the *Republic* makes appearances throughout antiquity. A few examples indicate how commonly the dialogue turned up, and how varied the contexts were that it appeared in.

One of the earliest anecdotes (if only we could know it to be true) concerns one of the several women who were said to have studied with Plato. Axiothea of Phlius, a small city near Corinth, supposedly read the *Republic* and moved to Athens to join the Academy, where she disguised herself as a man. The point seems to be that Axiothea was inspired by learning of the women guardians in the good city, which implies it was the *Republic*'s political program that had gripped her. Unfortunately although Axiothea was an early figure, the statement that she read the *Republic* comes from much later, in the fourth century AD, and does not prove anything about how the dialogue was known or how widely it was read in Plato's time. It might be a wry look back, with the suggestion that Plato ran his own school more conservatively than he wanted future philosophers to run the city: the *Republic* wants sexual difference out in the open for all to see, but in the Academy a woman had to wrap herself up as a man. And if the anecdote reflects more on the time in which it was written than on the time of Axiothea herself, it could be a later slap at Platonic politics, a kind of reminder to its audience about why not to take the *Republic*'s politics so seriously.

The Hellenistic historian Polybius lived a couple of centuries after Plato. His work *Histories* contains a sustained and serious discussion of political constitutions, and how one type of constitution transforms itself into another (Book 6). His own argument in favor of a mixed form, a constitution with both democratic and oligarchic elements, resembles parts of Aristotle's *Politics*, not anything in Plato. So it is all the more noteworthy that Polybius follows Plato's lead as a theorist of history. Polybius wants to explain how one constitution becomes another, and for causal principles he looks to *Republic* Book 8. He pinpoints *phthonos* 'malicious envy' as one of the operant forces behind the constitutional decline, as the *Republic* also does (and Plato's *Menexenus* too).

Writing some centuries after Polybius, within the first few hundred years AD, is Pseudo-Longinus, as he is called because nothing is known for certain about his name except that it was not Longinus. This author's work *On the Sublime* – more accurately *On Elevation*, as in 'high style' – describes the characteristics of fine writing. Pseudo-Longinus quotes from the *Republic*, and that would not be surprising for a book about the literary arts, except that he is interested in Plato as an example of elevated writing not as an authority about aesthetics. In fact *On the Sublime* contains antiquity's most unforgettable assessment of Plato as author, saying his life was an ongoing struggle to outdo Homer (13.4).

A bit after Pseudo-Longinus, Constantine ruled the Roman Empire. In the year 336 the bishop and scholar Eusebius wrote a tribute to him, *Praise of Constantine*, that drew on the *Republic* to portray the Emperor as a Platonic philosopher-king. Constantine of course had legalized Christianity – that is why a bishop would praise him – but one generation later the Empire was ruled by his nephew Julian, who tried to turn back the clock and reinstate Roman religion and culture at Christianity's expense. For this reason Christians call Julian 'the Apostate,' but he is also known as 'Julian the Philosopher' because of his extensive and enthusiastic studies. Julian immersed himself in neo-Platonism, using the Syrian philosopher Iamblichus as his guide. In his speech *The Sovereign Sun* Julian plays up the *Republic*'s analogy between the sun and the Good; he portrays himself as one who, having glimpsed that Good, now strives to serve the welfare of the Empire's people.

This is of course just what the Allegory of the Cave commands philosophers to do.

Here are two writers from the same century, one of them a Christian and the other Christianity's enemy, both finding their words for a ruler's enlightenment in the same Platonic dialogue. Because they are both figures of the court, it would be reckless to treat Eusebius and Julian as ordinary citizens who'd stumbled over a bit of Plato. Their positions would have made them look for Plato's political vision. Still they did find it. The *Republic*'s politics were available to its late ancient readers. That the dialogue also served as a theory of history to Polybius, and a sample of elevated writing to Pseudo-Longinus, suggests how many approaches to it were available to its audience in the eight or nine ancient centuries after Plato wrote it.

## THE *REPUBLIC* IN MODERNITY

Because western Europe passed through the Middle Ages mostly lacking Plato's works, the plot thins considerably for some centuries. Some Christian thinkers in the Byzantine Empire, such as pseudo-Dionysius, still took their inspiration from the neo-Platonists' Plato; and with the rise of Islam came Muslim readers of the years 900–1200. But even the energy and expertise of Muslim scholarship show the relative decline in Plato's influence, for the principal figures of this time tended to be Aristotelian philosophers.

The *Republic* occupies a place in Islamic philosophy that anticipates modern receptions of it. Al-Farabi, 'the founder of Islamic political philosophy', oriented his own philosophy toward Aristotle, especially regarding logic. But his political thought is inspired much more by Plato's *Republic* than by Aristotle's *Politics.* The great later philosopher Ibn Rushd, known in the West as Averroes, even more dramatically made an exception for the *Republic.* Averroes read Aristotle extensively, producing commentaries or synopses of Aristotle's works and most notably of his logical writings. Even when the subject was ethics, Averroes chose the *Nicomachean Ethics* as his subject. But when he wrote about political philosophy he passed over the *Politics* – if indeed that book was available to him – instead producing a commentary on Plato's *Republic.*

By this time, approaching the year 1200, all the generalizations about late antiquity seem to have been reversed. Aristotle is the preeminent figure for philosophers; of Plato's works, the *Republic* is read more widely than any other dialogue; and it is read as a work of political philosophy.

The Christianized, Latin-speaking western Europe did not simply follow Arab-speaking philosophers, though there is no doubt that Europe learned from them. And if Plato dominated Christian education as late as the year 500, some centuries later (around 1200 or 1300) it was Aristotle who did. Most of Plato's works simply did not exist in the West. The great leap in his availability to a Latin-speaking world came in 1484, when Marsilio Ficino published his complete Latin translation of the dialogues.

In the 500 years since Ficino's translation, the dialogues have been widely read and variously interpreted, both by experts in philosophy and classics and by general readers in most countries. This is not to say that currents of Platonism resurface in the modern world. People read the *Republic* without coming under its influence in anything like the way that Zeno or Plotinus came under its influence in antiquity. If anything the contrary is true about modern philosophy, that Plato tends to inspire rejection not agreement. It would not even be too hard to classify all modern thinkers as anti-Platonists of some stripe, categorizing them on the basis of which Platonic tenets they most insist on refuting. To paraphrase Alfred North Whitehead's respectful tribute, if philosophy has consisted of footnotes to Plato, they have been the kinds of footnotes that begin 'Yes, but … ' or 'This has now been disproved.'

As for the *Republic* in particular, probably a cluster of reasons explain its modern role as representative Platonic dialogue. It is Plato's second-longest work, much longer than the next in length. It ranges over a variety of philosophical areas, giving voice to all the essential features of Platonism. And it must be relevant that the *Republic* addresses the topics that appeal most to modern philosophical tastes. For in many cases, modern readers have not turned to Plato seeking discussions of the same themes that mattered in antiquity. Philosophers of history do not see historical change taking place as the *Republic* describes (and this was especially true when modern thinking about history was dominated by the anti-Platonic expectation of steady progress). The impulse toward skepticism is powerful in modern philosophy; but modern skeptics have not found their inspiration or their arguments in Plato. At the opposite extreme, speculative philosophy inclining toward mysticism has become all but impossible in philosophy, certainly in the years since Kant. Only a few writers sound like latter-day neo-Platonists – Emerson, for one, though he is a more nuanced thinker than the tag 'Yankee Plato' insinuates.

Although Plato does appeal to some readers who are drawn to magical philosophy and the occult, those readers gravitate to the *Timaeus* and *Critias* and the tales of Atlantis found there. The *Republic* has not encouraged neo-Platonic speculation even among people already inclined toward such thinking.

Finally, the normative ethics that inspired such admiration in antiquity strikes too many moderns as either undesirable or familiar. Plato's eye on the afterlife, and asceticism bordering on puritanical, may have led early Christian theologians to his dialogues. But today the pious have already heard this news, while those who reject such pieties coming from religion have no wish to reencounter them in philosophy.

The *Republic* intrigues modern readers for other reasons. If these are not entirely different reasons from the sources of its appeal in antiquity, they still indicate the distance that separates the two worlds. First come *politics*, including the problem of totalitarianism but also educational theory, and the *Republic*'s proposals regarding women and the family. Second is the theory of the *soul*, though now that theory stands apart from both religion and ethics. And third is the *Republic*'s gesture toward foundationalist *epistemology*.

## EPISTEMOLOGY

This book has said less about the *Republic*'s theory of knowledge than about other topics. Even modern foundationalist philosophers will not find this theory convincing. Here the *Republic* serves as inspiration rather than influence. And yet the passages in Books 5 and 6 that culminate in the Divided Line combine several powerful ideas, which do not occur together elsewhere in Plato or in any known work before him.

(1) An intelligible realm exists that contains entities more real than those found in the visible world.

(2) The cognitive states corresponding to this difference in reality also differ from one another, with some states superior to others.

(3) One level of understanding is better than another one, and the truth of one kind of statement better than another truth, according to a single criterion, call it clarity, certainty, or completeness.

(4) Among nonphilosophical statements, the best are those appearing in mathematics. Mathematical truths are more certain than empirical truths, and the concepts they contain are clearer.

(5) A method of analysis or method of proof (or some other method combining those two) can improve upon even the reliable knowledge found in mathematics.

(6) The ultimate result of applying the method is a single first principle from which all other true statements follow.

We should not claim more for the *Republic*'s system of knowledge than it can bear. Plato does not guess at the developments that would arrive in the late nineteenth century, such as the formalization of rules of inference. He would have been delighted to imagine the Form of the Good actually containing the steps by which other principles followed from the Good, but imagining such a thing was surely impossible in his day. And to a great extent the *Republic*'s theory of knowledge is 'generic Platonism,' which is to say a vague intuition about nonempirical truth. Tenets (1), (2), and (4) of the epistemological view might not imply more than the Platonism that many mathematicians still assume, when they think of mathematical truths as existing 'out there' waiting to be discovered, or when they say as Leopold Kronecker reportedly did, 'God made the integers; all else is the work of man.'

The Divided Line and the *Republic*'s elucidation of the Line go beyond generic Platonism when they identify a single criterion of epistemic superiority (3). Whether we call the better truths *clearer* than empirical observations or *more firmly true*, that one characteristic that Plato calls *saphêneia* can now be studied and pursued. (We not only know things now, we know that we know them, because now we know what knowing is like.) And (3) begets (5). Where a single criterion of knowledge exists, philosophers can hope to discover the method for achieving that quality. Finally the principle one arrives at (6) can be used to demonstrate the truth of all other true statements. That highest principle makes the others true, in a sense rendering them truer than they had been.

For Plato the interesting mathematics was geometry. As mathematics grew in power and elegance the Platonic hope for a great geometrical system in philosophy became all the more attractive. Arithmetic progressed in the Middle Ages; Arab scholars created algebra; and then in the seventeenth century the algebraic tradition joined with geometry in the form of analytic geometry. The math of Descartes's time went far beyond any math that Plato knew, but philosophical ambitions this math encouraged were already at work in the middle of Plato's *Republic*.

## POLITICS

If ancient authors played down the *Republic*'s politics because the classical city had disappeared from view, returning to emphasize the political theory luckily did not require the reinstatement of freestanding *poleis*. But something did return that the Roman Empire had suppressed: deliberations over how best to organize a society. Modern culture acknowledged that philosophers should address such issues. So even where the politics of the *Republic* are unacceptable to moderns, the dialogue is confronting the question of political legitimacy – What gives you a good reason to obey a state's laws? – as modern thought would do with new ferocity.

Modern political theorists, Thomas Hobbes for example, entered into debate with Plato despite rejecting his politics. Hobbes represents the modern turn away from first principles, philosophically ascertained, that will demonstrate how a community ought to govern itself. From his perspective Plato begins the inquiry too optimistically, with a fantasy of human beings' agreement to unite. In fact long-lasting violence and misery come before such union, according to Hobbes, and even organized communities live on with the threat of violence and misery always lying in wait. It is also a sign of Plato's optimism, from a Hobbesian point of view, that he expects philosophical inquiry to succeed where politics-as-usual has kept failing. Politics should begin by recognizing and seeking to describe the unsentimental reality of human actions, rather than by wishing it away.

For all the differences between Hobbes early in modernity and the recent liberalism of John Rawls, they would agree that beginning political discussion with philosophy is neither desirable nor possible. The content of justice, whether as a feature of communities or an individual's virtue, is not determined by aprioristic arguments for one conception of justice or another. Some manner of widespread consent is a necessary condition for the legitimate state. Plato sees the consent that is the disappearance of civil strife as the eventual by-product of a philosophically instituted political order. Construct the city rightly and the citizens who grow up in it and believe what they're told will approve of the constitution that governs them. But Hobbes and Rawls, like many thinkers in between, see the only possible consent as one that initiates the society and forms its conception of justice.

A more specific modern debate has concerned the best form of constitution, typically in a choice between democracy and some other kind of government. Rousseau is an early and surprising example of the modern figure who looks back more favorably on authoritarian Sparta than on Athens the allegedly irresponsible democracy. In Rousseau's case, at least, the *Republic*'s criticisms of democracy inform his assessment.

Marx (who, like Rousseau, genuinely studied antiquity) also shows his familiarity with the *Republic*. Consider the communistic life the guardians are said to live, without family or privacy or property. Plato is describing an elite class that will run his society, where Marx envisions some version of the same utopian arrangement for all people in a society; but there is a more fundamental insight at stake. Plato's reason for separating his guardians from property flows from his belief that unchecked economic power translates into the self-interested political power that Thrasymachus saw everywhere. Self-interested power makes justice impossible, according to the *Republic.* This so-called justice really is the advantage of the stronger, and Thrasymachus was correct to speak of that false virtue cynically; and in the end such justice is fated to produce class warfare. Marx understands the source and the extent of economic power very differently from Plato, but he too – under Plato's tutelage – sees how economic power skews a political order, and he too sees class warfare as the outcome of a social relationship to property that permits productive property to be held in private hands.

It goes without saying that Marx contemplates the arrival of outright civil strife more hopefully than Plato does. He is not a Platonist, after all, but a modern thinker who extends the *Republic*'s political analysis and definition of class into a response to the economic developments that came with modernity.

Comparisons between Marx and Plato could quickly say more: that both want to base the good society on 'ideology,' that both envision a plan of lifelong propaganda to produce enthusiastic citizens, and so on. And from such points of comparison it is a small step to calling both of them totalitarian thinkers. This book has already touched on the question of totalitarianism (see Chapter 10), which for a lifetime has lain at the center of political assessments of the *Republic.* There is no point regretting the persistence of the question. Totalitarianism is one of the worst conditions human beings can live under, and it only makes sense that thoughtful people should ask what brings totalitarian regimes into existence.

Nor is there any harm in asking whether the *Republic* fostered totalitarianism. Good answers to this question are bound to be complex, but the *Republic* will not be injured by an honest inquiry. It is the strongest exposition of utopian politics in Plato, and the liveliness of the contemporary debate has helped to cement the *Republic*'s place in the front rank of his writings: it is the dialogue that democracy's supporters must reckon with.

From our point of view the problem with asking about totalitarianism is that it can distract from other topics. The *Republic*'s advocacy of equal roles for men and women seems to have meant more in modern centuries than they did to an ancient Greek culture that would have seen such ideas as a curiosity. (That is, the men in the culture would have seen the ideas that way. Axiothea's story hints at how educated Greek women might have responded.) Even if modern feminism proceeds from basic premises about fairness for women, their rights, and their autonomy (premises of no importance to the *Republic*'s good city), and although Plato has no interest in such political goals as voting and property rights or equal pay, nevertheless these differences should not distract from the undoubted inspiration that modern feminists took from Book 5's arguments about women guardians. The *Republic* already achieves a great deal for modern feminism by demystifying gender difference. Comparing women and men to dogs of both sexes brings an air of rural common sense that ancient and modern discussions both benefit from (451d–e), and Plato refuses to call existing sex distinctions natural (456c) or to mind what public opinion says (452b). Citing the benefits to a city of producing fine women (456e), calling for equal educations (452a), and putting women naked in the gymnasium and armed into battle (452a–e), all suggest possibilities for women today regardless of Plato's wish for male and female citizens to surrender their happiness to the city.

As for education, that subject pervades the *Republic*. Plato would like to see the state design a coherent curriculum that is both challenging and pleasant. He would not leave education in the hands of parents, who want to reproduce their moral prejudices in their children. Nor does he approve of the endless rote learning that young Athenians were subjected to. Good health and integrity of character can and should be the result of large-scale, coordinated institutions. In this sense Ignatius of Loyola, founder of the Jesuits, spoke as a Platonist when he famously said, 'Give me the boy until he is seven and I will give you the man'; and Rousseau (who incidentally fumed at the 'promiscuity' in Book 5's proposals about women and family) can be seen as a modern inheritor of the *Republic*'s educational proposals.

Earlier chapters of this book covered these points. They are worth remembering in an assessment of Plato's legacy. We tend to forget that even theorists with ambitions as celestial as his can bring about practical reforms over the long haul (sometimes the very long haul). And as far as education goes, one more factor is relevant in explaining why modern readers responded to the

*Republic* more enthusiastically than ancient ones. By every measure, the modern industrialized world is more politically egalitarian than ancient civilizations were. Plato's Athens may have
operated with a radical and open form of democracy, but too
many of the city's inhabitants – all the slaves, the women, the
noncitizens – were more likely to suffer under the laws of that
democracy than to see their lives ameliorated. Many citizens were
too poor to think of sharing in Athenian culture by educating
their children even to the point of basic literacy. Ancient readers
who admired Plato's recommendations about education might
have applied the recommendations to their own children, not to
the young generation as a whole. But with the rise of compulsory
universal education, such recommendations could matter to
democracies – hence they could matter as public policy – instead
of just to aristocrats hoping to breed a fine next generation.

## SOUL

The *Republic*'s theory of soul has found a place in modern
thought, too – not its argument for immortality and the story
about reincarnation, certainly not the idea that the soul resembles
god. Even without the aspects of the theory that ground morality in
the soul's nature, Plato's way of accounting for human actions has
spoken to modern psychology. But practitioners of both traditional and innovative religions alike are drawn to the idea of self-
purification, while the secular spirit of psychoanalysis has a Platonic
aspect in its enterprise of clarification about the self. In both cases
the differences between modernity and the *Republic* must be kept in
mind; in spite of those differences however there is a real Platonic
spirit to much contemporary thinking about the soul.

Not only Christianity but many other religions too have resembled the *Republic*'s Platonism in promising to purify the soul, where
this means bringing a person peace of mind, even joy, with or
without a better fate after death. Knowledge can make the difference. The Gnostic sects that sprang up around the time of early
Christianity claimed to possess secret doctrines about heavenly
disputes over control of the earth. Whatever the teaching is, it
sets the soul along a new path. To this extent many cults and

religions would recognize themselves in the allegory of the cave, and the initiates' ascent to a superior state. It is no coincidence that Plato chose a cave to set his allegory in; for while our most common association with caves is primitive life ('cavemen'), in his Greece they symbolized cultic initiation.

But Plato adds an element to his vision of the soul's adventure that seems to be peculiarly his own, and is not found in religions. If many religions disclose inside knowledge about the soul's place in the universe and its future life, Plato makes this only a part of what the soul can learn. The soul's progress away from domination by the body is the effect of its mastering mathematics and then philosophical dialectic; that first separation from bodily concerns then makes more knowledge possible. The initiation that matters does not only show people their own natures and promise them future life. It brings them to abstract analysis of a kind that religions do not busy themselves with.

In a different way the knowledge pursued by the Platonic soul (the soul that improves itself) also goes beyond the knowledge that psychoanalysis pursues, in spite of the evident similarities to Plato that are at work here too.

Many readers have noted the affinities between the *Republic*'s tripartition of the soul (Book 4) and Freud's psychological structures, or between the bestial lust at work in the tyrannical soul (Book 9) and Freud's characterization of the id. More profoundly we can identify two psychoanalytic principles that the *Republic* also contains (and no other work of Plato's does, or not to the same degree):

(1) I am not one. Because of the plurality of motives that drive me, I do not always act as I want to.
(2) I do not know myself completely. Some of the motives that drive me are clear to me, but others need to be discovered and understood.

Both Freud and the *Republic* begin with the realization that people do not always carry out the actions they intend to. People explode with anger when they mean to stay calm, or blurt out an offensive thought; they try to quit a bad habit but they keep failing. Obsessive jealousy destroys a marriage and depressive languor hobbles the career. You have good reasons for acting a certain way, and you know what those reasons are – and yet you do not act on them.

Freud takes the difficulty of self-knowledge much further than Plato does, but I think Plato would accept this departure calmly enough, even seeing it as a natural development of his idea. The sharper difference between them might grow out of what they agree on, that people do not always do what they mean to. For modern psychology the soul is understood individualistically: both what you decide to do and what prevents you from doing it are facts peculiar to your life. Plato sees the soul as a normative concept, as all the ancient Greeks did. There is one healthy condition for the soul to be in, and the actions of one soul in that condition will be the same as those of all other souls in the same condition.

This is why the soul's justice, 'P-justice,' can issue in 'O-just' behavior: Plato thinks a good theory of the soul can do more for good behavior because there is a standard human soul, and in its healthy form it behaves according to human morals. For this reason, the knowledge that helps to bring the soul to self-recognition and self-mastery will be general knowledge about the human soul as such, not the idiosyncratic reading of oneself that many forms of modern therapy pursue. The goal is not special knowledge of yourself but general knowledge about human selfhood.

## A LAST WORD

One last word about the *Republic*'s legacy harks back to some of the issues raised in Chapter 1 of this book, regarding Plato's choice of a genre or a way of writing that would suit the philosophy he was trying to disseminate.

This might be a question that gained special force in the professionalized philosophical climate of the twentieth century, as philosophical writing tends to follow a single form: the 'article' or the book, typically footnoted, that speaks in sober tones about a single topic. A lot can be done with that mode of writing, as witness the wealth of philosophical books and shorter pieces published in the twentieth and so far in the twenty-first centuries. But some philosophers as well as nonphilosophers have wondered what other forms philosophical writing might take: fresher forms, livelier forms. For them Plato's dialogues continue to offer a special appeal, as Heidegger's gnomic lectures do, or Wittgenstein's later writings, or many of the books written by Nietzsche, Kierkegaard, Emerson, and other modernist thinkers. As a rule these philosophers are the most un-Platonic of recent philosophers. Platonism influences them in the attempt to write philosophy in something other than an impartial authorial voice.

Of course Plato wrote many dialogues besides the *Republic*. But one feature of the *Republic*, already mentioned, might make it the most inspirational work of Plato's for modern philosophers. The *Republic* gives us Socrates the cross-examining sharp thinker and also Socrates the moral leader, Socrates the intellectual speculator and Socrates the storyteller. This dialogue sometimes gives the impression of being able to encompass all philosophical thinking, without undue concern for uniformity of vision and tone. Modern philosophers in search of new ways of saying something in philosophy surely took heart in the *Republic*'s apparent ability to say everything.

## SUGGESTIONS FOR FURTHER READING

This chapter is thoroughly indebted to recent books that bring together the numerous details argued for by hundreds of scholars. Regarding the first generation after Plato the reader should begin with Dillon, *The Heirs of Plato: A Study of the Old Academy*, and Gottschalk, *Heraclides of Pontus*. Algra et al. have edited a massive, always helpful *Cambridge History of Hellenistic Philosophy*, which continues the story of philosophy from the time of the death of Alexander until the Roman conquest. Annas, *Platonic Ethics Old and New*, is a highly philosophical study of the Middle Platonists.

Political issues are at work, even if only in the background, in all the above. But some recent studies of later antiquity bring politics to the fore. O'Meara, *Platonopolis: Platonic Political Philosophy in Late Antiquity* – another invaluable source for this chapter – argues that politics mattered more to neo-Platonists than the stereotype of them would imply; Schofield, *The Stoic Idea of the City*, makes a similar case for politics and Stoicism. Also see Schott, 'Founding Platonopolis: the Platonic *Politeia* in Eusebius, Porphyry, and Iamblichus.'

And for the antidemocratic sentiments that distorted many modern readers' perceptions of Athens and Sparta, see above all Roberts, *Athens on Trial: The Antidemocratic Tradition in Western Thought*.

On contrasting the *Republic* with modern approaches to political philosophy, especially with Rawls, no discussion covers as much ground as Santas, *Understanding Plato's Republic*.

# APPENDIX

## FUNDAMENTAL PREMISES IN THE *REPUBLIC'S* ARGUMENT

① The unjust try to get the better of all others, the just only to get the better of the unjust (349b–c) – p. 65.

② Injustice is a force, with the power of promoting disunion, that can exist within an individual or a society (351d, e) – p. 67.

③ Everything has a work (*ergon*) that it alone can do, or that it does better than anything else can (352d–353a) – p. 67.

④ Justice is the virtue of the soul (353e) – p. 68.

⑤ Humans taken individually are not self-sufficient (369b) – p. 81.

⑥ People are naturally disposed to perform different tasks (370a–b) – p. 81.

⑦ The P-just soul = the soul of one who is most likely to perform O-just deeds – p. 122.

⑧ The P-just soul is the happiest possible soul – p. 121.

⑨ Virtuous and expert rule is possible if and only if the rulers are philosophers – p. 139.

⑩ The love of every kind of learning produces knowledge of ethical matters – p. 139.

⑪ The rational part of the soul has desires of its own (485d) – p. 143.

⑫ Every level of understanding requires a corresponding level of reality in the object of understanding – p. 158.

⑬ Poetry imitates appearance (595b–602c) – p. 204.

⑭ Poetry appeals to the worst parts of the soul (602c–606d) – p. 204.

# BIBLIOGRAPHY

This is a selection of books and articles for the reader who is getting to know Plato and the *Republic*, as well as an acknowledgment of the sources to which I have become most indebted in writing this book. An asterisk (*) indicates the works especially suitable to beginning students, while a dagger (†) indicates those with thorough references to other works on the *Republic*.

## PLATO AND SOCRATES: PLATO AS AUTHOR

Bambrough, R. (ed.), *New Essays on Plato and Aristotle*, London, Routledge & Kegan Paul, 1965.

†Benson, H. H. (ed.), *Essays on the Philosophy of Socrates*, Oxford, Oxford University Press, 1992.

Gadamer, H.-G., *Platons dialektische Ethik*, pub. in English as *Plato's Dialectical Ethics: Phenomenological Interpretations Relating to the Philebus*, trans. R. M. Wallace, New Haven, Yale University Press, 1991.

Goldschmidt, V., *Les dialogues de Platon: structure et methode dialectique*, Paris, Presses universitaires de France, 1947.

Griswold, C., 'Style and philosophy: the case of Plato's dialogues,' *Monist* 63 (1980): 530–46.

Grote, G., *Plato and the Other Companions of Socrates*, 3 vols., London, John Murray, 1975, originally pub. London, 1888.

Gulley, N., *The Philosophy of Socrates*, New York, St. Martin's Press, 1968.

*†Guthrie, W. K. C., *A History of Greek Philosophy*, vol. IV: *Plato: The Man and His Dialogues: Earlier Period*, Cambridge, Cambridge University Press, 1975.

Hyland, D., 'Why Plato wrote dialogues,' *Philosophy and Rhetoric* 1 (1968): 38–50.

Kahn, C., 'Did Plato write Socrates' dialogues?' *Classical Quarterly* 31 (1981): 305–20.

†Kraut, R., *Socrates and the State*, Princeton, Princeton University Press, 1984.

*Kuhn, H., 'The true tragedy: on the relationship between Greek tragedy and Plato,' *Harvard Studies in Classical Philology* 52 (1941): 1–40, and 53 (1942): 37–88.

McPherran, M. L., 'Socrates and the duty to philosophize,' *Southern Journal of Philosophy* 24 (1986): 541–60.

Moors, K., 'Plato's use of dialogue,' *Classical World* 72 (1978): 77–93.

Nails, D., 'The dramatic date of Plato's *Republic*,' *Classical Journal* 93 (1998): 383–98.

*†Nussbaum, M., *The Fragility of Goodness*, Cambridge, Cambridge University Press, 1986.

Patterson, R., 'The Platonic art of comedy and tragedy,' *Philosophy and Literature* 6 (1982): 76–93.

*Santas, G., *Socrates: Philosophy in Plato's Early Dialogues*, London, Routledge & Kegan Paul, 1979.

Saxenhouse, A. W., 'Comedy in Callipolis: animal imagery in the *Republic*,' *American Political Science Review* 72 (1972): 888–901.

Shory, P., *What Plato Said*, Chicago, University of Chicago Press, 1933.

Tarrant, D., 'Plato as dramatist,' *Journal of Hellenic Studies* 75 (1955): 82–9.

Taylor, A. E., *Plato: The Man and His Work*, London, Methuen, 1926.

*†Vlastos, G. (ed.), *Plato*, 2 vols., Garden City, Doubleday, 1971 (henceforth *Plato* I and *Plato* II).

——(ed.), *The Philosophy of Socrates*, South Bend, University of Notre Dame Press, 1971.

*†——, *Socrates, Ironist and Moral Philosopher*, Ithaca, Cornell University Press, 1991.

# HISTORICAL BACKGROUND

Algra, K., J. Barnes, J. Mansfeld, and M. Schofield (eds.), *The Cambridge History of Hellenistic Philosophy*, Cambridge, Cambridge University Press, 1999.

Blank, D. L., 'Socrates versus Sophists on payment for teaching,' *Classical Antiquity* 4 (1985): 1–49.

Cartledge, P., *Spartan Reflections*, Berkeley and Los Angeles, University of California Press, 2003.

——, *The Spartans: The World of the Warrior-Heroes of Ancient Greece*, Woodstock, Overlook Press, 2003.

Dillon, J. M., *The Heirs of Plato: A Study of the Old Academy (347–274 BC)*, Oxford, Oxford University Press, 2003.

Dover, K. J., *Greek Homosexuality*, London, Duckworth, 1978.

Gottschalk, H. B., *Heraclides of Pontus*, Oxford, Oxford University Press, 1980.

Hale, J. R., *Lords of the Sea: The Epic Story of the Athenian Navy and the Birth of Democracy*, New York, Viking, 2009.

Hanson, V. D., *The Other Greeks: The Family Farm and the Agrarian Roots of Western Civilization*, New York, The Free Press, 1995.

Kagan, D., *The Peace of Nicias and the Sicilian Expedition*, Ithaca, Cornell University Press, 1981.

O'Meara, D., *Platonopolis: Platonic Political Philosophy in Late Antiquity*, Oxford, Clarendon Press, 2003.

Ober, J., *Political Dissent in Democratic Athens: Intellectual Critics of Popular Rule*, Princeton, Princeton University Press, 1998.

Roberts, J. T., *Athens on Trial: The Antidemocratic Tradition in Western Thought*, Princeton, Princeton University Press, 1994.

Schofield, M., *The Stoic Idea of the City*, Cambridge, Cambridge University Press, 1991.

Schott, J. M., 'Founding Platonopolis: the Platonic *Politeia* in Eusebius, Porphyry, and Iamblichus,' *Journal of Early Christian Studies* 11 (2003): 501–31.

Sellars, J., 'Simon the shoemaker and the problem of Socrates,' *Classical Philology* 98 (2003): 207–16.

Vernant, J.-P., *Myth and Tragedy in Ancient Greece*, trans. J. Lloyd, Cambridge, Massachusetts, Zone Books, 1990.

Zhmud, L., 'Plato as "architect of science,"' *Phronesis* 43 (1998): 211–44.

## GENERAL WORKS ON THE *REPUBLIC*

Adam, J., *The Republic of Plato* (2nd ed.), 2 vols., Cambridge, Cambridge University Press, 1963.

*†Annas, J., *An Introduction to Plato's Republic*, Oxford, Oxford University Press, 1981.

Barney, R., 'Platonic ring-composition and *Republic* 10,' in McPherran (ed.), *Plato's Republic*, pp. 32–51.

* Blackburn, S., *Plato's Republic: A Biography*, New York, Atlantic Monthly Press, 2006.

Brann, E. T. H., 'The music of the *Republic*,' *St. John's Review* 39 (1989–90): 1–103.

*†Brown, E., 'Plato's ethics and politics in the *Republic*,' in E. N. Zalta (ed.), *Stanford Encyclopedia of Philosophy* <http://plato.stanford.edu/entries/plato-ethics-politics/>.

Crombie, I. M., *An Examination of Plato's Doctrines*, 2 vols., London, Routledge & Kegan Paul, 1962.

Cross, R. C. and A. D. Woozley, *Plato's Republic: A Philosophical Commentary*, New York, St. Martin's Press, 1964.

Ferrari, G. R. F., 'Socrates in the *Republic*,' in McPherran (ed.), *Plato's Republic*, pp. 11–31.

†—— (ed.), *The Cambridge Companion to Plato's Republic*, Cambridge, Cambridge University Press, 2007.

†Fronterotta, F., 'Plato's *Republic* in the recent debate,' *Journal of the History of Philosophy* 48 (2010): 125–51.

McPherran, M. (ed.), *Plato's Republic: A Critical Guide*, Cambridge, Cambridge University Press, 2010.

*Murphy, N. R., *The Interpretation of Plato's Republic*, Oxford, Oxford University Press, 1951.

Nettleship, R. L., *Lectures on the Republic of Plato* (2nd ed.), London, Macmillan, 1901.

†Ophir, A., *Plato's Invisible Cities: Discourse and Power in the Republic*, Savage, Maryland, Barnes & Noble, 1991.

Reeve, C. D. C., *Philosopher-Kings: The Argument of Plato's Republic*, Princeton, Princeton University Press, 1988.

Santas, G. (ed.), *The Blackwell Guide to Plato's Republic*, Malden, Blackwell Publishing, 2006.

*——, *Understanding Plato's Republic*, Oxford and New York, Wiley-Blackwell, 2010.

Sesonske, A. (ed.), *Plato's Republic: Interpretation and Criticism*, Belmont, California, Wadsworth Publishing Company, 1966.

*White, N., *A Companion to Plato's Republic*, Oxford, Blackwell, 1979.

## *REPUBLIC* BOOK 1

Adkins, A. W. H., 'The Greek concept of justice from Homer to Plato,' *Classical Philology* 75 (1980): 256–68.

Barney, R., 'Socrates' refutation of Thrasymachus,' in Santas (ed.), *Blackwell Guide to Plato's Republic*, pp. 44–62.

Boter, G. J., 'Thrasymachus and *pleonexia*,' *Mnemosyne* 39 (1986): 261–81.

Garnsey, P., 'Religious toleration in classical antiquity,' in W. J. Shiels (ed.), *Persecuting Toleration*, Studies in Church History 21, Oxford, Oxford University Press, pp. 1–27.

Gotoff, H. C., 'Thrasymachus of Calchedon and Ciceronian style,' *Classical Philology* 75 (1980): 297–311.

Hadgopoulos, D. J., 'Thrasymachus and legalism,' *Phronesis* 18 (1973): 204–8.

*Joseph, H. W. B., 'Plato's *Republic*: the argument with Polemarchus,' in Sesonske (ed.), *Plato's Republic*, pp. 6–16.

Kraut, R., 'Comments on Gregory Vlastos, "The Socratic elenchus,"' *Oxford Studies in Ancient Philosophy* 1 (1983): 27–58.

†Lycos, K., *Plato on Justice and Power*, Albany, SUNY Press, 1987.

Reeve, C. D. C., 'Socrates meets Thrasymachus,' *Archiv für Geschichte der Philosophie* 67 (1985): 246–65.

Roochnik, D. L., 'Socrates' use of the techne-analogy,' *Journal of the History of Philosophy* 24 (1986): 295–310.

*Sesonske, A., 'Plato's Apology: *Republic* I,' *Phronesis* 6 (1961): 29–36, and in Sesonske (ed.), *Plato's Republic*, pp. 40–47.

*Sparshott, F. E., 'Socrates and Thrasymachus,' *Monist* 50 (1966): 421–59.

Thayer, H. S., 'Plato: the theory and language of function,' in Sesonske (ed.), *Plato's Republic*, pp. 21–39.

*Vlastos, G., 'The Socratic elenchus,' *Oxford Studies in Ancient Philosophy* 1 (1983): 27–58.

——, 'Elenchus and mathematics: a turning-point in Plato's philosophical development,' *American Journal of Philology* 109 (1988): 362–96, and in Benson (ed.), *Essays on Socrates*, pp. 137–61.

Weiss, R., 'Wise guys and smart alecks in *Republic* 1 and 2,' in Ferrari (ed.), *Cambridge Companion to Plato's Republic*, pp. 90–115.

# POLITICS, ETHICS, AND PSYCHOLOGY

Annas, Julia, *Platonic Ethics Old and New*, Ithaca, Cornell University Press, 1999.

Bambrough, R., 'Plato's political analogies,' in P. Laslett (ed.), *Philosophy, Politics, and Society*, Oxford, Blackwell, 1956, pp. 98–115.

\*——(ed.), *Plato, Popper, and Politics*, Cambridge, Heffer, 1967.

Barker, E., 'Communism in Plato's *Republic*,' in Sesonske (ed.), *Plato's Republic*, pp. 82–97.

Blössner, N., 'The city–soul analogy,' trans. G. R. F. Ferrari, in Ferrari (ed.), *Cambridge Companion to Plato's Republic*, pp. 345–85.

Bobonich, C., *Plato's Utopia Recast*, Oxford, Oxford University Press, 2002.

†Cooper, J., 'The psychology of justice in Plato,' *American Philosophical Quarterly* 14 (1977): 151–57.

——, 'Plato's theory of human motivation,' *History of Philosophy Quarterly* 1 (1984): 3–21.

Crossman, R. H. S., *Plato Today* (2nd ed.), London, George Allen & Unwin, 1959.

Demos, R., 'A fallacy in Plato's *Republic*?' *Philosophical Review* 73 (1964): 395–98, and in Vlastos (ed.), *Plato* II, pp. 52–56.

Ferrari, G. R. F., *City and Soul in Plato's Republic*, Chicago, University of Chicago Press, 2005.

——, 'The three-part soul,' in Ferrari (ed.), *Cambridge Companion to Plato's Republic*, pp. 165–201.

Frede, D., 'Plato, Popper, and Historicism,' in J. J. Cleary and W. C. Wians (eds.), *Proceedings of the Boston Area Colloquium in Ancient Philosophy* XII, 1996, pp. 247–76.

Hitz, Z., 'Degenerate regimes in Plato's *Republic*,' in McPherran (ed.), *Plato's Republic*, pp. 103–31.

\*Irwin, T., *Plato's Moral Theory*, Oxford, Clarendon Press, 1977.

Klosko, G., 'Implementing the ideal state,' *Journal of Politics* 43 (1981): 356–89.

Leys, W. A. R., 'Was Plato non-political?' *Ethics* 75 (1965): 272–76, and in Vlastos (ed.), *Plato* II, pp. 166–73.

Lorenz, H., *The Brute Within: Appetitive Desire in Plato and Aristotle*, Oxford, Oxford University Press, 2006.

Mabbott, J. O., 'Is Plato's *Republic* utilitarian?' in Vlastos (ed.), *Plato* II, pp. 57–65.

McPherran, M., 'The gods and piety of Plato's *Republic*,' in Santas (ed.), *Blackwell Guide to Plato's Republic*, pp. 84–103.

Moline, J., 'Plato on the complexity of the psyche,' *Archiv für Geschichte der Philosophie* 60 (1978): 1–26.

\*Morrow, G. R., 'Plato and the rule of law,' *Philosophical Review* 59 (1941): 105–26.

Moss, J., 'Appearances and calculations: Plato's division of the soul,' *Oxford Studies in Ancient Philosophy* 34 (2008): 35–68.

Neu, J., 'Plato's analogy of state and individual: the *Republic* and the organic theory of the state,' *Philosophy* 46 (1971): 238–54.

\*†Nussbaum, M., 'The *Republic*: true value and the standpoint of perfection,' in *The Fragility of Goodness*, pp. 136–64.

Ostwald, M., 'The two states in Plato's *Republic*,' in J. P. Anton and G. L. Kustas (eds.), *Essays in Ancient Greek Philosophy*, vol. I, Albany, SUNY Press, 1972, pp. 316–27.

Pierce, C., 'Equality: *Republic* V,' *Monist* 57 (1973): 10–11.

*Popper, K., *The Open Society and Its Enemies*, London, Routledge & Kegan Paul, 1945.

Rankin, H. D., *Plato and the Individual*, London, Methuen Press, 1964.

Reeve, C. D. C., 'Blindness and reorientation: education and the acquisition of knowledge in the *Republic*,' in McPherran (ed.), *Plato's Republic*, pp. 209–28.

*Robinson, R., 'Dr. Popper's defence of democracy,' in *Essays in Greek Philosophy*, Oxford, Clarendon Press, 1969, pp. 74–99.

Russell, D., *Plato on Pleasure and the Good Life*, Oxford, Oxford University Press, 2007.

*Sachs, D., 'A fallacy in Plato's *Republic*,' *Philosophical Review* 72 (1963): 141–58, and in Vlastos (ed.), *Plato* II, pp. 35–51.

Schofield, M., 'Music all pow'rful,' in McPherran (ed.), *Plato's Republic*, pp. 229–48.

Shields, C., 'Plato's divided soul,' in McPherran (ed.), *Plato's Republic*, pp. 147–70.

*Shorey, P., 'Plato's ethics,' in *The Unity of Plato's Thought*, Chicago, University of Chicago Press, 1903, and in Vlastos (ed.), *Plato* II, pp. 7–34.

Singpurwalla, R., 'Plato's defense of justice in the *Republic*,' in Santas (ed.), *Blackwell Guide to Plato's Republic*, pp. 263–82.

†Smith, N., 'Return to the cave,' in McPherran (ed.), *Plato's Republic*, pp. 83–102.

Sprague, R. K., *Plato's Philosopher-King*, Columbia, University of South Carolina Press, 1976.

Thayer, H. S., 'Models of moral concepts and Plato's *Republic*,' *Journal of the History of Philosophy* 7 (1969): 247–62.

*Thorson, T. (ed.), *Plato: Totalitarian or Democrat?* Englewood Cliffs, Prentice-Hall, 1963.

Vasiliou, I., *Aiming at Virtue in Plato*, Cambridge, Cambridge University Press, 2008.

Versenyi, L. G., 'Plato and his liberal opponents,' *Philosophy* 46 (1971): 222–37.

*Vlastos, G., 'Justice and happiness in the *Republic*,' in Vlastos (ed.), *Plato* II, pp. 66–75.

Whiting, J., 'Psychic contingency in the *Republic*,' in R. Barney, T. Brennan, and C. Brittain (eds.), *Plato and the Divided Self*, Cambridge, Cambridge University Press, 2011.

## WOMEN AND FEMINISM

*†Bluestone, N. H., *Women and the Ideal Society: Plato's Republic and Modern Myths of Gender*, Amherst, University of Massachusetts Press, 1987.

Calvert, B., 'Plato and the equality of women,' *Phoenix* 28 (1975): 231–43.

Halperin, D., *One Hundred Years of Homosexuality and Other Essays on Greek Love*, New York, Routledge & Kegan Paul, 1990.

Irigaray, L., 'Plato's *hystera*,' in *Speculum of the Other Woman*, trans. Gillian C. Gill, Ithaca, Cornell University Press, 1985, pp. 243–364.

*Keuls, E., *The Reign of the Phallus: Sexual Politics in Ancient Athens*, New York, Harper & Row, 1985.

Lesser, H., 'Plato's feminism,' *Philosophy* 54 (1979): 113–17.

Smith, N., 'Plato and Aristotle on the nature of women,' *Journal of the History of Philosophy* 38 (2000): 145–68.

Vlastos, G., 'Was Plato a feminist?' *Times Literary Supplement*, March 17–23 (1989).

# METAPHYSICS, EPISTEMOLOGY, AND DIALECTIC

*Allen, R. E., 'The argument from opposites in *Republic* V,' in Anton and Kustas (eds.), *Essays in Ancient Greek Philosophy* I, pp. 165–75.

Benson, H. H., 'Plato's philosophical method in the *Republic:* the Divided Line (510b–511d),' in McPherran (ed.), *Plato's Republic*, pp. 188–208.

Brentlinger, J. A., 'Particulars in Plato's middle dialogues,' *Archiv für Geschichte der Philosophie* 54 (1972): 116–52.

*Cherniss, H., 'The philosophical economy of the theory of ideas,' *American Journal of Philology* 57 (1936): 445–56, and in Vlastos (ed.), *Plato* I, pp. 16–27.

Elias, J. A., '"Socratic" vs. "Platonic" dialectic,' *Journal of the History of Philosophy* 6 (1968): 205–16.

Ferejohn, M., 'Knowledge, recollection, and the Forms in *Republic* VII,' in Santas (ed.), *Blackwell Guide to Plato's Republic*, pp. 214–33.

†Fine, G., 'Knowledge and belief in *Republic* V,' *Archiv für Geschichte der Philosophie* 60 (1978): 121–39.

——, 'Separation,' *Oxford Studies in Ancient Philosophy* 2 (1984): 31–87.

Gosling, J. C. B., '*Republic* Book V: *ta polla kala* etc.,' *Phronesis* 5 (1960): 116–28.

Gulley, N., *Plato's Theory of Knowledge*, London, Methuen Press, 1962.

Hamlyn, D. W. '*Eikasia* in Plato's *Republic*,' *Philosophical Quarterly* 8 (1958): 14–23.

Irwin, T. H., 'Plato's Heracleiteanism,' *Philosophical Quarterly* 27 (1977): 1–13.

Joseph, H. W. B., *Knowledge and the Good in Plato's Republic*, Oxford, Clarendon Press, 1948.

Kahn, C., 'The Greek verb "be" and the concept of being,' *Foundations of Language* 2 (1966): 245–65.

Malcolm, J., 'The Line and the Cave,' *Phronesis* 7 (1962): 38–45.

Moravcsik, J., 'Understanding and knowledge in Plato's philosophy,' *Neue Hefte für Philosophie* 60 (1978): 1–26.

Morrison, J., 'Two unresolved difficulties in the Line and the Cave,' *Phronesis* 22 (1977): 212–31.

Nehamas, A., 'Confusing universals and particulars in Plato's early dialogues,' *Review of Metaphysics* 29 (1975): 287–306.

*——, 'Plato on the imperfection of the sensible world,' *American Philosophical Quarterly* 12 (1975): 105–17.

——, 'Self-predication and Plato's theory of Forms,' *American Philosophical Quarterly* 16 (1979): 93–103.

Patterson, R., *Image and Reality in Plato's Metaphysics*, Indianapolis, Hackett Publishing Company, 1985.

Raven, J. E., 'Sun, Divided Line, and Cave,' in *Plato's Thought in the Making*, Cambridge, Cambridge University Press, 1965.

Rickless, S., *Plato's Forms in Transition*, Oxford, Oxford University Press, 2007.

*Robinson, R., *Plato's Earlier Dialectic* (2nd ed.), Oxford, Clarendon Press, 1953.
——, 'Analysis in Greek geometry,' in *Essays in Greek Philosophy*, pp. 1–15.
Ryle, G., 'Dialectic in the academy,' in Bambrough (ed.), *New Essays on Plato and Aristotle*, pp. 39–68.
*Santas, G. X., 'The Form of the Good in Plato's *Republic*,' in J. P. Anton and A. Preus (eds.), *Essays in Ancient Greek Philosophy*, vol. II, Albany, SUNY Press, 1983, pp. 232–63.
Smith, N., 'Plato's Divided Line,' *Ancient Philosophy* 16 (1996): 25–46.
Vlastos, G., 'Degrees of reality in Plato,' in Bambrough (ed.), *New Essays on Plato and Aristotle*, pp. 1–19.
Wedberg, A., *Plato's Philosophy of Mathematics*, Stockholm, Almqvist & Wiksell, 1955.


## POETRY AND ART

Annas, J., 'Plato on the triviality of literature,' in Moravcsik and Temko (eds.), *Plato on Beauty, Wisdom and the Arts*, pp. 1–27.
†Belfiore, E., '"Lies unlike the truth": Plato on Hesiod, Theogony 27,' *Transactions of the American Philological Association* 115 (1985): 47–57.
Burnyeat, M. F., 'Culture and society in Plato's *Republic*,' *Tanner Lectures on Human Values* 20 (1999): 217–324.
Deleuze, G., 'Plato and the simulacrum,' *October* 27 (1983): 45–56.
Fitzpatrick, K., 'Soul music in Plato's *Republic*,' *Journal of the Utah Academy of Sciences, Arts, and Letters* 84 (2007): 104–16.
Gadamer, H.-G., *Dialogue and Dialectic*, trans. P. C. Smith, New Haven, Yale University Press, 1980.
Griswold, C., 'The Ideas and the criticism of poetry in Plato's *Republic*, Book 10,' *Journal of the History of Philosophy* 19 (1981): 135–50.
*†Halliwell, S., *Plato: Republic 10*, Warminster, Aris & Phillips, 1988.
——, *The Aesthetics of Mimesis: Ancient Texts and Modern Problems*, Princeton, Princeton University Press, 2002.
*Havelock, E. A., 'Plato on poetry,' in Sesonske (ed.), *Plato's Republic*, pp. 116–35.
Lodge, R. C., *Plato's Theory of Art*, London, Routledge & Kegan Paul, 1953.
Moravcsik, J. and P. Temko (eds.), *Plato on Beauty, Wisdom and the Arts*, Totowa, Rowman & Littlefield, 1982.
Murray, P., 'Poetic inspiration in early Greece,' *Journal of Hellenic Studies* 101 (1981): 87–100.
†Nehamas, A., 'Plato on imitation and poetry in *Republic* 10,' in Moravcsik and Temko (eds.), *Plato on Beauty, Wisdom and the Arts*, pp. 79–124.
Pappas, N., 'The *Poetics*' argument against Plato,' *Southern Journal of Philosophy* 30 (1992): 83–100.
——, 'Plato's aesthetics,' in Edward N. Zalta (ed.), *Stanford Encyclopedia of Philosophy* <http://plato.stanford.edu/entries/plato-aesthetics/>.
Partee, M. H., 'Plato's banishment of poetry,' *Journal of Aesthetics and Art Criticism* 29 (1970): 209–22.

——, 'Plato on the rhetoric of poetry,' *Journal of Aesthetics and Art Criticism* 33 (1974): 203–12.

Tate, J., '"Imitation" in Plato's Republic,' *Classical Quarterly* 22 (1928): 16–23.

——, 'Plato and imitation,' *Classical Quarterly* 26 (1932): 161–69.

*Verdenius, W. J., *Mimesis*, Leiden, E. J. Brill, 1949.

Woodruff, P., 'What could go wrong with inspiration? Why Plato's poets fail,' in Moravcsik and Temko (eds.), *Plato on Beauty, Wisdom and the Arts*, pp. 137–50.

## THE MYTH OF ER

*Annas, J., 'Plato's myths of judgment,' *Phronesis* 27 (1982): 119–43.

Ferrari, G. R. F., 'Glaucon's reward, philosophy's debt: the myth of Er,' in Partenie (ed.), *Plato's Myths*, pp. 116–33.

Frutiger, P., *Les mythes de Platon*, Paris, Alcan, 1930.

Halliwell, S., 'The life-and-death journey of the soul: interpreting the myth of Er,' in Ferrari (ed.), *Cambridge Companion to Plato's Republic*, pp. 445–73.

Lear, J., 'Allegory and myth in Plato's *Republic*,' in Santas (ed.), *Blackwell Guide to Plato's Republic*, pp. 25–43.

McPherran, M., 'Virtue, luck, and choice at the end of the *Republic*,' in McPherran (ed.), *Plato's Republic*, pp. 132–46.

†Partenie, K. (ed.), *Plato's Myths*, Cambridge, Cambridge University Press, 2009.

*Stewart, J. A., *The Myths of Plato*, Sussex, Centaur Press, 1905.

Tate, J., 'Plato, Socrates and the myths,' *Classical Quarterly* 30 (1936): 142–45.

# INDEX

**Hegel in *Routledge Guides to the Great Books***

# The Routledge Guidebook to Hegel's Phenomenology of Spirit

**Robert Stern,** University of Sheffield

The *Phenomenology of Spirit* is arguably Hegel's most influential and important work, and is considered to be essential in understanding Hegel's philosophical system and his contribution to western philosophy. The *Routledge Guidebook to Hegel's Phenomenology of Spirit* introduces the major themes in Hegel's great book and aids the reader in understanding this key work, examining:

- The context of Hegel's thought and the background to his writing
- Each separate part of the text in relation to its goals, meaning and significance
- The reception the book has received since its publication
- The relevance of Hegel's ideas to modern philosophy

With a helpful introductory overview of the text, end of chapter summaries and further reading included throughout, this text is essential reading for all students of philosophy, and all those wishing to get to grips with Hegel's contribution to our intellectual world.

February 2013 – 276 pages
Pb: 978-0-415-66446-2| Hb: 978-0-415-66445-5

Available from all good bookshops

## Locke in *Routledge Guides to the Great Books*

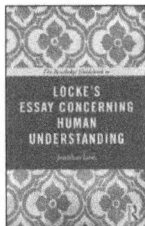

## The Routledge Guidebook to Locke's Essay Concerning Human Understanding

**E.J. Lowe**, Durham University

John Locke is widely acknowledged as the most important figure in the history of English philosophy and *An Essay Concerning Human Understanding* is his greatest intellectual work, emphasising the importance of experience for the formation of knowledge. The *Routledge Guidebook to Locke's Essay Concerning Human Understanding* introduces the major themes of Locke's great book and serves as a companion to this key work, examining:

- The context of Locke's work and the background to his writing
- Each part of the text in relation to its goals, meaning and impact
- The reception of the book when it was first seen by the world
- The relevance of Locke's work to philosophy today, its legacy and influence

With further reading suggested throughout, this text follows Locke's original work closely, making it essential reading for all students of philosophy, and all those wishing to get to grips with this classic work.

February 2013 – 288 pages
Pb: 978-0-415-66478-3| Hb: 978-0-415-66477-6

**Wittgenstein in *Routledge Guides to the Great Books***

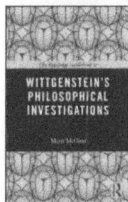

## The Routledge Guidebook to Wittgenstein's Philosophical Investigations

**Marie McGinn**, University of York

Wittgenstein is one of the most important and influential twentieth-century philosophers in the western tradition. In his Philosophical Investigations he undertakes a radical critique of analytical philosophy's approach to both the philosophy of language and the philosophy of mind. *The Routledge Guidebook to Wittgenstein's Philosophical Investigations* introduces and assesses:

- Wittgenstein's life
- The principal ideas of the Philosophical Investigations
- Some of the principal disputes concerning the interpretation of his work
- Wittgenstein's philosophical method and its connection with the form of the text.

With further reading included throughout, this guidebook is essential reading for all students of philosophy, and all those wishing to get to grips with this masterpiece.

February 2013 – 352 pages
Pb: 978-0-415-45256-4 | Hb: 978-0-415-45255-7

For more information and to order a copy visit
http://www.routledge.com/books/details/9780415452564/

Available from all good bookshops

ROUTLEDGE

## Wollstonecraft in *Routledge Guides to the Great Books*

# The Routledge Guidebook to Wollstonecraft's A Vindication of the Rights of Woman

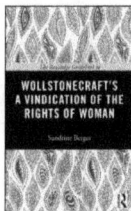

WOLLSTONECRAFT'S
A VINDICATION OF THE
RIGHTS OF WOMAN

Sandrine Berges

**Sandrine Berges,**
Bilkent University, Turkey

Mary Wollstonecraft was one of the greatest philosophers and writers of the Eighteenth century. During her brief career, she wrote novels, treatises, a travel narrative, a history of the French Revolution, a conduct book, and a children's book. Her most celebrated and widely-read work is *A Vindication of the Rights of Woman*. This Guidebook introduces:

- Wollstonecraft's life and the background to *A Vindication of the Rights of Woman*
- The ideas and text of *A Vindication of the Rights of Woman*
- Wollstonecraft's enduring influence in philosophy and our contemporary intellectual life

It is ideal for anyone coming to Wollstonecraft's classic text for the first time and anyone interested in the origins of feminist thought.

February 2013 – 272 pages
Pb: 978-0-415-67414-0 | Hb: 978-0-415-67415-7

Available from all good bookshops

## Aristotle in *Routledge Guides to the Great Books*

# The Routledge Guidebook to Aristotle's Nicomachean Ethics

**Gerard J. Hughes**, University of Oxford

Written by one of the most important founding figures of Western philosophy, Aristotle's *Nicomachean Ethics* represents a critical point in the study of ethics which has influenced the direction of modern philosophy. The *Routledge Guidebook to Aristotle's Nicomachean Ethics* introduces the major themes in Aristotle's great book and acts as a companion for reading this key work, examining:

- The context of Aristotle's work and the background to his writing
- Each separate part of the text in relation to its goals, meanings and impact
- The reception the book received when first seen by the world
- The relevance of Aristotle's work to modern philosophy, its legacy and influence.

With further reading included throughout, this text is essential reading for all students of philosophy, and all those wishing to get to grips with this classic work.

February 2013 – 336 pages
Pb: 978-0-415-66385-4 | Hb: 978-0-415-66384-7

Available from all good bookshops

For Product Safety Concerns and Information please contact our EU
representative GPSR@taylorandfrancis.com
Taylor & Francis Verlag GmbH, Kaufingerstraße 24, 80331 München, Germany